Property Development

Property Development

David Cadman
B.Sc. (Estate Management) F.R.I.C.S.
Property Market Analysis
Fellow, Wolfson College, Cambridge

Leslie Austin-Crowe
B.Sc. (Estate Management) F.R.I.C.S.
General Manager,
Northampton Development Corporation

SECOND EDITION

LONDON   NEW YORK
E. & F. N. SPON

First published 1978 by
E. & F. N. Spon Ltd
11 New Fetter Lane, London EC4P 4EE
Second edition 1983
Published in the USA by
E. & F. N. Spon
733 Third Avenue, New York NY10017

Printed in Great Britain by J. W. Arrowsmith,
Bristol

ISBN 0 419 12820 4

British Library Cataloguing in Publication Data

Cadman, David
  Property development. — 2nd ed.
  1. Real estate investment — Great Britain
  I. Title   II. Austin-Crowe, Leslie
  333.3'8   HD598

  ISBN 0-419-12820-4

Library of Congress Cataloging in Publication Data

Cadman, David.
  Property development.

  Includes index.
  1. Real estate development — Great Britain. 2. Real property—
Valuation — Great Britain. 3. Real estate investment — Great Britain.
4. Real property — Great Britain. I. Austin-Crowe, Leslie. II. Title.
HD596.C27 1983   333.73'15'0941   83-10581
ISBN 0-419-12820-4 (pbk.)

To our families

Contents

Preface to the first edition

The collapse of the property market in 1973/74 was a shattering experience for all those involved with property development and finance. As chartered surveyors, one in the private sector and the other in the public sector, we were able to observe that event closely. Now that the dust has begun to settle we are anxious to contribute to a better understanding of the risks and pitfalls that face the developer, whether he be a property company, a builder, an institutional investor, an occupier, a local authority, a government department or a statutory undertaker.

Very little has been written on the subject of property development, in part no doubt because the traditional developer has been reluctant to record his attitudes and methods. We believe that there is a need, particularly at a relatively practical level, for some guidance to be given and so we have prepared this book as a basic study of the process of property development. Because we had to start from scratch and because we wished, so far as we were able, to encompass the entire process of development, we have had to be selective on matters of detail. We are aware that we have omitted some matters and only touched upon others. No doubt our choice of priorities will not be accepted by everyone but we hope that we have done enough to alert the reader to some of the dangers and to encourage him to scrutinize all estimates and evaluations with great care. We hope that we will also foster new ideas and stimulate others to fill in the gaps that we have left.

Because the book is based upon the experience of public service and private practice, we hope that it will go some way to improve mutual understanding between public and private sectors and encourage better communication between them.

Too often, we believe, an impasse has appeared because the two sides have seen their relationship as one of confrontation and not as one of co-operation. If we have been able to do anything to change such attitudes, we will be satisfied.

Despite the attempts of the government to encourage metrication and even though architects now use metric dimensions, the majority of those concerned with property development, including financial institutions, valuers and selling/letting agents still use square feet and rates per square foot. Throughout the book, therefore, we have used Imperial units.

London   D.C.
Northampton   L.A-C.
November 1977

Preface to the second edition

In the period 1978—80 the property market recovered from the slump of the mid-1970s. This revival occurred despite an economic recession, underlying the increasing influence of the 'weight' of institutional money on the market. In the last two years, however, markets have faltered once again. In the residential sector price increases have failed to keep pace with inflation and in many cases have been virtually static. In the commercial and industrial sectors the gap between 'prime' property and the rest has widened. According to the *Investors Chronicle/Hillier Parker Rent Index* average commercial and industrial rents have shown no real growth since 1969 and questions are being raised about the level of prime investment yields and their implicit rates of rental growth.

A change in government has also brought a number of changes, including a cut-back in public-sector expenditure, the removal of Office Development Permits and Industrial Development Certificates, the repeal of the Community Land Act and amendments to the Development Land Tax. Some amendments have also been made to the planning system and two new Urban Development Corporations have been established along the lines of new town development corporations.

The growing importance of the financial institutions and the development of computer technology are encouraging the provision of more and better information about property. Some of the analysis that is emerging may, in the next five years, lead institutions to question their own criteria more

carefully than they have in the past. This, together with continuing economic uncertainty, is likely to make property
development more selective.

London   D.C.
Northampton   L.A-C.
August 1982

Acknowledgements

In producing the book we have been greatly assisted by discussion with professional colleagues, developers and financial institutions and we thank them for their comments and advice.

In particular in preparing this second edition we would like to thank Nick Griffiths, David Simms and Ian Bond for their help in updating the material, and Margaret Sutton and Pat Rice for typing and retyping the drafts of additional material.

CHAPTER 1

Introduction: the development process

1.1 INTRODUCTION

This book provides an introduction to the process of urban property development in the United Kingdom. It is concerned with both public authority and private enterprise development. It is essentially a practical book and describes the principal steps in the development process, drawing attention to certain important matters such as the concept of risk and project control. It is not intended to be a book for those who have already learnt the lessons of development by hard experience. Nor is it concerned with personalities, myths or legends. It is intended to provide a basic grounding from which further, more searching study can be undertaken.

As the term 'property development' has such an emotive connotation, it must be defined for the purpose of this book. First, in so far as property development is beset with uncertainty we accept that it involves 'speculation'. We do not, however, use this word in a derogatory sense. All business ventures which involve uncertainty are, to a degree, speculative and those involved in them are, in that sense, speculators. Second, property development is not 'land-dealing'. There may be those who call themselves property developers, who buy and sell land in a rising market. But as they seldom place one brick upon another, their business does not come within our definition of property development.

Property development is an industry that produces buildings for occupation by bringing together various raw materials of which land is only one. Others are building materials, public services, labour, capital and professional expertise. The completed building may be let or sold to an occupier. If it is let, it can be held as an investment or sold to an investor. It is

Table 1.1 Value of output at current prices (£m)

Year	New housing	Other new work	All new work	Repair and maintenance		All repair and maintenance	All work
				Housing	Other		
1969	1 470	2 292	3 762	639	800	1 439	5 201
1970	1 427	2 542	3 969	686	865	1 551	5 520
1971	1 628	2 794	4 422	765	929	1 694	6 116
1972	1 915	3 053	4 968	946	1 051	1 997	6 965
1973	2 539	3 808	6 347	1 279	1 251	2 530	8 877
1974	2 589	4 456	7 045	1 504	1 483	2 987	10 032
1975	3 025	4 976	8 001	1 658	1 759	3 417	11 418
1976	3 593	5 186	8 779	1 788	1 976	3 764	12 543
1977	3 618	5 668	9 286	2 106	2 302	4 408	13 694
1978	4 210	6 454	10 664	2 616	2 861	5 477	16 141
1979	4 478	7 648	12 126	3 242	3 417	6 659	18 785
1980	4 405	9 159	13 564	4 114	4 359	8 473	22 037
1981	3 787	8 905	12 692	4 130	4 428	8 558	21 250

(Based on *Housing and Construction Statistics, 1969–1979 and March 1982* HMSO, London.)

a venture in which losses as well as profit are made. Success depends upon the attention given to the detail of the development process and the quality of judgment that guides it.

The development industry employs substantial resources of capital and labour. Some idea of its size can be obtained from Table 1.1 and Figs 1.1 and 1.2.

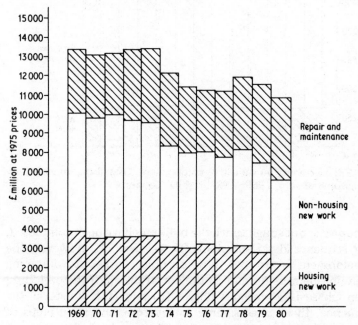

Fig. 1.1 Construction industry: value of output at 1975 prices. (Based on *Housing and Construction Statistics, 1969—1981*, HMSO, London.)

1.2 THE DEVELOPMENT PROCESS

The development process may be divided into four phases:

 (i) Evaluation
 (ii) Preparation
(iii) Implementation
(iv) Disposal

The phases may not always follow this sequence and may overlap. If the development is truly speculative and an

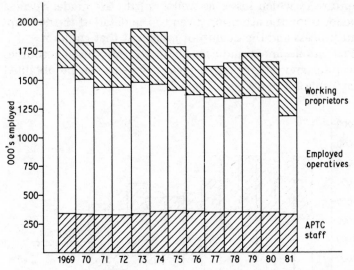

Fig. 1.2 Construction industry: employment. (Based on *Housing Construction Statistics, 1969—1981*, HMSO, London.)

occupier is not sought until the buildings have been completed, the sequence described above is followed. If, however, the development is pre-sold to an occupier, subject to obtaining planning permission and to the construction of the buildings, then phase (iv) precedes phases (ii) and (iii). Whatever the sequence, these phases serve to illustrate the main steps of most residential, commercial and industrial development projects.

1.2.1 Evaluation

No phase of the development process is more important than the phase of evaluation. Indeed it is so important that we have devoted a separate chapter to it (Chapter 2).

Evaluation encompasses both the analysis of the market place in general and in particular — market research — and the financial assessment of the project. It should be carried out before any commitment is undertaken and while the developer retains flexibility. The methods of assessing the financial viability of the particular projects are well established.

However, traditionally, much less attention has been given to detailed market research.

Evaluation involves the combined advice of the development team but in the end the responsibility for interpreting that advice rests with the developer who has to decide whether or not to bear the risk of the project.

It is not always understood that the public sector is responsible for a substantial proportion of new development. As Fig. 1.3 shows, until quite recently that proportion was 50% or more. However with the latest cut-back in public expenditure that has fallen. In 1980 it fell to some 40%.

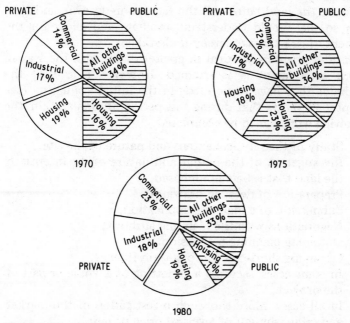

Fig. 1.3 Construction work: value of new orders. (Based on *Housing and Construction Statistics, 1969–1981*, HMSO, London.)

1.2.2 Preparation

Once the decision to proceed with a particular site has been made, there are many things that have to be done before the site can be purchased and the development started. In describing the initial evaluation (see Chapter 2), we list the factors that have to be estimated. Before committing himself to a project by the purchase of the site and the signing of a building contract, the developer must try and quantify these items more precisely. As he does so the initial evaluation may need to be revised and if, in the event, the figures indicate an unacceptable return the project may have to be abandoned.

The developer should attempt to delay any substantial commitment, such as the purchase of the land, until such time as the greater part of the initial evaluation has been thoroughly tested. It may well be, however, that he has to purchase the land before all the factors are known, and if he does so, he should understand, evaluate and allow for the element of risk that is thereby undertaken.

In later chapters we deal in greater detail with the way in which each factor is ascertained. However, a look at the estimates that have to be made in the initial evaluation (see Chapter 2) shows that during this period of 'preparation' the following work has to be completed:

(a)   Study of the physical extent and nature of the site.
(b)   Investigation of the extent and nature of the interest in the land that is being purchased.
(c)   Preparation of detailed drawings.
(d)   Submission of a planning application.
(e)   Negotiations with the planning authority.
(f)   Obtaining planning permission.
(g)   Obtaining short- and/or long-term finance.
(h)   In some cases, securing a preletting of a whole or part of the project.
(i)   In all cases, more thorough investigation of the market and establishment of levels of price or rent.
(j)   Preparation of more detailed estimates of cost and possibly Bills of Quantities.
(k)   Some discussion as to the contractor to be selected and possibly some preliminary negotiations with one or more contractors.

When the preparatory work has been completed, the project must be evaluated once again. It may be that the preparation has taken some time and the economic circumstances which determine the success of the development have changed. It is of the utmost importance, therefore, that the developer refrains from committing himself until he is satisfied that his initial evaluation is correct or that any revised evaluation produces a viable scheme. Until the land is acquired, the costs involved are unlikely to be substantial. Thereafter, however, the developer is committed not only to a purchase price, but a particular location. Many developers will only commit themselves to a purchase subject to obtaining the appropriate planning approval and the negotiations with the planning authority take up a considerable proportion of the total preparation time.

As a general rule the developer should at all times refrain from over optimism and retain a 'healthy scepticism' for the advice that he is given. He should prevent himself from envisaging unduly high levels of rent and price and unduly low levels of cost. He should always allow some contingency for unforeseen hazards. If he does so, he may miss some opportunities but he should also avoid many catstrophes.

At some stage the land is purchased and the final part of the preparation phase is undertaken — the settlement of detailed drawings and Bills of Quantity and the negotiation and signing of the building contract. We look at this in Chapter 5, but it must be remembered that this work takes time to complete and this must be allowed for in preparing the project evaluation.

Finally, before the development starts the strategy for monitoring and controlling it must be settled. The programme for site and project meetings must be arranged. The initial development timetable and estimated cash flow must be prepared. A final check must be made to ensure that all working drawings are ready, and if not, that they will be completed within an agreed period of time. The stage is then set for construction to start.

1.2.3 Implementation

The third phase, implementation, brings together at one point in space and time all the raw materials of the development process. A commitment has now been made to a particular site and to particular buildings at a particular cost spread over a particular time. The flexibility that was possible in the earlier phases has been lost. In many small projects there is virtually no opportunity for change once the building contract has been signed. This emphasizes once again the importance of careful evaluation and preparation and of maintaining flexibility for as long as possible.

However, the possibility of additional unwarranted cost and delay remains. The developer must take as much interest in the running of the project as in its promotion. He must, at all times, monitor the detailed progress of construction. This inevitably involves regular visits to the site and regular meetings with his team of advisers. He must be able to question advisers on technical matters on which, of necessity, he cannot have full knowledge. He must, therefore, have a sufficient understanding of the entire process of development to be able to judge whether or not the advice that he is given is good. We look at this in more detail in Chapter 8.

1.2.4 Disposal

At the end of the project estimates become reality. It can be seen whether or not estimated costs have been exceeded, or whether the development took longer to construct than was planned. Now it is necessary to see whether or not an occupier can be found at the estimated rental or price and within the period originally forecast. In some cases the occupier is found before the development starts, but in many cases it is necessary, and indeed advisable, to complete or virtually complete the development before seeking an occupier. The disposal may take the form of a letting, or it may be the outright sale of the freehold interest. In the case of a residential development there are many sales, while in that of an office building the property may be disposed of in one major letting.

Although this phase usually comes at the end of the development process, it is of the utmost importance that the selling strategy forms part of the original project evaluation and that the agent responsible for selling, whether he be a member of the developer's staff or an outside agent, is included from the start as a part of the development team.

Once the development is let, the developer has to decide

whether or not he wishes to hold the investment or sell it. He may, of course, have already made this decision and arranged his finance accordingly; but even if he has not, he should have given careful thought to the investment value of the property and ascertained which investors, be they pension funds, insurance companies or private individuals, would be likely to wish to acquire it. Selling is considered in some detail in Chapter 6, and the methods of obtaining long-term funding in Chapter 7.

1.3 OBJECTIVES

It is very difficult to set down a short list of 'objectives' for development. In simple terms the purpose of development is to provide accommodation for occupation for the person carrying out the development, or for someone else. Beyond this, the objectives vary. As an example, consider the following list. Each can act as a developer, that is, be responsible for promoting development, but each is likely to have quite different objectives:

(a)   An occupier
(b)   A property company
(c)   An investor
(d)   A builder
(e)   A local authority

1.3.1 An occupier

An occupier tries to provide a building best suited to his particular needs. These may be very specialized as, for example, where some highly specialized industrial process is involved. The building that the occupier seeks to provide may have little or no general market value. His prime objective is to provide a building within which he can best carry on his business. Profit is taken indirectly in the benefits derived from occupation, and it may be of no concern that the open-market value of the completed building is less than the total cost of construction. The occupier may be persuaded to compromise and modify his plans to provide a more standard type of building on the basis that such a building has a more established market value and permits greater flexibility in the event of a disposal, or the necessity of raising a loan on the basis of the security of the building. To the extent, however, that he varies his plans, he does not achieve his prime objective.

Many commercial and industrial companies become involved in schemes for development for their own occupation either as extensions to their existing premises, or on entirely new sites. The efficient control of the process of development is as important to them as it is to the property company. Although one of the main factors of risk — the finding of an occupier — is absent, most of the other factors of risk are there — such as, for example, possible variations in cost and in time. Indeed in some ways the risks are greater. An industrialist may decide to expand his accommodation in order to house a new process. The cost of the building may be only a small part of the total cost of the project but a delay of two months in obtaining planning permission may, as a result, delay the new production line and lead to loss of orders and missed opportunities. It is, therefore, important that occupiers carrying out their own development should:

(a) Have a thorough understanding of the time taken in arranging for and carrying out projects of development.
(b) Have a thorough understanding of the sequence of events in the development process and the way in which these events have to be co-ordinated.
(c) Be aware of the possible variations in building costs and of the methods used to control development expenditure.

1.3.2 A property company

The prime objective of a property company, whether it is a small, local one-man-band or a multinational, is to make a direct financial profit from the process of development. In this the company is no different from any other company making a product for sale. The property company brings together raw materials and processes them into a product to be sold in the marketplace. The process is often long. It is invariably carried out on a specific location. Production is normally based upon an external labour force, the 'in-house' staff being kept as small as possible. The customer may be known beforehand, as when a building is prelet, or entirely unknown.

The company normally produces and sells direct to the customer without a 'middle-man'.

Within the overall objective of profit, however, the aims of property companies vary. Some specialize in terms of location, such as the local company developing in and around a particular town and restricting itself to the area it knows well, or a large company deciding to concentrate on a regional area, say, Scotland or the South East of England. Some companies specialize in a certain type of property. Some, for example, concentrate on industrial development and others on offices or houses. Some specialize in a particular kind of development process such as altering or improving existing buildings, known as 'refurbishment'. Specialization enables the companies to acquire above-average knowledge and experience of a particular market, often enabling them to succeed where others would fail.

On the other hand, some companies deliberately avoid specialization, trying to spread their risks, either geographically or in terms of the type of property that they handle. They try to achieve a balance within their development programme between, for example, offices, factories, warehouses and shops or between one town or region and another. They may, perhaps, decide to cover both residential and commercial development.

Financial objectives also vary. Some companies seek to sell each project as and when it is completed, making an immediate capital profit. Others try to retain an interest in the property and look for a stream of income related to holding costs that enables them to enjoy future growth in rental income. There is no golden rule. It is, however, important that each company formulates objectives, adopts a policy and does not dart from one course to another on the basis that the grass always looks greener on the other side of the fence.

1.3.3 An investor

As with a property company the prime objective of an investor is direct financial gain. Investors, however, tend to take a longer view and are more concerned with the flow of income over an extended period of time. When they become involved in development itself, they do so as a means of producing an asset with an income stream which gives them an adequate return on capital invested and an opportunity to see that income and capital grow. In order to be persuaded to take on the risks associated with development, rather than acquiring a property when it is completed and let, they need a higher return. They can, however, afford to accept a lower immediate return than a property company.

The policies of investment companies differ. However, they all tend to seek a balanced portfolio of uses, rather than specializing in one particular use. Most companies also try to spread their investments geographically, although some, particularly the smaller locally based investors, concentrate on the area that they know and can manage best.

Investors tend to be cautious and dislike unconventional buildings and uses, and indeed unconventional lease terms. They generally avoid properties which involve substantial management and often prefer, for instance in the case of offices, a building let to a single tenant.

1.3.4 A builder

Unlike a property company which promotes a development and arranges for its construction by employing a building contractor, a builder can extend his contracting role and take on the additional risk of development, buying the land, arranging the finance and organizing sales or lettings. When a builder acts merely as a contractor, he takes a profit related to building cost and time. If he also undertakes the promotion of the development and the risk that is associated with it, he requires a larger return, but even so he can afford, by combining the building and development profit, to accept a lower overall profit.

Although the prime objective is direct financial gain, there are other objectives as well. The builder who retains a substantial labour force, skilled or otherwise, wishes to see continuing employment of that labour force and this may be an important objective in times when the general demand for building work is slack. In order to achieve this objective a building company, in periods of slump, may substantially cut its tendering rates and therefore its profits.

1.3.5 A local authority

There has been a considerable increase in the involvement of public authorities with property development during the nineteenth and twentieth centuries. However, until recently most public authority activity has been directly related to and ancillary to their statutory public duties as, for example, housing authority, highway authority, or the like. It is only in recent years that there has been a considerable increase in the activities of public authorities in property development as a self-contained enterprise.

The basic characteristics of the property market and the economic principles underlying the operation of the market apply both to public authority and private enterprise activities. However, there are ways in which the objectives of local authorities differ from those of the private developer. Quite apart from the political considerations there are certainly two matters which are peculiar to local authorities: (i) public accountability, and (ii) the need to have regard to the overall needs of the community and the effect upon it of development proposals.

Public accountability often influences the methods of operation, although not necessarily the ultimate results. It is essential for a local authority to be able to demonstrate that all its dealings are free from suspicion of intrigue or corruption, that all with whom it does business are treated with equal fairness and that the local authority in its capacity as custodian of the public purse has exercised prudent financial and aesthetic judgement. These are all matters in respect of which criticism is frequently levied, sometimes to the point of ill-feeling.

Public accountability often involves some element of public participation. Local authorities should take a comprehensive view of the effect of development on the community. A proposed development may affect the character of a whole residential neighbourhood. A shopping development may affect the balance of the town's shopping pattern. It may be highly desirable to attract a certain type of employment.

Early public consultation can often save a good deal of delay and frustration at a later and more critical stage.

The philosophical objectives underlying the actions of a local authority are the improvement of the environment and the quality of life of the community within the framework of the available resources. The practical objectives of the local authority are largely determined by its policy with regard to the future size and character of the community for which it is responsible. The objectives of an authority which has a vigorous growth policy, anxious to expand the population and attract new employment, are very different from those of an authority whose policy is to preserve the existing character and scale of the community. An authority might have differing policies in different parts of its area. Ideally objectives should be clearly set out in the structure and local planning policy documents although in practice such documents are not always available in a final form and some of the economic assumptions on which they have been based will often be found no longer valid. However, the objectives should be essentially concentrated on ensuring the availability of an adequate supply of accommodation of all types to meet the reasonable demands expected to arise within the foreseeable future.

When preparing the planning framework for future development the local authority is usually faced with a number of alternatives which make differing demands on local and national resources and confer varying benefits on the whole community and different groups within the community. How is the choice to be made?

The physical costs of development can be estimated with reasonable accuracy. It is common practice to provide estimates of the total overall cost of new town development proposals or major town expansion schemes. Such estimates are given in considerable detail, showing for example the cost of land acquisition and the cost of the different physical components of the plan, such as roads, housing, industry, open space, education and so on. The total overall development costs will broadly indicate the division between public and private expenditure and the development cost per head of population provides a simple and effective cost comparison.

But the total capital cost of the physical development is

only part of the financial story. The 'cost in use' is of equal importance. Alternative road networks will differ both in capital cost and in the travelling cost imposed upon the road users. When considering the number, distribution and capital cost of new schools, the travelling costs of pupils should be taken into account. Similar considerations apply to many other facets of the development. Estimates of cost in use, by their very nature, depend upon a number of assumptions about the behaviour of the users. The costs incurred by road users depend upon the number of people travelling between different origins and destinations, their mode of transport and value judgments concerning the cost of travelling time for different types of user. When simply comparing one road network with another, common assumptions enable effective comparisons to be made. It is when the total cost in use of a road network is included in a total assessment of the cost in use of a particular development proposal that differing value judgments relating to the various facets might produce a distorted picture.

Comparisons must also be made between the aesthetic and the social development aspects of alternative development proposals. These are matters which cannot be reduced to monetary terms and attempts to make comparisons quantified on a financial basis are likely to prove highly misleading.

Various techniques have been developed in an attempt to enable an overall assessment of development proposals to be made in a meaningful way and to allow valid comparisons between alternatives. None has yet been evolved which provides an entirely satisfactory method of both assessing cost in use and quantifying aesthetic and social benefits.

Cost benefit analysis seeks to provide an overall evaluation of development proposals in financial terms. The best-known example is probably that used in the Roskill Report on the proposals for a third London airport. The limitations of the cost benefit technique, particularly with regard to aesthetic and social value judgments, were widely debated at the time the report was published. The closely related technique of preparing a planning balance sheet recognizes that certain costs and benefits cannot be reduced to monetary terms and that it is impossible to quantify others in a positive way. In the planning balance sheet mathematical techniques are used to compare the relative advantages and disadvantages to different sections of the community of various aspects of alternative development proposals. An overall assessment of the costs and benefits of each development proposal is then produced in relative terms.

The techniques of cost benefit analysis and the preparation of planning balance sheets are usually associated with large-scale planning proposals. But the same basic principles apply to the consideration of development proposals on a much smaller scale. For example one could use these techniques to analyse alternative proposals for the provision of new shopping accommodation when considering whether it is better to enlarge a town centre or to provide district shopping centres in the suburbs. The extent to which the various costs and benefits are to be included in the analysis must be defined with great care. Some will be directly relevant and immediately apparent, such as building costs and land values and infrastructure costs, whereas others will be too 'remote' for inclusion in the analysis, such as the possible financial gain to the shopping public from lower prices attributable to the likelihood of greater competition created by one pattern of shopping development as compared with another.

The use of sophisticated techniques to make an overall evaluation of development proposals should not be allowed to obscure the practical difficulty of assessing many aspects of cost in use and of making aesthetic and social value judgments. An assessment of the total physical costs of development proposals, coupled with a written statement setting out in simple commonsense terms the extent to which the proposals meet the objectives of the local authority, is perhaps the best way of presenting analyses of development proposals and making comparisons between alternatives, bearing in mind that the members of a local authority have to make a democratic decision on behalf of all the people in the community.

This list of five different types of developers is not intended to be exclusive but merely to illustrate the fact that objectives vary, depending upon who takes on the role of the developer. It should also be understood that identities can overlap. We have already described how an investor can take on the role of a developer. Equally a property company may take on the role of investor and seek to combine within its portfolio profits from development and the creation and holding of property investments. An owner occupier may combine the role of the developer with that of occupier and, indeed, with that of the investor. The man building his own house may not see himself as a developer but, in essence, he is, for a developer is one who promotes the development process providing buildings for his own or another's occupation and for investment or sale.

1.4 RISK

Because property development is by its nature uncertain, it involves an element of risk. In this it is similar to many other business ventures. During the property boom of 1971–3, however, many serious-minded people began to discount this factor almost entirely. It seemed that each enterprise was bound to succeed, that rents would always be higher than expected, that capital values could be relied upon to increase as more and more institutions entered the property market. Caution was regarded as old fashioned and optimism was the order of the day. But in late 1973 and early 1974 this optimism proved to be false. Interest rates rose, prices fell, properties took longer to let or did not let at all, building costs were exceeded and estimated profits became actual losses. Suddenly the element of risk became a reality and a generation of developers, institutions and professional advisers learnt the hard but important lesson that the prudent developer should never underrate the element of risk. In each project he should try to identify it and contain it.

Conventional methods of evaluation tend to belie the true uncertainty that is an inherent part of the property development process. In the last five or so years some attempts have been made to develop better methods and one example is given in Section 2.3 below.

1.4.1 Time and place

It may be simplistic but nevertheless true to say that a development must be carried out at the right place and at the right time. Indeed it has been said that there are only three rules for successful development — location, location and location. This adage draws attention to the fixed nature of development and to the care that must be taken in deciding in which part of the country, in which town, in which street or in which part of a street to develop. Certain types of use are more dependent upon their precise location than others. A shop may be out of position by being twenty yards away from a particular part of the street or by being separated from the best retail area by a cinema. On the other hand, a warehouse may be well located, provided it is within a mile or two of a particular motorway junction. Two houses on the same estate may be very comparable in value, but the same house in a different part of the same town may have a quite different value.

However, despite the adage, it is not enough to select only the correct location. It is also necessary to ensure that the development is produced at a time when there is a demand for it. As the process of development itself takes several months, or even years, this inevitably means forecasting demand. It also means that any delays that occur are crucial. Time lost in acquiring a site, in obtaining planning permission or in coping with an unforeseen constructional problem may delay the project to such an extent that by the time that it is ready for occupation the market has changed adversely. Again this is more important for some types of development than for others. The completion date of an estate of warehouses, for example, may be less significant than the completion date for a shopping centre, which may be timed to coincide with a particularly active trading month. But all markets can change and the control of the timing of development is always important.

1.4.2 Preproject evaluation

We have already referred to four phases of development (Section 1.2) and the way in which, at each phase, the developer's commitment increases and the possibility of variation decreases. Once the land is purchased, the developer is committed to a particular location and, to a large degree, to a particular type of development. Once the planning permission has been given, the nature of the development is further restricted. Once the building contract is signed, the developer is committed to a development cost that, if it varies at all, is likely only to increase. It is, therefore, essential that the project is thoroughly evaluated and prepared before these commitments are made and while there is a possibility of changing course, of reducing cost or even abandoning one location in favour of another. Such an exercise takes time and has to be paid for, but expenditure incurred at this early stage may save much more expenditure later on. This is not to say that the preproject evaluation should be pursued in a leisurely or ponderous fashion — to do so might well mean missing valuable opportunities — but the evaluation should be thorough and should be approached from the point of view of 'what is wrong', rather than by trying to justify a course of action which at first seems attractive. The characteristics of the evaluation are described in Chapter 2 and referred to again in Chapter 8.

1.4.3 Project control

Throughout this book (and particularly in Chapters 5 and 8), we refer to the importance of project control — the tireless attention to detail is necessary to produce a successful development. Given able advisers and a determination to scrutinize and question every aspect of a project, a developer can identify and substantially contain the risk that he takes. For example, if he thoroughly tests the market, his estimates of rent and price will be sound. If he thoroughly investigates the building cost, negotiates the building contract with care and adequately monitors the project, he will be able to control and contain the cost and will not be embarrassed by sudden and unexpected increases.

1.4.4 Agreement prior to commitment

The principal parts of the financial evaluation of development are as follows:

(a)   Land cost
(b)   Building cost
(c)   Rent/price levels

(d)   Length of the development/selling period
(e)   Short- and long-term finance

Each of these is unknown when the developer first considers a project. Indeed some may remain unknown until the project is completed. The extent to which they are uncertain fundamentally affects the degree of risk undertaken by the developer. If he can determine any of them before committing himself to the land and building cost, he can substantially reduce his burden of risk.

(a) *Land cost*

The purchase price of the land is the first main financial commitment. Ideally the land should not be purchased until the appropriate planning permission has been obtained and the detailed building cost established. If this is not possible, the developer should try to negotiate and sign a contract that is subject to his obtaining an appropriate planning permission. Normally such a contract specifies a time by which the permission must be obtained. Where the extent of the planning permission is uncertain, it may be necessary to agree that the price of the land be calculated by reference to a formula related to the eventual planning permission.

Sometimes it is possible to purchase an option to acquire the land at an agreed price by a future date. During the intervening period the developer can then try to obtain a planning permission and establish the building cost and level of rent or price.

A further method of reducing the risk related to land cost is to enter into a joint venture with the landowner, whereby his share of the eventual profit is related to an agreed value for the land plus notional interest on that 'cost' during the period of development. The developer thereby reduces his commitment to the project and, in return, shares the profit with the landowner. Great care must be taken with such agreements to make sure that the clauses that describe the control of the development and the method of sharing any profit are clearly worded and quite unambiguous.

(b) *Building cost*

Building cost is the second main financial commitment and

there are a number of ways in which it can be made more certain. These are described in Chapter 5. It is only by careful selection of the contractor, negotiation of the contract and the tightest project control that unwarranted increases in building costs can be prevented.

(c) *Rent/price levels*

Any temptation to overestimate future levels of rent or price should be firmly resisted. During the boom period of 1971—3 there was an increasing tendency to evaluate development projects on the basis of 'today's costs and tomorrow's rents'. The danger of such an approach is obvious, particularly at a time when inflation is likely to have its impact upon costs more directly than upon rents and prices. Estimates of rents and prices must be as realistic as possible and based upon a thorough analysis of present and future market trends. In some cases where there is very little evidence of market conditions, a full market-research exercise needs to be carried out.

In recent years, several attempts have been made to improve the information base in both residential and commercial/ property markets. These include regular surveys and indices of performance including information on house prices prepared by the Abbey National and the Nationwide Building Societies and information on rents and yields provided by the larger firms of estate agents such as Hillier Parker and Jones Lang Wooton who produce indices of rents and Healey and Baker who produce a yield graph. A more recent series is a regular survey of national office and industrial rents and market conditions published jointly by Property Market Analysis and Property Agents International.

(d) *The length of the development/selling period*

Once again, in evaluating a project, the developer should not allow himself to be over optimistic on the time that it will take to build and let or sell the development. He should, of course, take the advice of his advisers but he must question them closely to ensure that he is quite satisfied with that advice. The estimation of the length of the building period is comparatively straightforward but the length of the letting/selling period has to be based on opinion and past experience, and is much more difficult to determine. The length of time that it takes to agree terms and sign a lease or contract should never be underestimated.

The element of risk related to finding an occupier can be reduced or entirely removed by preletting or preselling the development in part or in whole. A house can sometimes be sold 'off the plan' or perhaps, where several similar houses are being built, by reference to a single show-house. It is sometimes possible to secure the occupier of an office building before building starts. Similarly it may be possible to prelet an industrial building, although the smaller warehouse and industrial units are often difficult to prelet, occupiers being reluctant to commit themselves to new accommodation until it is virtually complete. Some shopping schemes are based upon two or three main prelettings to major tenants one of which will often be a supermarket operator. But it is unusual for all the shops to be let prior to the start of the project, and indeed while to do so would reduce risk, most developers would argue that it would not produce the highest rent-roll.

While preletting or preselling a development adds to security and reduces risk, in a rising market it restricts the level of profit that can be achieved. Because of the time that it takes to build, the rents or prices that are negotiated prior to the development starting are likely to be below the levels prevailing at the time that the building is completed. Care must, therefore, be taken to ensure that a commitment is not given to rent or price until the building costs have been carefully determined and agreed.

Where a preletting has been agreed, it is necessary to define the time from which the rent will run and to ensure that this is clear and unambiguous. In most cases the occupier will require a period for his own fitting-out work. This period should be agreed as part of the preletting negotiations and the date of the start of the occupational rent should be fixed by reference to the date of the architects' certificate of practical completion (if necessary, for the relevant part of the building).

(e) *Short- and long-term finance*

Unless a project is being built entirely with the developer's own funds — unlikely except in the smallest projects —

arrangements to borrow money have to be made before the project can start. This may involve arranging a complete package of short- and long-term finance or it may mean only securing short-term finance to acquire the land and build, the long-term finance being left until the project is further advanced. As with a preletting, the long-term finance terms negotiated prior to a project starting are likely to be less favourable to the developer than those than can be negotiated at the end of the project, when most, if not all, of the uncertainties have been removed. In some cases it may not be possible to obtain short- or long-term finance until the building contract has been agreed and the tenants' secured. The availability of long-term finance and the yield required by investors are crucial factors affecting the profitability of development.

In deciding how much to reduce the element of risk, a balance has to be found between reward and security. Generally speaking, the reward that the developer can obtain reduces with greater security, but in uncertain economic times, it is a brave man or a fool who does not forego some of the possible reward for some element of security. This is particularly so where the developer's prime objective is not the taking of development risks as such. An occupier, a contractor/ developer, an investor/developer or a local authority each have a different prime objective and where they act as the developer the balance should swing firmly towards security and away from risk.

The extent to which a local authority wishes to accept the risk of carrying out speculative development as against development for their own use or public-sector housing, is a matter of policy to be decided by each authority. Before accepting that risk, however, it is prudent to ask at least the following questions:

(a) Is there a shortage of a particular type of accommodation?
(b) Is the private sector responding to that shortage by providing accommodation on terms acceptable to occupiers?
(c) Is the provision of such accommodation on acceptable terms viable?

(d)   What is the degree of risk involved?
(e)   Are the necessary resources available in terms of manpower and finance?

The degree of risk is usually directly related to the complexity and scale of the proposed development. At one extreme the acquisition of a small parcel of fully serviced residential land and its resale for private-sector development only involves a very limited degree of risk. At the other extreme a substantial degree of risk is involved in the assembly, over a period of time, of a large town-centre site and its development, requiring extensive infrastructure provision and the construction of a large amount of shop, office and other commercial buildings. At present, many authorities are reluctant to engage in speculative private-sector development and prefer to restrict their activities to ensuring an adequate supply of land. Thereafter they either rely upon the private sector to carry out the development, or enter into some form of development partnership — thereby reducing the burden of risk while at the same time enjoying substantial control over the development, some interest in its profit and probably a guaranteed return on the site-assembly cost.

1.5 GOVERNMENT ACTION

Property development is highly sensitive to the effects of government action. The building industry is often used by government as an economic regulator. Property is a major tax base for both central and local government. Various aspects of the occupation and ownership of property are the subject matter of political controversy. A wise property developer has regard to government policies and attitudes and endeavours to evaluate their possible impact.

Individual government actions must be viewed in their context as part of the whole policy framework. Rarely is any action entirely self-contained and unrelated to other matters. The government may intervene directly in development activity by such measures as the creation of New Town Development Corporations or Special Development Agencies.

The Location of Offices Bureau was established to actively encourage office occupiers to move out of London and during the period of its existence achieved considerable success. Recently under the Local Government Planning and Land Act 1980 Urban Development Corporations have been set up to promote the re-development of the docklands at London and Liverpool and if these are successful it is no doubt possible that others might be set up to deal with intractable inner area problems elsewhere. The development activities of nationalized industries and statutory undertakers and local authorities are subject to government control or influence. But property developers will be to a greater extent affected by fiscal measures, population and planning policies, and general and politically motivated legislation.

Fiscal measures depend not only on general government policy objectives, but also on the state of the national economy. A vigorous expanding economy provides increasing resources and thus growing scope for government action. The government decides what proportion of the total national income must be appropriated to public expenditure and how total public expenditure is allocated between competing demands; it ensures that expenditure remains under control, often by the imposition of strict cash limits. The total amount of public money available for the provision of infrastructure has an important impact on development, as explained in Chapter 7. At the end of 1976 the need to reduce public expenditure led to the issuing of guidelines to local authorities concerning land acquisitions and disposals under the Community Land Act, which placed severe constraints on local-authority activities.

Grants and subsidies of various kinds influence the demand for property both directly and indirectly. Government grants led to an increase in the construction of new hotels at the end of the 1960s. Housing improvement grants and grants in aid of local authority expenditure incurred within housing improvement areas are material considerations affecting the decision whether to improve or demolish and redevelop. In 1982 there has been some re-shaping of the derelict land reclamation programme so as to provide for government grants of up to 100% towards the cost of reclamation and infrastructure carried out by local authorities in pursuance of an agreement for the sale of land for private developments in circumstances where the development value is insufficient to cover the infrastructure cost. Other types of grant and subsidy have an indirect effect. The extent to which public transport is subsidized might affect the demand for property in different locations. The rapidly increasing cost of daily commuting into London is leading many large employers of office workers to worry about their ability to attract people to work in the centre of London and to consider the advisability of decentralizing the whole or part of their office organization. Substantial reductions in rail subsidies might lead to increased office decentralization, thus reducing the demand for offices in the centre of London and increasing the demand in provincial towns. Reductions in subsidies are, in many areas, leading to the severe curtailment of rural bus services, coupled with sharp increases in fares. In the long term this tends to increase the demand for housing in towns at the expense of the more remote country areas, particularly at the cheaper end of the housing market.

Industrial expansion and investment is encouraged in various ways. Grants are given towards the cost of modernizing specific industries including the cost of new buildings. Grants may offset the cost of bringing forward industrial investment earlier than would normally be required, in order to take advantage of slack conditions and surplus capital manufacturing capacity. Buildings erected for manufacturing operations qualify for substantial investment allowances for tax purposes. Measures such as these clearly enhance the demand for industrial buildings and sites.

Discriminatory taxation might be used to influence employment in particular sectors of the economy. For example, Selective Employment Tax was intended to discourage the expansion of employment in the service industries in the hope that this would result in more employment in the manufacturing industries.

The size and demographic characteristics of the population exert an influence on the property market. A stable and ageing population requires different housing and leisure facilities than a vigorous expanding young population. The extent to which government population policy can alter the birth rate is a matter of speculation but it is as well to study changes in population policy.

General planning and population distribution policies have a significant impact. Regional development policy is implemented in many ways. For many years the distribution of new industrial development was controlled by the Industrial Development Certificate system. Substantial financial incentives are offered in respect of new developments which will create employment in the 'special development areas', 'development areas' and 'intermediate areas'. For some years office development in Greater London and a limited number of other areas was subject to direct government control under the Office Development Permit system. The restriction of new office development in London in the 1960s led to a sharp increase in the value of existing office premises and to an increase in demand for offices in convenient provincial towns. The abolition of Industrial Development Certificates and Office Development Permits leaves the control of industrial and office development subject to the normal planning process.

Priorities in the allocation of public expenditure take account of regional development policy. The building of new motorways and the provision of other transportation facilities can help to open up a region for development. Increased public expenditure on social amenities and adjustments to the Rate Support Grant help to encourage development. Recent changes in government policy will encourage redevelopment of the inner cities and reduce the volume of development in new and expanding towns.

General legislation relating to the construction and occupation of buildings often exerts an important influence on development decisions. The stringent application of Building Regulations, particularly those concerned with the adequacy of access and fire precautions, might so increase the building cost as to result in a proposed new building becoming quite uneconomic. Similarly, the cost of converting old buildings to different uses is often prohibitive. It has been suggested that the requirements of the Health and Safety at Work legislation have given additional impetus to the closure of small businesses in the inner city areas. Antipollution legislation improves the environment and also places restraints on certain types of development.

The business rents freeze and the subsequent proposals for a swingeing tax on development gains in 1973 undoubtedly hastened the collapse of the speculative development market. Many developers argued that the provisions of the Community Land Act and the high level of development land tax inhibited confidence in property development. No tax is ever popular, but following the repeal of the Community Land Act and with the passage of time which leads to increasing familiarity, there are signs in 1982 that developers are becoming reconciled — or maybe resigned — to development land tax. No doubt the reduction in the rate of tax to 60%, together with certain other concessions has helped to gain a measure of acceptance.

The designation of Enterprise Zones under the powers in the Local Government Planning and Land Act 1980 is an imaginative and innovative attempt to stimulate industrial and commercial activity to bring about the renewal of worn out urban areas. The incentives include a relaxation of planning control so that most developments within the Enterprise Zone will not need individual planning permission, exemption from rates on industrial and commercial property, exemption from development land tax and 100% capital allowances for corporation and income tax purposes. Enterprise Zones are designated for certain periods of time, although the time may be extended by order made by the Secretary of State. Generally the Enterprise Zones have been welcomed as a bold experiment which might succeed in re-invigorating areas where so many other courses of action have failed. Some fears have been expressed that the designation of the Zones will not create any new activity but merely attract industry and commerce from adjoining areas so that ultimately prosperous Enterprise Zones might be encircled by depressed areas from which industry and commerce has been sucked into the designated zone. Cynics argue that the main beneficiaries will be the landowners within the Zones. (If this proves to be true landowners in the areas immediately outside might suffer.) The government is monitoring the effect of the Enterprise Zones. Time will tell.

The private housing market depends on the availability

and cost of mortgage finance. The net cost of finance depends upon the extent of tax reliefs. Substantial changes are reflected in market demand, with consequent repercussions on the house-building industry and the residential land market. The private market is also affected by the availability of public authority rented accommodation and the extent to which it is subsidized.

Local authorities are becoming increasingly active in encouraging economic growth. Many carry out or promote industrial and commercial development. Planning and housing policies reflect the needs of industry and commerce. Various statutory powers — perhaps the most important being Section 137 of the Local Government Act 1972 — enable local authorities to give limited financial assistance to industry in their areas. Some authorities are establishing Enterprise Agencies which although benefitting from local authority support are separate corporate bodies not subject to the same tight government control.

The European Economic Community is likely to become of increasing importance. All public authorities and property developers should acquaint themselves with the Community's policies with regard to regional and industrial development and the assistance which the Community is prepared to give to further their implementation.

It must be remembered that the strength of normal market forces may wholly or partially counter the effects of government action.

CHAPTER 2

Evaluation

2.1 INTRODUCTION

Although rigid thinking is always dangerous, both public- and private-sector developers should formulate policies to direct their activities. In the public sector the policy is often restricted by a particular geographical area — the boundary of an authority. In the private sector there is more choice. The developer may decide to concentrate on some particular type of property use such as industrial or residential, or on some particular location such as the Midlands or the South East of England. He may prefer a mixed-development portfolio and seek a balance between different types of property use, location, tenure, and so on.

The ability to formulate a policy, however, requires a proper understanding of the economic, fiscal and social trends at national, regional and local level — and an understanding of their effect on price levels. No development should be undertaken without a proper analysis of the market for which the buildings are constructed. This may seem so obvious that it is hardly worth stating but historically too little effort and expenditure has been spent on such analysis and too many projects have been undertaken entirely on 'hunches', or on the basis that someone else has carried out a similar project successfully elsewhere. All too often development projects have been undertaken on the basis of a superficial knowledge of the market and, while in some cases a general rise in the level of rents has 'saved' a development, it cannot be assumed that rents will always rise more rapidly than costs. Developers should be wary of relying too greatly on their own or someone else's past experience and ensure that they are always aware of the present demand pattern for the product that they are producing.

But a general understanding of the market is not enough. In order to make a proper evaluation, a developer must also have an understanding of the essentially practical aspects of construction, such as building costs, time scale, building contracts, and so on. He must also be thoroughly informed of the availability of development finance, both short and long term, the rates of interest that are charged and the terms that are likely to be imposed.

The developer must know the professional skills he will need to employ to carry through the development. He must decide whether he wishes to provide these skills from within his own staff or to hire them. The skills that he needs vary with the particular project but, bearing in mind that throughout the project he has to rely heavily upon the guidance of professional advisers, it is of the utmost importance that he selects a team which he can trust and which will work together successfully (see Chapter 8).

Traditionally the development team has comprised an architect, a quantity surveyor and an estate agent. If, however, greater thought is to be given to the precommitment, policy-forming phase of development — the phase that we call 'evaluation' — other skills may be needed, particularly those of the land economist, the architect/planner and the valuer. Evaluation can be divided into two parts: market research, and financial evaluation.

2.2 MARKET RESEARCH

Market research is carried out to establish the nature of the property market at a particular time. In most cases it is directed at a particular type of development and a particular location, in order to establish whether or not a demand exists and whether or not that demand is being matched by an existing or proposed supply of accommodation.

It is especially important where:

(a) The developer is proposing to undertake a development of which he has little or no previous experience.
(b) The developer is proposing to undertake a development that will take place over several years.

(c)   Market conditions are particularly uncertain.
(d)   The developer is entering into a specialized market for which there is little existing evidence.

Market research is concerned, first, with general factors that affect the property market as a whole, and second, with factors related to the particular type of development or location with which the client is concerned.

2.2.1 General factors

First, consideration must be given to the characteristics of the economy at national and regional level and to whether the economy as a whole or within the particular region is expanding or declining. Some thought should also be given to the general level of interest rates, the availability of money and the prospects of inflation.

Given the general state of the national economy, the characteristics of the region can be considered in more detail. It is almost certain that its characteristics will not coincide entirely with the national characteristics. It will have its own physical characteristics, such as road layout, ports, airports, railway network and the availability of labour and raw materials. It may have a population which is growing at a time when the national population is declining and may be affected by government restrictions or incentives. Since the war, there has been a long-standing attempt to persuade industry to relocate in Development Areas and move out of the South East. More recently the government has adopted a policy of persuading commerce and industry to return to the inner-city areas.

Having established the characteristics of the region, the research must have regard to the characteristics of the particular town or district within which the development is planned. Regard must be had to the structure of the local economy, the state of employment, population, the availability of schools, the local preferences for one location as against another, the state of the supply of competitive accommodation and the attitude of the local authority and other government bodies to the kind of development that is proposed. It is not until this general background has been established that the more detailed work related to the particular type of development or particular locations can properly be carried out.

2.2.2 Factors related to a particular type of property or particular location

In most cases market research is concerned with a particular type of property, for example, houses or offices. Once the developer has decided on the general area in which he wishes to work, the research has to establish, in more detail, the particular characteristics of the market for that kind of property in that location.

The research that is done depends on the type of property involved. If it is housing, it includes discussions with local estate agents and building society managers and the questioning of occupiers of other houses in the area, trying to establish the characteristics that they find attractive and, perhaps more importantly, the characteristics that they find unattractive. In some cases it may be clear that the development is likely to attract people living outside the area, perhaps in a nearby city. Their attitudes and preferences must be established and, in such cases, the research must ensure that their views are known.

The questioning is normally carried out by specialist staff on a questionnaire or form, and the formulation of the questions and the analysis of the form requires careful thought. A badly phrased question often produces an inaccurate answer. The method of questioning varies but it is sometimes found that a more accurate answer is obtained by asking people what their existing housing lacks, or what they would not like to see in the new development, rather than asking them what they want or particularly like.

Where the client is considering industrial or warehousing development, particular regard must be had to available employment, transport routes, raw materials and, in some cases, the supply of specialized kinds of labour. Occupiers' preference for particular design features must also be considered. These might include sprinkler systems, eaves-heights, insulation, the proportion of offices to production or storage space and the suitability of the building for large articulated vehicles.

So far as shopping is concerned, regard must be had to the catchment area of the proposed development and the competition from other shopping centres and individual shops. Shopping development is one of the most specialized forms of development and before entering into it the particular demands of the retail trade must be thoroughly understood.

Where an office development is proposed, the research has regard to the availability of transport, the supply of labour and the relationship of the proposed site to shopping facilities. Consideration is also given to the extent to which design features such as air conditioning are demanded in the particular area and, in this instance, people from outside the area may need to be questioned. This would certainly be the case where a provincial town is attracting firms relocating from London.

2.2.3 The special needs of a local authority

A local authority has special needs and responsibilities but, when acting as a developer, it too must have a thorough understanding of the market place. Ideally surveys should be made at regular intervals to ascertain the total amount of property on the market. This enables a judgement to be made as to whether there is a shortage or surplus and whether it is increasing or decreasing. Normally there is always a certain amount of empty property of all types and it is desirable that there should be, in order to give the market 'elbow room' to operate. Market price movements are important indicators. The valuers and planners must keep a finger on the pulse of the market and this can only be done satisfactorily by constantly meeting and engaging in discussion with those who are active in the market, such as estate agents, builders, developers, building societies, financial institutions, and the like.

It is important that market research is carried out in a way which produces information that is capable of meaningful analysis. Statistics relating simply to the total amount of factory and warehouse floor space are of very limited value — how much is modern, what proportion is single- and multi-storey, how much of the warehouse space could be used for manufacturing without expensive conversion costs, is there a good selection of different units available. Without such information, it is impossible to make an accurate assessment.

Similarly the results of surveys of the housing market should be broken down at least into price ranges and localities and coupled with information about the total amount of undeveloped residential land for which planning permission exists.

There is no easy or foolproof way of collecting information about the total amount of property on the market nor is it likely that statistics will ever be entirely comprehensive, but provided they are always collected in the same way, relative movements between one time and another should be reliable. Perhaps the simplest statistical base is the total amount of property within the research area (whether vacant or not) in the hands of estate agents and developers — due care being taken to avoid double-counting.

When interpreting the results of local market research, a local authority must also have regard to the general economic background and national property-market trends. If the local property market appears to be moving against the broad national trends, it is important to identify the reason — perhaps one or two large employers have moved in taking up factory space and creating a demand for houses — so as to be sure that the market research is not producing an artificial picture.

The state of the property market at any one time is not an infallible guide to future demand. Experience in recent years has shown how volatile the market can be and how susceptible it is to changes in general economic conditions and interest rates. However, it is a useful indicator when interpreted correctly. Careful market research and skilful interpretation of the results help an authority to match supply to demand and achieve an optimum cash flow when programming land acquisitons and sales and the provision of infrastructure.

2.3 FINANCIAL EVALUATION

2.3.1 The conventional technique

Conventional techniques of evaluation are comparatively straightforward. As might be expected, total costs are compared with total revenue to discover whether the project produces an adequate rate of return, either in terms of a trading profit or in terms of an investment yield. The main variables are:

(a) Land price
(b) Building cost
(c) Rents/prices
(d) Interest rates
(e) Investment yields
(f) Time

The way in which these variables are brought together in an evaluation or development appraisal can best be shown by an example. Let us assume that a developer is considering the development of an acre of land which has planning permission for the development of 20 000 square feet of warehousing; interest rates are at 15%; building costs are £20 per square foot; the estimated rental value of the completed development is £65 000 per annum; and the asking price for the freehold interest in the land is £200 000. A typical conventional evaluation might be as follows:

Land Cost	£	£
Land price	200 000	
Cost of acquisition (i.e. agents and legal fees plus stamp duty) @ 3.5%	7 000	
Total land purchase price	207 000	
Interest on land purchase price from date of purchase to completion and disposal of development, 18 months @ 15%	49 000	
Total land cost		256 000

Building Cost

Estimated building cost
20 000 sq ft
@ £20 per sq ft   400 000

Architect's and
Quantity Surveyor's fees
@ 12½ %   50 000
                                         450 000

Interest over the building
period of 12 months assuming
cost spread evenly over the
period; and for the letting
period of 3 months
@ 15%   50 000

Total building cost   500 000

Letting Cost

Agent's fees @ 15% estimated
rental of £65 000   9 750

Advertising, brochures, etc.   5 250

Total letting cost   15 000

Total Development Cost (TDC)   771 000

Estimated Rental Value (ERV)
20 000 sq ft @ £3.25 per
sq ft p.a.   65 000 pa

Estimated Capital Value (ECV)
(ERV capitalized @ an
investment yield of 7% net,
i.e. allowing for investors'
costs of purchase)   say   900 000

Developer's Profit (DP)	£	£
ECV	900 000	
Less developer's cost of disposal @ 2%	18 000	
	882 000	
Less TDC	771 000	
Developer's Profit on Cost		111 000
DP as a percentage of TDC		14.4%

In this example, the land price is taken as fixed or invariable but in many cases the developer may need to determine the land price that can be afforded in order to enjoy a fixed target rate of profit. If, therefore, in this example, we assume that the developer wishes to ensure a rate of profit of 25% on total development cost, a *residual land evaluation* to determine the affordable land price can be carried out as follows:

	£
Estimated capital value (as above)	900 000
Less developer's costs of disposal @ 2%	18 000
Net ECV	882 000
Less Total Development Cost excluding total land cost, but including 25% profit on cost	643 750
Residue	238 250

This residue is made up of:

Land price =	1.0
Ancillary costs of purchase @ 3.5% =	+ 0.035
	1.035
Cost of interest in holding land for 18 months @ 15% pa	x 1.236
Total land cost =	1.279
Profit on total land cost @ target rate of 25% =	x 1.25
	1.599

The residual land value, that is the price that the developer can afford to pay to ensure the target rate of profit, is, therefore, arrived at as follows:

	£
Residue	238 250
Divided by factor to take account of land price, cost of purchase, interest and profit	1.599
Residual land value	148 999
say	150 000

This calculation can be checked as follows:

Land price	150 000
Cost of purchase @ 3.5%	7 500
Total land purchase price	157 500

		£
Interest for 18 months @ 15%	37 200	
Total land cost		194 700
Total building and letting cost (as above)		515 000
Total development cost		709 700
Net estimated capital value (as above)		882 000
Developer's profit		172 300
Developer's profit on cost		24.3%

Given the 'rounding' errors in the calculation, this result confirms that at a land price of £150 000 the target level of profit of 25.0% can reasonably be expected to be achieved.

Although this method or some simple variation of it is the one most used in practice, it has two basic weaknesses. First, it is inflexible in its handling of the timing of expenditure and revenue. Secondly, by relying on single-figure 'best estimates' it hides the true uncertainty that lies behind the calculation.

2.3.2 Cash flow method

The first of these problems can be overcome by adopting a method of appraisal known as the cash flow method.* This method enables the flow of expenditure and revenue to be spread over time thereby presenting a more realistic and accurate assessment of development costs and income. Thus the typical conventional evaluation described above can be presented as a cash flow appraisal as shown on pages 42—43.

Whilst this form of appraisal gives a clearer insight into the structure of the evaluation its real advantage only becomes apparent when an attempt is made to allocate expenditure

---

*see Baum and Mackmin, *The Income Approach to Valuation*, 2nd Edn, Chapter 18.

and revenue more accurately over time. The conventional method described on pages 36—38 above does not do this. For example, the building cost is normally treated as being spread evenly over the building period whereas in practice this is seldom so. The cash-flow method enables us to allow for an irregular pattern of cost giving a more explicit presentation of the flow of expenditure and a more accurate assessment of the cost of interest. Thus, we can take our basic example and assume the following flow of building cost:

Months	4	5	6	7	8	9
% Total costs	3.80	4.70	5.80	6.90	8.60	10.30

Months	10	11	12	13	14	15
% Total costs	12.70	13.50	11.90	8.50	6.80	6.50

The revised appraisal can now be carried out and presented as shown on pages 44—45.

The outcome of this revised appraisal is an increase in developer's profit which is a result of the fact that the appraisal now reflects a spread of expenditure which is lower than average in the early months, thereby reducing the burden of interest overall. The revision has also now taken account of the standard contractual practice of some 5% of the contract sum being retained for three months after the completion of the project whilst the building is checked for defects. The retention sum and period may vary.

2.3.3 Identifying uncertainty

Although the cash flow method provides a more accurate and explicit form of calculation, it still relies upon a set of fixed variables. That is to say the elements that make up the calculation, such as building cost and rent, are presented as selected 'best estimates' without giving a true impression of the range from which they have been selected. If we look more closely at the basic example of a conventional evaluation set out in Section 2.3.1 above, we can see that it is based upon a considerable number of variable factors. To illustrate

Development Appraisal (Cash Flow Approach)*
Phased construction cost instalments

CALCULATION

Months:	0	1	2	3	4	5	6	7	8
Land price	200 000								
Acquisition costs	7 000								
Construction costs					14 440	17 860	22 040	26 220	32 680
Professional fees					1 805	2 233	2 755	3 278	4 085
Agent's fees									
Advertising costs									
Subtotal	207 000	0	0	0	16 245	20 093	24 795	29 498	36 765
Balance b/f		207 000	209 425	211 878	214 360	233 116	255 940	283 733	316 554
Total	207 000	207 000	209 425	211 878	230 605	253 209	280 735	313 230	353 319
Interest		2 425	2 453	2 482	2 511	2 731	2 998	3 324	3 708
Balance c/f	207 000	209 425	211 878	214 360	233 116	255 940	283 733	316 554	357 027

* The subtotals, totals, balances and interest have been rounded by the computer to give an integer.

Months:	9	10	11	12	13	14	15	16	17
Land price									
Acquisition costs									
Construction costs	33 333	33 333	33 333	33 333	33 333	33 333	33 333		
Professional fees	4 167	4 167	4 167	4 167	4 167	4 167	4 167		
Agent's fees									
Advertising costs							5 250		
Subtotal	37 500	37 500	37 500	37 500	37 500	37 500	42 750	0	0
Balance b/f	419 158	461 568	504 475	547 885	591 803	636 236	681 189	731 919	740 493
Total	456 658	499 068	541 975	585 385	629 303	673 736	723 939	731 919	740 493
Interest	4 910	5 407	5 910	6 418	6 933	7 453	7 980	8 574	8 674
Balance c/f	461 568	504 475	547 885	591 803	636 236	681 189	731 919	740 493	749 167

Months:	18	Total
Land price		200 000
Acquisition costs		7 000
Construction costs		400 000
Professional fees		50 000
Agent's fees	9 750	9 750
Advertising costs		5 250
Subtotal	9 750	
Balance b/f	749 167	
Total	758 917	
Interest	8 776	95 693
Balance c/f	767 693	767 693

Total Development Cost	767 693
Rental income	65 000
Developer's yield	8.47%
Capital value	880 458
Developer's profit	112 765
DP as % TODC	14.7%

Development Appraisal (Cash Flow Approach)*
Equal construction cost instalments

CALCULATION

Months:	0	1	2	3	4	5	6	7	8
Land price	200 000								
Acquisition costs	7 000								
Construction costs					33 333	33 333	33 333	33 333	33 333
Professional fees					4 167	4 167	4 167	4 167	4 167
Agent's fees									
Advertising costs									
Subtotal	207 000	0	0	0	37 500	37 500	37 500	37 500	37 500
Balance b/f		207 000	209 425	211 878	214 360	254 371	294 851	335 805	377 239
Total	207 000	207 000	209 425	211 878	251 860	291 871	332 351	373 305	414 739
Interest		2 425	2 453	2 482	2 511	2 980	3 454	3 934	4 419
Balance c/f	207 000	209 425	211 878	214 360	254 371	294 851	335 805	377 239	419 158

* The subtotals, totals, balances and interest have been rounded by the computer to give an integer.

Months:	9	10	11	12	13	14	15	16	17
Land price									
Acquisition costs									
Construction costs	39 140	48 260	51 300	45 220	32 300	25 840	24 700		
Professional fees	4 893	6 033	6 413	5 653	4 038	3 230	3 088		
Agent's fees									
Advertising costs								5 250	
Subtotal	44 033	54 293	57 713	50 873	36 338	29 070	33 038	0	0
Balance b/f	357 027	405 242	464 282	527 433	584 484	627 669	664 092	704 909	713 166
Total	401 060	459 535	521 994	578 306	620 822	656 739	697 129	704 909	713 166
Interest	4 182	4 747	5 439	6 179	6 847	7 353	7 779	8 258	8 354
Balance c/f	405 242	464 282	527 433	584 484	627 669	664 092	704 909	713 166	721 520

Months:	18	Total
Land price		200 000
Acquisition costs		7 000
Construction costs	20 000	400 000
Professional fees	2 500	50 000
Agent's fees	9 750	9 750
Advertising costs		5 250
Subtotal	32 250	
Balance b/f	721 520	
Total	753 770	90 223
Interest	8 452	
Balance c/f	762 223	762 223

Total Development Cost	762 223
Rental Income	65 000
Capital Value	880 458
Developer's Profit	118 235
DP as % TDC	15.5%

this we repeat the example below in an abridged form, numbering the variable factors 1—14.

Land Cost	£	£
Land price	200 000 (1)	
Cost of acquisition @ 3.5%	7 000 (2)	
Total land purchase price	207 000	
Interest on land purchase cost for 18 months (3) @ 15% (4)	49 000	
Total land cost		256 000
Building Cost		
Estimated building cost 20 000 sq ft (5) @ £20 per sq ft (6)	400 000	
Architect's and Quantity Surveyor's fees @ 12½% (7)	50 000	
	450 000	
Interest for 15 months (8) @ 15% (9)	50 000	
Total building cost		500 000
Letting Cost		
Agent's fees @ 15% ERV	9 750 (10)	
Advertising, brochures, etc.	5 250 (11)	
Total letting cost		15 000
Total Development Cost (TDC)		771 000

Estimated Rental Value (ERV)	£
20 000 sq ft @ £3.25 per sq ft pa (12)	65 000 pa

Estimated Capital Value (ECV)
(ERV capitalized at a net
investment yield of 7% (13)   say   900 000

Developer's Profit
(allowing for 2% developer's
disposal costs) (14)   111 000

Developer's Profit on Cost   14.4%

The fourteen variables that have been identified are as follows:

(1)   Land cost
(2)   Ancillary costs of acquisition
(3)   Pre-building contract, building and letting periods
(4)   Short-term rate of interest
(5)   Area of building
(6)   Building cost
(7)   Professional fees related to construction
(8)   Building and letting periods
(9)   Short-term rate of interest
(10) Agent's fees
(11) Advertising costs
(12) Rental value
(13) Investor's yield
(14) Developer's costs of disposal

As we shall see in the next section in most cases these can be reduced to the following four main variable factors:

(i)   Short-term borrowing cost
(ii) Building cost
(iii) Rental value
(iv) Investor's yield

It is the variation of these factors that most affect the outcome of the development. Although this example is based upon a warehouse development it can be applied to most other forms of commercial and industrial development. Whilst it would require some modification for a residential scheme, the underlying principles are universally applicable.

In the end, developers must form their own judgement about the estimates that are made of the variable factors. However, they normally rely to some extent upon the expert advice of the development team, with the architect and quantity surveyor advising on building cost and the estate agent advising on rental value, selling price and likely investor's yield.

In the past, many decisions in the development industry have been based almost entirely upon 'hunch' and entrepreneurial 'feel'. As a general rule, very little effort has been made to analyse markets methodically. However, it may be that as a result of the collapse of the property market in 1973—4, developers, whether they be property companies, occupiers, institutions or local authorities, will in the future adopt a more cautious, thoughtful and 'professional' approach to the development of land. Greater attention needs to be given to pre-project evaluation. We have already referred to this and will refer to it again but it cannot be emphasized too often. The cost of such work and the time that it takes often leads to greater savings of cost and time later on in the project. Furthermore, it is most important to establish the economic viability of the scheme and the particular characteristics of the market place before being committed to the major financial burdens of land and building costs. Only when the evaluation has been prepared and discussed by the development team can a decision be made as to whether or not it is prudent to purchase or lease a particular site and, if so, on what terms and subject to what caveats.

2.3.4 Sensitivity

In the previous section certain variable factors were referred to as being more significant than others. This is to say that in most cases the financial outcome of the development is more sensitive to their variability than to the variability of the other factors. A 10% increase in building costs, for example, is likely to have a more significant impact on profitability than a similar increase on marketing costs. The name given to the procedure for testing the affect of variability is *'sensitivity analysis'*. One or more factors in the evaluation or appraisal can be varied and the effect on viability measured and recorded. The procedure can then be repeated and the different results compared. Before the development of computers such analysis was rather cumbersome and time consuming but now that computers and, in particular, microprocessors, are more commonly available such analysis can be carried out rapidly and with ease. If, for example, we take the cash flow appraisal set out in Section 2.3.2, we can carry out the sensitivity analysis shown in Table 2.1.

Table 2.1 Variation in developer's profit (%)

Variable (original value)	Original value − 10%	Original value + 10%
Land price (£200 000)	+ 27.31	+ 25.57
Interest rate (15%)	+ 10.16	− 9.94
Building costs (£20 per sq ft)	+ 55.04	− 48.37
Rent (£3.25 per sq ft)	− 77.41	+ 79.57
Gross area (20 000 sq ft)	− 28.91	+ 25.30
Professional fees (12.5%)	− 5.77	− 5.70
Investors yield (7%)	+ 88.33	− 72.27
Agent's fees (15%)	+ 0.97	− 1.04
Advertising (£5250)	+ 0.56	− 0.55
Land acquisition costs (3.5%)	+ 10.90	− 0.90
Investor's purchase costs (3.5%)	+ 2.85	− 2.92
Developer's disposal costs (2.0%)	+ 1.60	− 1.70

This analysis shows that the outcome of the appraisal is most sensitive to changes in investment yield, rent and building cost. If, for the purpose of our example, we now assume that a change in investment yield is unlikely within the timescale of the appraisal, we can concentrate upon the affect of possible variations in rent and building cost. Let us suppose that the range of possibilities that the development team think appropriate is a range of rent of £3 to £4 per sq ft per annum and a range of building cost of £18.50 to £25 per sq ft. Remember that, at this stage, we are talking about *possibilities* and not *probabilities* and, therefore, that the range is likely to be rather wide. The following matrix can now be prepared showing the level of developer's profit expressed as a percentage (i.e. rent as a percentage of total development cost).

Building cost (£ per sq ft)	Rent (£ per sq ft pa)					
	3.00	3.15	3.25	3.50	3.75	4.00
18.50	11.09	16.58	20.23	29.34	38.44	47.52
20.00	5.69	10.91	14.39	23.07	31.73	30.37
21.50	0.79	5.77	9.09	17.37	25.64	33.89
23.00	−3.68	1.09	4.26	12.18	20.08	27.98
25.00	−9.05	−4.55	−1.55	5.93	13.40	20.86

The total range of possible outcomes can be seen to be −9.05% to +47.52%.

The next step for the developer is to narrow the focus of attention by concentrating on the most probable outcomes. Let us suppose that as a result of discussion amongst the development team the outer limits of the ranges of rent and building cost are excluded as being possible but unlikely. The developer can now concentrate on a narrower range of outcomes as follows:

Building cost (per sq ft)	Rent (per sq ft pa)		
	3.15	3.25	3.50
18.50	16.58	20.23	29.34
20.00	10.91	14.39	23.07
21.50	5.77	9.09	17.37

Although this represents a substantial focus of probability, the range of possible outcomes still remains wide, a developer's profit that ranges from +5.77% to +29.34%, giving an indication of the real uncertainty that lies behind the appraisal. The developer must now try and weigh up the possible outcomes, assigning either objectively or subjectively, some probability to each estimate of rent and building cost. In the end, the original 'best estimate' of £3.25 per sq ft per annum rent and £20 per sq ft building cost may be selected, but the context of possibility and uncertainty in which it lies should now be better understood. On the other hand an attempt may be made to fix one of the variables. Let us assume, for example, that a preletting is agreed at £3.25 per sq ft per annum. This now narrows the range of likely outcomes to +9.09% to +20.33%. On these figures, a maximum profit of 29.34% has fallen to 20.33%, but, as a trade-off, the minimum level of profit has risen from 5.77% to 9.09% and the degree of uncertainty has been reduced. It is just this kind of trade-off that is made possible by sensitivity analysis and an understanding of probabilities, particularly when it is matched to the use of cash flow appraisals and incorporates the facilities of computer technology.

This is no more than a brief introduction of the idea of sensitivity. A more detailed treatment of this is contained in Peter Byrne and David Cadman *Risk and Uncertainty in Property Development* (to be published 1984, E. & F. N. Spon) and *Valuation and Development Appraisal* (ed Clive Darlow, published 1982 by *Estates Gazette*).

2.4 REHABILITATION AND CONSERVATION

In many cases a developer has to consider open land, a cleared site or a site covered by thoroughly outmoded or derelict buildings. There are, however, occasions when consideration has to be given to the possibility of rehabilitating or 'refurbishing' existing buildings. Sometimes this is because the planning authority has imposed a restriction upon development by listing the building as being of architectural or historic importance. At other times the possibility is considered because it is thought that the value of the existing buildings for refurbishment exceeds that of the land as a site for complete redevelopment. This is not the place to consider the matter in detail but some of the more obvious advantages and disadvantages of rehabilitation as against redevelopment are shown in the following sections.

2.4.1 Residential property

The rehabilitation of existing houses can sometimes enable housing conditions to be improved without disrupting the social cohesion of the area. The post-war policy adopted by some urban local authorities of wholesale demolition and clearance followed, often after considerable delay, by un-sympathetic new houses or tower blocks of flats has now been severely criticized. As a consequence many authorities are considering more schemes of refurbishment on a street by street basis. In the private sector and particularly in certain parts of London such as Islington, Pimlico and Fulham, such a process has taken place where developers and indeed owner-occupiers have refurbished old terraced buildings, thereby extending their economic life. This process can sometimes so alter the character of an area that it disrupts the existing social pattern. When it does so, its critics refer to it as 'gentrification' and complain that, whilst it does much to improve the physical fabric of the area, the existing population are 'expelled' by their inability to outbid the more affluent newcomers.

2.4.2 Offices

Within the commercial and industrial sector office buildings are often the most suitable for refurbishment. Indeed some property companies have specialized almost exclusively in such development. Where a building has outstanding architectural features and is perhaps surrounded by similar buildings, it may be particularly attractive to those occupiers that seek prestigeous accommodation of special character. If no change of use is intended, the developer may avoid the problems of having to obtain a planning permission and may thereby be able to reduce total development time. If the building is partly occupied and the refurbishment does not include substantial structural work, it may be possible to carry out a partial scheme thus avoiding the necessity of 'buying out' the existing tenant.

There can, however, be disadvantages. The layout of the building may be unsuitable for modern use and in particular the relationship of the gross area of the building to the net lettable area may be unfavourable because of unavoidable 'dead space' such as corridors and landings. The total capital commitment may be less than a comparable new building but the nature of the work may require costly specialist craftsmen and there may be quite unforeseen structural problems. It may prove difficult to provide such a building with modern services such as central heating, air conditioning and lifts and future costs of maintenance may be high.

2.4.3 Factories and warehouses

Old industrial and warehouse buildings do not lend themselves readily to refurbishment. Changes in technology and methods of working, to say nothing of the statutory requirements of the Health and Safety at Work legislation, mean that such buildings are often unsuitable. This is not to say that industrial companies do not occupy old buildings — they do — but when they are seeking new accommodation the advantages to be gained from modern buildings normally outweigh the possible savings in rent to be obtained from refurbished premises. The additional costs of heating and lighting, the lack of clear open space, the poor ancillary office accommodation, poor floor loadings, inadequate eaves heights for storage, inadequate space for lorry circulation and access, and high costs of maintenance are just some of the factors that make older buildings unsuitable. Some attention has recently been given, particularly in the inner-city areas, to the possibility of converting older industrial and warehouse buildings to provide cheap accommodation for the small 'one-man-band' company which may be unable to afford a modern building. But as a general rule the cost of accommodation is seldom a major item of industrial costs and modern buildings facilitate efficient production and storage space.

2.4.4 **Shops**

Although shopping habits have changed quite dramatically over the last thirty years and new shopping centres, super-markets and out-of-town stores have been built, many high streets and traditional shopping centres have maintained their basic structure and fabric. However, the shops them-selves have been altered and enlarged, often by the traders. Some areas, such as Carnaby Street in London, have, of course, fundamentally changed their character by altering the facade and interiors within the shell of the old buildings. Shopping as a use is very sensitive to location and provided buildings are well located their economic life can be com-paratively long, albeit subject to fairly frequent alteration, much of which may be quite superficial. Those property companies who have specialized in shopping development have been almost entirely concerned with new buildings. However, existing buildings have been incorporated within new schemes where land has been opened-up at the rear of an established shopping area. In such cases it is often found that the value of the shops as they stand, subject only to some alteration, exceeds their value as the site for com-pletely new buildings. In a number of cases local authorities have insisted upon the retention of an existing facade because of its architectural or historic importance and it has, there-fore, been incorporated into new buildings constructed behind it.

2.4.5 **Yield**

In assessing the economic viability of a commercial or in-dustrial refurbishment scheme, it is most important to consider carefully the yield that is appropriate in calculating the capital value of the completed building. The difference between a new and a well-refurbished office building in a prime location may not be very large but the difference in yield between a modern and a refurbished old industrial building is likely to be considerable. There is no general rule to apply and an investigation must be made in each case.

CHAPTER 3

Making the land available

3.1 INTRODUCTION

The implementation of development plans and individual development projects is impossible without the necessary land. When the market research and other preliminary studies have been made and the evaluation completed, the first practical step in the implementation process will be to make the land available.

It is likely that the development activities of public authorities within the foreseeable future will be concentrated — although not necessarily exclusively so — on making land available, while the activities of private developers will be directed to the acquisition of sites for their own developments. For the purpose of studying this particular aspect of property development, it is thought that the most logical sequence is to examine the land acquisition and disposal activities of public authorities and then the acquisition of sites by developers. This does not imply that this is the order of things in all or even the majority of developments, because large amounts of land are acquired by developers on the open market despite the increasing involvement of public authorities. But there has to be a beginning and an end and this is the chosen sequence.

3.2 PUBLIC AUTHORITY LAND ACQUISITION

3.2.1 What, where and when to buy

What is the purpose for which the land is being acquired? How may the optimum cash flow be achieved? In the majority of cases public authorities involved in the development process will be acquiring land with a view to its subsequent disposal to developers. These factors must always be clearly borne in mind.

Where acquisition takes place against the background of an approved structure or local plan, it will often be found that land-use allocations have been made for some years ahead and the total land allocated to the particular use for which the land is required is more than initially needed. In such cases the choice of which land to buy will be influenced by the availability of existing infrastructure. Not only roads and services, but also the availability of schools and other community facilities and public transport should be taken into account. Other things being equal, land already provided with physical and social infrastructure will be the most economic to develop and normally the first to be developed. Once major infrastructure has to be provided, it will usually be necessary to arrange for the progressive and continuous development of such land in order that there might be some possibility of making the overall development economically viable.

The individual land holdings might also influence the order of acquisition. If one large landowner is prepared to sell by agreement, the acquisition will be more expedient than if the required land is held in small parcels by numerous owners, in which case it would be rare to find them all of one opinion and prepared to sell so that compulsory powers would have to be exercised. Once compulsory powers have to be used, then of course it makes little difference whether or not ownership is fragmented.

Another aspect to be considered is the possibility of being faced with the necessity to acquire a much larger parcel than required, because the part which could otherwise be left in the hands of the owner is not a self-contained, viable unit. If such extra land could be disposed of only at a substantial loss, the cost of development would thus be increased and the overall cash flow worsened. Similarly if large amounts of compensation have to be paid for severance.

The need to provide alternative accommodation could influence the programming of land acquisition. Even in cases where there is no absolute legal requirement, local authorities are reluctant to evict occupiers unless alternative accommodation is available. Dwelling accommodation is not difficult to provide but small businesses often face considerable difficulties not only in finding other accommodation, but also in being able to pay for it. This is particularly so in the case of small retail or manufacturing businesses which for many years have been conducted in old premises, where costs of occupation are low and turnover and profit margins do not cover the cost of occupying new premises at current market values. It is always helpful to allow such occupiers as long as possible to look for their own alternatives even when the acquiring authority is able to make new premises available. Undoubtedly this problem will be to some extent eased by the new attitudes favouring refurbishment and improvement of old urban areas rather than large-scale clearance and comprehensive redevelopment. Many old properties which in the comprehensive redevelopment era would have been demolished will now be available for occupation, although it might be found that if the various statutory legislation is applied too rigorously to these old industrial and commercial premises, the statutory requirements will prove more effective in preventing occupation — because it is often uneconomic to meet the required standards — than large-scale clearance.

If it is not possible to acquire by agreement — always the ideal — and it is necessary for a compulsory purchase order to be made, the prevailing government attitude towards acquisitions must be taken into account. If development land is owned by a builder who has every intention of proceeding with development — housing, factories or whatever — which will meet a local need, a compulsory purchase order is likely to be confirmed only in exceptional circumstances, whereas an order relating to land whose owner has no intention of developing or selling and is frustrating local need is much more likely to be confirmed.

On the face of it, the justification for land acquisitions under Section 19 of the Local Government, Planning and Land Act, 1980 should be relatively straightforward. However, at times when the government is trying to reduce public expenditure and encourage private investment, a much less enthusiastic response will be shown to attempts to acquire land and it will be more difficult to obtain the Secretary of State's authorization.

Some thought should always be given to future market-price movement, even though it is difficult to predict. However, there are occasionally times when there is a strong possibility of a rise or fall, and the timing of acquisitions should be adjusted accordingly. In 1973 the prices paid for residential land were impossible to justify by reference to current house prices and building costs, and once the market broke it was obvious that the prices of development land had a long way to fall. Many purchasers of land in 1973 — public as well as private — no doubt later wished they had paid more attention to the basic economics and remembered that the value of development land is essentially a residual value.

Movements in interest rates are of some importance, particularly in cases where land might be held for several years or where money has to be borrowed on a long-term basis — new-town development corporations have to borrow for 60 years at fixed rates — but where land can be disposed of quickly and loans repaid, interest rates will not normally be a major factor.

Changes in legislation are sometimes easier to predict than changes in market prices or interest rates. Obviously if it is fairly certain that the statutory basis of compensation is likely to be changed so as to benefit the acquiring authority then land acquisitions should be postponed for as long as practicable, and vice versa.

If a development project is held up because of delays in land acquisition the financial consequences can often be serious, quite apart from any other consequences. The fact that land acquisition is a means to an end, rather than an end in itself, should not be lost sight of.

All the factors have to be carefully evaluated when deciding what land to buy. Last but by no means least, is the need to consider all the property already in the ownership of the authority. Can any be made available for development? Perhaps a valuable housing site acquired for local authority housing which has been deferred can be sold for private housing and other land acquired at a later date for local authority purposes. Such an arrangement might work wonders for the cash flow. Of course, the whole of a local authority's property holdings have to be managed and constantly revalued on a corporate management basis, and consideration of possible disposals even if additional land has to be bought at a later date is a vital aspect of the management process.

3.2.2 Green fields or redevelopment sites

Ease of dealing with land acquisition and its subsequent development and cash-flow considerations are bound to tempt authorities to deal with 'green-field' sites on the urban perimeter, particularly where physical infrastructure is available. Many fears have been expressed that this could lead to the neglect of inner areas badly in need of redevelopment. Undoubtedly this is a possibility. However, where social infrastructure in the form of schools and community buildings and the like is available in the central areas, authorities will be reluctant to embark on peripheral expansion if — as is often the case — the necessary social infrastructure does not exist. Furthermore the cost of travelling from a peripheral site to the centre will result in a growing tendency for many who work in the centre wishing to live nearby.

It is in this type of situation, when faced with a choice between a green-field site and an inner-area redevelopment, that a local authority might take a view which would not normally be that of the private developer. Apart from questions of economic viability, the local authority must consider the effects of its decision on the life of the community as a whole.

The dilemma is often heightened by the anomalous effects which the statutory basis of compensation can sometimes have upon acquisition costs. In the inner areas the statutory basis of compensation for a large number of small parcels of land in some circumstances will result in a total compensation cost which exceeds the value of the whole area for redevelopment in accordance with a reasonable development brief. Recently it has been made clear that government policy will be to increase the financial resources for inner area development. The intelligent application of grants and the like should help to bring about redevelopment of areas which have been run down and derelict for far too long.

3.2.3 Conservation or redevelopment

How is a local authority to decide whether to conserve and rehabilitate, or to clear and redevelop? Factors affecting this decision with regard to individual buildings are referred to in Chapter 2. The practicability of restoring and finding suitable uses for individual buildings figures largely in the assessment of a possible improvement area. But there are additional factors to be taken into account when considering an area as opposed to individual buildings. Sometimes the answer is obvious. Few would dispute the desirability of conserving, almost irrespective of cost, an area containing a substantial proportion of seventeenth- and eighteenth-century buildings so grouped and interrelated as to make the area one of outstanding architectural merit. Conversely an area of poor quality, small, back to back mid-Victorian terraced houses, fronting directly onto the pavements, in very bad structural condition, will almost certainly be demolished in a locality where there are many other similar houses more worthy of preservation. These are extreme examples. Decisions are often difficult and will ultimately depend on subjective value judgment. The climate of public opinion is now more favourably inclined to the retention and improvement of what exists. There is a greater general appreciation of old buildings, including those of the once despised Victorian and later construction. Maybe this is because so many old buildings have been demolished since 1945 and replaced with new buildings generally thought to be of less aesthetic value.

Urban areas vary enormously in character and complexity. It is impossible to devise a universal set of standards upon which to base a judgment as to whether to improve or to demolish and redevelop, but there are a number of general considerations. The overall layout is often outmoded; old urban areas were designed and built for a way of life quite different from that which prevails today. Car parking, open space and other amenities are often non-existent and the roads may be inadequate. Detailed surveys will show whether there are sufficient buildings worthy of preservation and improvement; it is not necessary to retain all. Buildings not worth keeping may be demolished and replaced by buildings of a scale and character in sympathy with those to be retained.

Other uses for cleared sites might provide desirable amenties within the area.

When considering the whole or part of a town centre, the authority must decide whether the existing commercial buildings are capable of meeting the current requirements of potential occupiers, particularly in terms of size. It is often impossible to fit large superstores into old shopping streets without radically altering the street pattern and destroying the scale and character of the existing locality. But will the old shopping streets remain viable if the large modern stores are developed elsewhere? Is it likely that the pattern of retail trading will adapt to changing conditions, so that, for example, old shops too small to provide the floor space needed by the large multiples will, over a period of time, be gradually occupied by specialist traders for whom smaller premises are quite suitable? Will traffic management schemes provide adequate service access and make the shopping streets safe and pleasant for the shopping public? Is it possible to provide adequate car parking in convenient locations? Is public transport adequate?

Old industrial areas present difficulties quite apart from those inherent in the buildings themselves. The solution of access and parking problems will almost certainly necessitate some demolition. The majority of industrial and service industry occupiers are heavily dependent on road transport, so that good road access is essential. However, the provision of an adequate road network often detracts from the environmental quality of adjoining areas. Many old industrial areas are in close proximity to residential accommodation, so that care has to be taken to ensure that the occupation and use of any refurbished industrial or service industry buildings do not negate attempts to improve the quality of adjoining residential accommodation. The rehabilitation of old industrial property in inner areas of mixed development needs sensitive handling. It must be remembered that land occupied for many years for non-residential purposes might be heavily polluted and unfit for building.

When considering the improvement of residential areas, the essential question is whether the improved area will provide an environment of a sufficiently high standard to give an acceptable quality of life to the inhabitants. Where it is impossible to improve the whole of an extensive area in one operation, it is important that confidence is created in the overall improvement programme. The attitude of mind of the inhabitants and their desire to remain or move elsewhere will have a major influence on the overall success.

Clearance and total redevelopment is unavoidable in many areas. Improvement is only worthwhile if it results in attractive conditions for those who live or work in the improved area. Much of the criticism of clearance and redevelopment is due to the inhuman scale and unsuitable character of the new development.

The statutory powers available to a local authority to promote the improvement of an area and the availability of government grants will affect the decision whether to improve or to acquire, clear and redevelop. The powers to establish General Improvement Areas and Housing Action Areas and the range of financial grants available for the improvement and repair of dwellings and in aid of the local authority expenditure in the area generally are important factors. Historic buildings grants might be available, albeit on a limited scale. The attention of a number of local authorities is now turning to the possibilities of Industrial Improvement Areas.

The cost of acquisition, the cost of improving the existing buildings and their market value when improved are the tangible factors which are capable of being quantified by traditional and accepted methods. The aesthetic and social aspects are the intangible and yet vitally important factors. Of course it is not necessary for an authority to acquire property simply to bring about the improvement of an area However this section is essentially concerned with the matters which will be examined by a local authority when deciding whether to acquire land in existing areas of urban development with a view to making it available for redevelopment.

3.2.4 Planning and practical availability

An important distinction must be drawn between planning allocations and the actual availability of land for development. This is frequently a bone of contention between planners and developers and can lead to a shortage of land for development in the absence of a careful analysis of the land-use allocations.

Frequently development land is not able to be developed because adequate sewerage or water supplies are not available or can only be provided at prohibitive cost. Planning consent may be refused for development proposals on allocated land because existing road access is inadequate. Development may not fit into the framework of an approved programme map. Perhaps the owner of development land does not wish to sell either because he does not wish to see development on his land or because he thinks that by waiting a few years he will obtain a much better price. The land might already be owned by a builder for development over a period of years. For these and other reasons developers may be frustrated, and planners must realize that putting annotations on maps is not quite the same thing as making land available for development.

3.3 LAND DISPOSALS

In the United Kingdom few private enterprise developers as such are content to limit their activities to land operations. Usually a developer acquires land because he himself wishes to carry out the development of the land. But it is in the sphere of land operations, i.e. the acquisition, servicing and disposal of land for others to develop, that the speculative development activities of local authorities are likely to be concentrated for some years to come. Quite apart from any desire on the part of the authorities, the difficult economic climate and the resulting government anxiety to reduce public expenditure will make it so. These notes are, therefore, written essentially to describe the operations of a local authority, although many of the comments would be equally applicable to the activities of a large private estate owner or a large private enterprise developer who acquires larger areas of land than he needs in order that he may dispose of some part of it to other developers.

The ownership of land and the power to decide how it should be sold or leased, and the manner of its development, are the fundamental issues which will enable the authorities to exercise great influence over the development within their sphere of control. Ownership of the land should give the authorities all the power necessary to bring about positive planning and implementation, provided that land-disposal policies are carefully thought out and skilfully put into practice. Ill-conceived policies and disposal methods could do great harm to a community. When local authorities venture into the world of speculative property development, the responsibilities can be onerous. Their first duty is to clearly understand all the implications of their policies and methods.

3.3.1 Land for residential development

The local authority should constantly monitor the overall situation. Is the land already in the ownership of the authority adequate for the council-house building programme? Can any land be sold? Is there a need for land for housing associations catering for general rented housing needs, or for special categories of tenants, such as students or single people requiring hostel accommodation or the retired or those in need of sheltered accommodation?

What is the demand for land for speculative private housing? Is there a demand for individual private building plots? How much land is allocated by the planning authority for housing use and how much of that is available for development? Does the supply match the demand? All these matters must remain constantly under review to enable the authority to take a positive role rather than simply react to the pressure of events.

Decisions must be made as to the allocation of the various areas of residential land between the different types of residential development. The relative attractions of the different sites must be assessed, such as location, aspect and physical features — shape, slope, landscaping, character of adjoining properties, proximity to transport, schools, shops and other amenities.

The overall social balance of the community must be taken into account. It would be a mistake in a town of any size to group all rented council houses together in one location and to segregate private houses strictly in accordance with their market values. A reasonable balance must be achieved. On the other hand, it is perhaps a peculiarity of life that in villages people are normally quite happy to live cheek by jowl, irrespective of income groups, and yet in towns it is normally difficult to persuade anyone to build expensive individual houses next to large areas of low-cost rented housing. Perhaps this is another example of the way in which the scale of development affects human behaviour.

When disposing of land for private residential development, the effect on the character of the locality and the value of adjoining land should be borne in mind. It is unlikely that any authority will wish to concern itself with very small, infilling development which can prove time-consuming and vexatious in the case of claims that the values of adjoining properties have been depreciated. This type of development, however, is a good illustration of the way in which the character of a locality can be slowly and subtly but nevertheless substantially changed over a period of years. Such changes are not always slow or subtle. However, other than in exceptional circumstances this type of infilling is best left to private enterprise activity subject to normal planning controls.

Land disposal for private residential development falls into one of two broad categories: individual building plots, and parcels for speculative development.

(a) Individual plots

The opportunities for private purchasers to buy an individual plot on the open market are limited. Speculative builders do not normally wish to sell plots: when they do so, it is usually a condition that the purchaser will also commission the builder to erect the dwelling whether it be designed by the builder or by the purchaser's own architect and this can hardly be described as a genuine plot sale. Another source of private plots is the sale of parts of gardens of existing dwellings so that infilling takes place: this often brings into the market attractive plots in mature areas, although in many localities the supply of surplus garden land is drying up. An authority might wish to increase the supply by constructing the necessary estate roads and services in order to break up a parcel of land into individual plots.

The development of land in the form of individual building plots can be a troublesome business and is rarely profitable. Doubtless this is why private enterprise seldom considers it a worthwhile activity. However, a local authority might undertake this work, perhaps to encourage higher-quality development in a particular locality or as an attraction to business people who might also locate their business in the area. The availability of individual plots certainly widens the choice available and gives a prospective owner the opportunity of building a house which will have its own character and individuality.

The first essential is to determine the size of plots, the quality and character of the dwellings to be built and the number of plots to be provided. These decisions will be taken in the light of the results of market research. The precise development solution will be tailored to fit local requirements, but a number of basic considerations will always be present. There is a minimum size of plot which it will be practical to provide. The larger the plot the greater the freedom of design which can be given to the purchaser, which is the underlying purpose. The number of storeys to be built on the individual plots must be determined. Often it is desirable to group bungalows together.

Landscaping requirements should be specified for each plot and related to the landscaping of the whole estate. It may be advantageous to stipulate that buildings should be a minimum distance inside the plot boundaries. To give a degree of privacy, any firstfloor living or bedroom windows should be a certain distance from any boundary which they overlook.

It is helpful to prepare a design guide for purchasers and their architects. In all cases purchasers should be asked to discuss designs at the outline sketch stage, much difficulty and frustration will thereby be avoided. The most satisfactory arrangement is to make it clear that contracts for sale will not be exchanged until the design has been approved and that contracts will require the dwelling to be built in accordance with the approved design. The usual arrangement is for the legal estate to be conveyed and the purchase price paid before the purchaser takes possession of the plot to enable mortgages to be obtained from building societies, but it is quite possible to make other arrangements for the payment of the purchase price — for example, in instalments subject to the payment of interest on the outstanding balance.

Nowadays the majority of sales are freehold, although sometimes plots are offered on a leasehold basis in areas where leasehold is customary. It is difficult to see the advantage to the authority of holding a leasehold building estate of this type, bearing in mind the possibility of leasehold enfranchisement leaving the authority with a fragmented holding. Ground rents do not rank for tax relief so that anything more than a nominal ground rent is disadvantageous to the purchaser in this respect. Ground leases — perhaps at a premium with a nominal ground rent — might be useful in cases where plotholders are required to contribute to the maintenance of common parts of the estate not adopted or taken over by the local authority. The maintenance contributions from each plotholder can then be recovered as if they were additional ground rent. This overcomes difficulties which might otherwise arise if the plots were sold freehold, and positive convenants to pay maintenance contributions would then not run with the land on resale.

In some localities local builders have difficulty in finding plots for individual, high-quality speculative houses. A small number of plots on this type of development might be sold to builders on condition that they build high-quality houses all of different designs. Such arrangements can help get development started and assist the cash flow.

The authority will usually build the estate roads to adoption standards complete with all the necessary services. Economic considerations dictate that whenever possible development should take place on both sides of the roads. A common practice is to lay only the base of the road in the first instance, leaving the final surface to be put on when housing development is completed to avoid damage from building contractors' vehicles. Similarly the provision of footpaths is often left until the houses have been built not only to avoid damage, but also to allow the plot-purchaser to decide the position of crossovers.

All communal landscaping and open space should ideally be designed in such a manner as to ensure it will be taken over and maintained by the local authority responsible for highways or parks and open spaces. If landscaping and open space provisions exceed the standards normally taken over, a capital payment might be required to cover future maintenance.

Suitable restrictive covenants should be imposed to prevent subsequent alterations or additions to properties which would detract from the overall environment and to limit the use of properties to private residences only. Most purchasers realize that covenants are in the common interest and readily accept them. Covenants to enforce the principle of open-plan front gardens without fences will usually be the ones most often broken. It is worthwhile giving a good deal of thought to this particular aspect of development policy at the outset. It is certainly the one which gives rise to most difficulties.

A disclaimer is usually inserted into the legal contracts to the effect that the common restrictive covenants do not imply that the land is part of a building scheme which might otherwise restrict the authority's freedom to develop the land as it wishes. However, an authority would no doubt feel morally obliged not to detract from the original concept on the basis of which the first plots are sold.

(b) Residential land — sale of speculative parcels

Once the land suitable for speculative residential development has been identified, how should it be sold? What are the various aspects of the disposal process and the ways of dealing with their implementation?

(i) Size of parcels

This will be decided in the light of market reaseach. For the general run of low-cost speculative housing at twelve to sixteen dwellings per acre, the large national house-builders wlll rarely be interested in less than 5 acres, will probably prefer between 10 and 20 acres and might be interested in considerably larger parcels — up to 100 acres or more — for development over a period of years. Small local builders seek anything from a single plot to a few acres. Density is an important consideration when determining the size of site; many builders ask for land in terms of housing units rather than acres.

(ii) Servicing

If one self-contained parcel of land is to be sold and the authority does not own any adjoining land, the usual practice is to leave the developer to provide all necessary roads and services: he buys the land as it stands. Where the authority owns a substantial acreage which has to be divided up into separate parcels, a decision has to be made as to who will be responsible for access roads and the services.

When a large area has to be broken down into parcels, it is normally best for the authority to provide the minimum length of roads (with services) to give reasonable access to the boundary of each parcel. It would be only in exceptional circumstances that an authority would carry out any works inside the individual parcels. Circumstances may arise in which it is convenient to place the responsibility for building the access roads on one of the developers. The cost incurred by the developer on access roads will obviously affect the price at which the land is sold. This type of arrangement is useful when the authority wishes to reduce capital expenditure to the minimum. The programme for the construction of the access roads must be clearly defined and the necessary rights reserved for the authority to carry out or complete the works and recover the cost from the developer in the event of his own failure to meet his obligations. Such a situation could cause a great deal of delay and difficulty and it is advisable to contemplate arrangements of this type only with developers of undoubted standing and probity.

When access will be needed at a future date over the estate roads within the parcel of land to open up other land for development, care must be taken to reserve the necessary rights of way over the estate roads — at any rate, until they are adopted as public highways — and to provide that the roads will be built to an agreed timetable.

(iii) Tenure

Normally land for residential development is sold freehold with adequate provisions in the legal document to enable the authority to ensure that the developer meets all his obligations.

However, when the Community Land Act came into force government policy was that freeholds should be sold only to

house purchasers and house builders had in the first instance
only a licence to carry out the development with the right to
require the authority to convey freeholds to individual house
purchasers. Although this is no longer so nevertheless licence
arrangements are often made to facilitate payment for the
land in stages to enable the house builder to improve his
overall cash flow or other special price or payment arrangements which might be agreed for one reason or another.

An authority should not convey all the house plots and
then find itself left owning the freehold of numerous small
areas of no value which are a maintenance burden. This is
dealt with at greater length in connection with the development brief.

(iv) Development finance

The developer is usually entirely responsible for financing all
of the development. Some find the necessary finance from
their own cash flow, others will rely on bank overdraft or
merchant bank facilities. A few might obtain finance from
building societies. Financial institutions will rarely be happy
to advance money to a developer who simply holds a licence,
but this difficulty is overcome by providing that in the event
of the failure of the developer, the institution shall have the
right to nominate others to take over the licence and complete the work and call on the authority to convey the freeholds in accordance with the licence terms.

The building societies may only lend on the security of a
legal estate, so that a developer relying on this source for
finance will need the freehold or leasehold in the first instance.

(c) The residential development brief

The purpose of the development brief is to set out the
requirements of the authority with regard to the development
to be carried out on the site. There are three principal issues.
When is a development brief necessary? What matters should
be included in the brief, and in what degree of detail and
with how much flexibility? What are the advantages and
disadvantages of using the development brief?

When promoting the development of a large area of land
on a comprehensive basis with the intention of disposing of a
number of parcels of land to different developers, it is

necessary to give a clear indication of the type of development expected on each of the parcels. Road and footpath points in the various developments must link up sensibly, and major landscaping, open spaces, and the like should be designed on a comprehensive basis. A sensible overall balance of house types, sizes and prices has to be achieved. By using development briefs, the authority can ensure that all the different developments will fit together happily and safeguard the value of the land remaining in its ownership. When preparing each brief, the authority will have regard to the likely effect of the development upon the value of the adjoining land. From the developer's viewpoint it is important for him to know what development is to take place in the vicinity in order to satisfy himself that nothing is likely to detract from his own proposed development. In a large new development area the developer will often find himself purchasing land when the only indication of the development likely to take place on adjoining parcels will be that contained in the relevant development briefs. In such circumstances the degree of flexibility with regard to the possible amendment of the development briefs must be made clear. Otherwise there is a danger that a developer buying one parcel might feel that he has been misled by the authority, if the development briefs for the adjoining parcels are substantially modified. When dealing with disposals in a large comprehensive development area over a period of time, an authority should not rigorously bind itself to development briefs which changing fashions or economic circumstances will render obsolete.

Often an authority will wish to see development which will fit in happily with the surrounding environment. Maybe an authority will wish to see a particular type of development carried out on a site in order to satisfy some pressing local need. The preparation of a suitable development brief will be the best way of making its wishes clear. When competitive bids are invited, the amount of the bids will be greatly influenced by the development which will be permitted; the possible consequences of subsequent departure from the terms of the brief are dealt with in the later examination of methods of sale.

Care must be taken to avoid the creation of a 'building scheme', which might enable the purchaser of a parcel of land to take legal action against an authority or a subsequent developer purchaser who seeks to modify the content of the 'building scheme'.

The content and degree of detail must be carefully tailored to the circumstances of each disposal. Above all, ensure that every development brief is based on common sense and related to practicality and reality. The more important matters which must be considered for inclusion are described in the following sections.

(i) Density

The number of dwellings to be built will influence both the value of the land and the layout. The simplest brief will specify the total number of dwellings to be built on the site. Alternatively the brief might specify a certain number of habitable rooms or bed spaces per acre, thus giving greater flexibility. Maybe the developer will be given some discretion as to how many dwellings he puts on to the site. If the site is in a transitional position between sites for low-density, high-cost housing and sites for higher-density, lower-price dwellings, the former site might be protected by stipulating different densities for different parts of the site to be sold.

(ii) Dwelling types

Usually the stipulations will be related to the size of dwellings and to the storey-heights of the buildings. Circumstances may arise in which it will be considered desirable to stipulate a range of sizes with the number of each size to be built. Sizes may be stipulated very precisely by quoting superficial floor areas, or more loosely by the number of bedrooms or the number of bed spaces in each type of dwelling. Any firmly held views about storey-heights should be made clear, particularly when flats or maisonettes are to be built. If an authority is anxious to meet a demand in its area from retired people, for example, perhaps only bungalows will be permitted, or at any rate a proportion of the dwellings be provided in that form. It is a matter of some delicacy as to how requirements concerning quality are introduced. The developer must be able to understand easily at the outset what is required. The brief might specify a standard represented by a certain minimum building price per square foot. Another method is to indicate that the dwellings should be of an equivalent standard to those selling within certain price brackets in the locality. The latter method enables the developer to use his initiative in working out the most successful combination of design and construction standards, building materials and floor space to meet the market requirements. A distinction must be drawn between using price ranges as indicators and any attempt to control the selling price of the dwellings built on the land.

(iii) Building materials

It is common practice to indicate ranges of external cladding materials which will be acceptable. In the absence of strong views about cladding materials, it should be left to the developer to put forward proposals. If there are very decided views about the use of certain materials, perhaps because the development is to take place in or adjoining a conservation area or an area of outstanding natural beauty, then the preferred materials and how they are to be used should be precisely stipulated. The materials to be used inside the dwellings which will not be seen externally are normally left entirely to the developer, who must of course satisfy building regulations and the like. It is always preferable to refer to a range of certain cladding materials rather than to specify one particular material, in order to leave as much freedom of choice as possible to the developer.

(iv) Design styles and standards

Only in exceptional circumstances should the design brief be used to control the aesthetic design beyond dealing with cladding materials. In sensitive localities it might be stipulated that the new buildings shall be of the same character and scale as those in the immediate vicinity. Otherwise the developer should be left free to provide what he considers will be most attractive to the house-buying public, remembering that he will be subject to planning, building regulation and other public authority controls quite outside the terms of the development brief. Parker Morris design standards should be imposed only when there is clear evidence of a ready market demand for houses of such a standard.

(v) Layout

Road and footpath access points into the site will usually be marked on the plan attached to the brief. It should be made clear whether a traditional layout, or one which will result in pedestrian and vehicular segregation, is required or whether that is a matter which will be left entirely to the decision of the developer. Are open fronts required, or will low boundary walls or hedges be permitted? Are grass verges and trees required within the highway boundary, and will they be adopted by the highway authority? Is any provision to be made for children's play spaces within the housing areas, and will they be taken over by the local authority? Are major landscaping areas to be provided, and are sites to be set aside for public leisure and recreational purposes? If so, will they be taken over by the local authority? Ideally all the areas of land outside the actual dwelling curtilages should be taken over by the local authority and the developer should be placed under an obligation to put the areas into the condition required by the local authority immediately prior to takeover. If there are areas outside the dwelling curtilages which will not be taken over, then the developer must produce practical proposals for the general maintenance and upkeep of those areas.

It may be necessary to impose conditions for the benefit of adjoining parcels of land. For example, particular landscaping requirements along one or more boundaries and variations in the densities or reservation of access.

(vi) Completion time

It is desirable to include a condition that the whole of the development must be completed by a certain date. A speculative developer is very much at the mercy of the vagaries of the market and allowance has to be made for this. If it is expected that speculative housing-estate development will be completed within two years, it would not be unreasonable to provide that the development shall be completed within three years and allow further extension of time, provided the developer has used every reasonable endeavour. It would be impractical to expect a developer to carry on completing houses, if he is unable to sell them. Should the developer be in breach of the completion condition, the authority will usually be able to take back the undeveloped land. In that event there may be a provision for the authority to pay to the developer the cost or the value, whichever is the lesser, of any uncompleted work on the land which they repossess.

The advantage of using a development brief is the ability to clearly convey requirements with regard to the development of the site and, thus, reduce to a minimum the time needed for discussion and the risk of abortive design work on the part of the developer, who can see at the outset whether what is required by the authority is the type of development that he wishes to carry out. The disadvantage is that an authority might produce a development brief which is far too detailed and inflexible and an unreasonable restriction upon the developer's freedom of action to react to market conditions.

An authority could indeed use a development brief as almost a new system of development control on the basis that developers would either buy the site subject to the brief, or not buy at all. The normal operation of the property market will, of course, exercise some influence on those authorities anxious to see development taking place. Unreasonably onerous conditons in the development brief will reduce the market price of the land and in certain situations will render the land unsaleable. Speculative housing development is a highly competitive business. When preparing a development brief, an authority must have regard to the likely market reaction which, although not an infallible indicator, does represent the sum total of a wide cross section of views and is not to be lightly ignored. The developer is at risk if he fails to produce what house purchasers want and can afford, and he should be given reasonable freedom to utilize his own specialized knowledge of market requirements and building techniques.

The use of a development brief is not essential. When an authority is disposing of a site by direct negotiation, the details of the development can be worked out by amicable discussion. This is often a more sophisticated and satisfactory process than the somewhat arbitrary production of a development brief. Often occasions will arise when an authority selling a site has no very strong feelings about what development should take place on the land. In that event there is nothing inherently wrong in offering the land on the open market to the highest bidder for whatever development for which planning consent can be obtained. This might well be regarded as the most traditional of all the methods of land disposal.

(d) Method of sale

Regard must be had to prevailing market conditions and the question of public accountability. If it is necessary or desirable to introduce competitive bidding, auction or some form of tender is the answer. If not, straightforward negotiation might produce the best results.

When the market is buoyant and there is a keen demand for land, and the number of developers anxious to buy exceeds the number of sites available, some form of competitive bidding is probably the only way to satisfactorily meet the requirements of public accountability. When market prices are fluctuating wildly, the invitation of competitive bids might be the only way to determine the price with confidence. Competitive bids will be invited either by auction, or some form of tender.

Auction is self-explanatory. It is customary to employ a professional auctioneer and the expense is normally higher than when an authority uses its own staff to deal with the sale by tender. At the auction each bidder will proceed to make one bid higher than his rivals, whereas when submitting tenders each bidder will submit his highest offer because he will not know what bids are being submitted by his rivals. For example, if four bidders are prepared to pay £10 000, £20 000, £30 000 and £40 000 respectively at auction the top bidder would have to pay £31 000, whereas he would tender £40000. On the basis of this example it is clear that the invitation of bids by tender would produce the best price.

Tenders may be 'open' so that anyone may submit a bid, or 'selective' so that the category of potential bidders is in some way limited. Careful thought needs to be given to any proposal to limit the category of bidders. This question frequently arises when land is being sold by tender and yet never — or hardly ever — when land is to be sold by auction. If good reasons can be adduced for limiting the category of bidders there is no reason why this should not be done, although it will normally be difficult to justify any limitation other than that the land will only be sold to builders registered with the National House-Building Council. If an authority has a monopoly in supply of land, limitations will not only to some extent distort the market but will also have serious effects upon the business propects of those who are excluded from the bidding, at any rate within the local authority area.

Tenders may be invited on a variety of bases. The simplest is competitive price bids subject to approval of the detailed development scheme at a later date. When it is considered that excellence of design or the type or quality of a development is of paramount importance, the price of the land might be fixed and tenders invited on the basis of competitive designs. Tenders may be invited on the basis of competitive price bids coupled with competitive designs and the authority will choose the bid which gives the best combination of the two: this makes the selection of the best bid that much more difficult, but it is not impossible to invite tenders on a basis that involves the consideration of more than one factor. Competitive design bids necessitate time and expense on the preparation of the designs and for that reason are less attractive to developers. When the property market is slack, many reputable developers will only consider competing on the basis of competitive designs in the most exceptional circumstances. Tenders involving the preparation of competitive designs should not be indiscriminately used. Design drawings should be requested with the minimum degree of detail necessary. Tender documents must be clear and precise and comprehensive. If a design brief is included in the tender documents, allegations of bad faith will often follow any significant modification after the acceptance of the winning tender. When tenders are invited, it is important to make it clear that the authority is not bound to accept any of the bids that might be submitted.

Straightforward negotiation is often the best method of disposal when the land market is relatively quiet and prices reasonably stable and there is ample land available to meet the requirements of all prospective developers. At times when conditions in the development industry are very slack negotiation might be the only practical method, because developers might not be interested in competitive bidding. This was the case in many localities during 1974 and 1975. However, it is important that adequate evidence is available in the shape of market transactions (to which the local authority has not been party) to prove the prices obtained by the local authority are reasonable. If the local authority is in a monopoly position, then from time to time it will be necessary to invite competitive price bids in order to establish the fair open market value. If the District Valuer does not have to frank every sale, it is nevertheless advisable to obtain his agreement from time to time in order that the authority shall be in a position to demonstrate fairness and impartiality in the fixing of the disposal terms.

(e) Special price arrangements

In recent years unusual conditions in the residential land market have resulted in a sharp increase in the number of special arrangements for fixing the price of residential land. During the boom which lasted from the beginning of 1971 until the end of 1973 landowners who obtained the market price at the time of sale were aggrieved when they realized that within six or twelve months the value of the land had doubled and they began to search for ways of ensuring that they would benefit from any rapid increase in land values between the date of sale and the completion of the development on the land. The subsequent recession resulted in land prices falling almost as quickly as they had risen and on the falling market builders were reluctant to commit themselves to firm prices for parcels of any substantial size, and in many cases severe cash-flow problems precluded them from paying for land outright. The special arrangements devised at the outset to enable the landowners to share in the rapidly increasing land values were subsequently modified with a view to making the land deals more attractive to builders and, thus, tempting them to buy on a very difficult market.

Always remember than many of the special price-fixing arrangements were devised to cope with unusual market conditions. Where it is possible to fix the price and arrange for payment in the usual simple, straightforward manner, it will often be in the interests of both parties to do so. Before entering into special price-fixing arrangements, examine the justification for so doing and ensure that the arrangements will be easy to implement and all the implications fully understood by both parties.

One simple method which has been often used is to quote the price of the land in terms of a percentage of the total selling prices of the dwellings built with a minimum figure for the land quoted as a safeguard. For example, if a parcel of land is to be sold for development at ten houses to the acre and each house is estimated to sell at £28 000, the price might be quoted as £40 000 per acre freehold or 15 per cent of the total selling price of the houses whichever is the greater. The landowner will be certain of receiving his £40 000 per acre and will automatically benefit from any increase in the selling prices of the houses. Without adequate safeguards the builder could easily find himself in difficulties. If house-purchasers ask for additional works to be carried out which will increase the selling price of the houses, then the landowner will automatically take part of that increase unless the cost of additional works is ignored for the purpose of calculating the land value. A more serious problem occurs when the selling prices of the houses rise more slowly than building costs. The landowner is entitled to a part of the increase in the house prices even though the increase will not cover the builder's extra costs. To safeguard the builder, it is possible to provide that the landowner shall only share in the net increases in house prices after deducting increasing building costs during the development period: if provision is made for the increase in building costs to be calculated by reference to one of the standard indices, lengthy argument can often be avoided. But this example shows how a simple price arrangement might contain a serious trap for one of the parties — in this instance, the builder — and how the agreement quickly becomes more complicated with the introduction of adequate safeguards.

It is quite possible to devise other arrangements. A price might be agreed with a proviso that on completion of the development the builder shall pay to the landowner a proportion of the net development profit. It would be necessary to agree the precise basis for the profit calculation and a time for the development. The ability to negotiate special price arrangements will be entirely dependent upon prevailing market conditions.

(f) The method of payment

The simplest and most advantageous to the landowner's cash flow is for the total price for the land to be paid at the outset, that is, on completion of the legal transaction or on taking possession whichever is the earlier. There are many alternatives. When builders are anxious to safeguard their cash flow, arrangements are commonly made for the purchase price to be apportioned and a payment made each time a dwelling is sold, or the purchase price might be paid in several instalments during the development period. It is important to ensure that there is an ultimate time limit within which all payments must be made. In some special price arrangements it may not be possible for the ultimate purchase price to be calculated until the completion of the development, but such arrangements will usually include for a substantial part of the price to be paid either at the outset or during the development period. It is essential to evaluate carefully the various alternatives. Special arrangements for the fixing of the land price and the method of payment must be capable of being reduced to a common basis so that both the landowner — particularly a local authority having to meet the requirements of public accountability — and the developer will be able to compare easily one land transaction with another and also with normal open market value. Usually it is best to reduce all transactions to a common basis by calculating the effective purchase price on the assumption that the whole price is to be paid at the outset. Arrangements which are unduly complicated and difficult to evaluate are best avoided unless there is some compelling justification for them. Public authorities should avoid arrangements which unduly distort normal market prices and place them in danger of producing hypothetical values in an unreal world of assumptions and expectations which might never be fulfilled.

(g) Unusual transactions

On occasions local authorities wishing to solve accommodation problems peculiar to their own area might make unusual arrangements when selling residential land. A special price might be agreed on condition that there is some restriction on the selling price of the dwellings. It might be agreed that in the first instance the dwellings shall be sold only to people within a restricted group — perhaps the inhabitants of the local authority area or people on the housing waiting list. The full implications and the ultimate beneficiaries of such arrangements need careful study. Frequently they will be accompanied by provision for the authority to buy the dwellings from the first purchasers, if they wish to sell within a certain period of time.

3.3.2 Land for industry, warehousing and associated developments

The quality of the employment structure affects all aspects of life in the community. A well-balanced, prosperous employment structure gives economic stability and good job prospects for the people and their children living in the community. The general level of prosperity in turn affects various aspects of life, such as shopping and entertainment facilities, educational provision and the quality of housing.

The industrial development policy of any authority will be very much influenced by its general attitude to population growth and the need or desirability of attracting new industry into the area. Those living in a pleasant dormitory town or living a pleasant rural existence in an area of outstanding natural beauty might well prefer to see the general character of their area remain unchanged and, if so, will resist any attempt to introduce new industrial development.

However, there are many localities which for a variety of reasons are faced with difficult unemployment problems. Maybe employment in the traditional industries is shrinking rapidly either because of a falling off in the demand for their products as a result of the development of alternatives, or competition from international manufacturers. The introduction of labour-saving methods and machinery often substantially reduces the demand for workpeople. In some areas now somewhat euphemistically referred to as Development Areas, problems of unemployment have been endemic for many years. The bulge in the number of school-leavers in recent years has created unemployment problems in many localities which might well persist even after an improvement in the general economic climate in the country as a whole. The lack of adequate employment opportunities is regarded as one of the major reasons for the social and economic decline experienced in many inner-city areas.

In general terms it is, therefore, likely that the majority of local authorities throughout the country will be anxious to attract employment of a type which they consider suitable for their own locality and the attraction and development of employment is rapidly growing into a specialized career occupation.

Local authorities are not the only public bodies active in the field of industrial development. The new towns and the English Industrial Estates Corporation and Welsh and Scottish Development Agencies have built or made available sites for substantial amounts of factory space, and others such as the Council for Small Industires in Rural Areas promote industrial development albeit on a smaller scale. There is a long history of public authority activity in this field.

A local authority wishing to attract industry must first of all decide its overall industrial development strategy. Where is the new industry to be located? Will the activities of the local authority be restricted to making available suitable sites or will the authority erect factory buildings? If so, how will they be financed? Will the sites or buildings be made available only to prospective occupiers or will some land be made available to speculative developers? What other facilities will be offered to attract industry? Will local authority housing to rent be made available for employees and will the local authority provide other services, such as staging exhibitions, giving talks and providing coach tours for the employees of industrial firms thinking of moving into the area? Will social development staff be available to help overcome the personal and family difficulties of the employees so that they will be able to settle down happily in the new location? A local authority must think very carefully before attempting to attract industry on any scale, if it is not prepared to develop a comprehensive strategy embracing all these matters. The amount of mobile employment able and willing to move to new locations is limited and there is fierce competition to attract it.

The strategy of the local authority will be greatly influenced by the likely size of the development programme, which will be decided in the light of market research into how much industry it is reasonable to expect to be attracted to the area and over what period of time. The market-research basis will be much more extensive than for most other types of development, because it is possible to attract industry from a very considerable distance. Indeed by a vigorous promotional campaign the local authority might create a market for its industrial land and buildings where one did not previously exist.

(a) Location

Ideally a choice of location should be offered. Small business and those employing mainly female labour will often prefer sites adjoining a town centre, if they can be made available. Small groups of small factories might be built in or adjoining residential areas for light industry, although it must be remembered that many light-industrial firms receive deliveries from very large vehicles so good road access is essential. The possibility of redeveloping the sites of old, outmoded factories and warehouses should not be overlooked. However, it is likely that with a development programme of any size the greater part will take place on new industrial estates.

The new industrial estates will be carefully located with regard to the town road pattern. Maybe several estates will be developed in different parts of the town to avoid undue concentration of traffic and to facilitate the provision of public transport for the journeys between home and work. At least one estate ideally should have a lettable net area of at least 100 acres so as to give flexibility in the provision of sites of different sizes and also to help with the overall economics. If the development programme is extensive, one or more of the industrial estates will probably have an area of 200 or 300 acres or more.

It is almost impossible to say with certainty at the outset precisely how a large industrial estate should be subdivided. Certain main roads might have to be built to fit in with the overall town road pattern and if so main roads, or at least a substantial length of them, will be built in the first instance with a limited number of estate roads to provide a variety of sites. Additional estate roads can be built later when the pattern of demand for sites of different sizes becomes clear.

In most localities it will probably be found in practice that the great majority of inquiries will probably be for sites of between 1 and 5 acres and it is unlikely that there will be many serious inquiries for sites of more than 20 acres. However, it is advantageous to retain a number of very large sites for as long as possible, and there is no point in putting more estate roads than are essential to provide the number of small sites to meet the expected demand for the next two or three years. Interest charges on estate roads and services rapidly mount up, although if engineering costs are rising this is an offsetting factor. So is the possibility of building the roads more cheaply, if they are included in a larger contract.

(b) Development brief

Attractively laid out and landscaped industrial estates with good road access well served by public transport will be one of the major inducements to industrial employers to move into the locality.

The authority will decide the broad estate development policy. Nowadays a variety of employment will be found and often the term Industrial Estate is replaced by the term Employment Area, which will be used for the remainder of this commentary. It is often desirable to zone parts of large employment areas for the different types of employment. While it is not essential to distinguish between industrial and warehousing development, it is important to set aside certain areas suitable for research development or office development. Some office employers prefer a campus-style development rather than a town centre location, and if the employment area adjoins open countryside or an educational campus or maybe a high-class housing area, then part of the employment area might well be suitable for meeting the requirements of office employers. Normally research laboratories may be associated quite happily with office development.

For the guidance of developers it is useful to produce a design brief covering such matters as plot-development ratios, building heights if it is necessary to control them, minimum car-parking requirements, landscaping requirements within the site boundaries, boundary fencing requirements and the type of fencing which will be permitted, and minimum distances of buildings from the site boundaries. The degree of control to be exercised over the design of the buildings is a matter of judgment and common sense. Although it is often useful to specify in the brief a range of external cladding materials which will be acceptable — and the range will be wide because on large, well-landscaped sites buildings of quite different materials can sit together side by side quite happily — the most practical arrangement is for the architect to meet whoever is responsible for building design control at the outset and discuss the proposed building design when it is still at the 'back of an envelope' stage. Flexibility will have to be the keynote in any control system, but a reasonable quality of design must be insisted upon in the interests of all the occupiers on the estate. Certain uses are by their nature of a less attractive appearance and it is advisable to set aside land for them in an unobtrusive position. Concrete batching plants or uses involving a large amount of open storage are examples.

(c) Basis of site disposal

A local authority does not develop an industrial estate solely as a property-development exercise: the essential reason is to attract employment. To this end, sites should always be available for disposal direct to the industrialist. Even if the industrialist does not wish to design and build and finance his premises, the possibility of taking a site will enable him to shop around and obtain the best possible terms — maybe on a package-deal basis. When dealing with an industrialist proposing to erect buildings for his own occupation, the matters to be mainly considered are as follows.

Although subject to the consent of the Secretary of State local authorities are able to sell freehold a building agreement and lease will usually be the basic method of disposal. Initially a licence is granted and when development has been completed the formal lease is granted. Opinions as to the best length of lease on a modern industrial estate vary. A 99-year term is probably the one most widely used and is on the whole generally acceptable. Some of the financial institutions who might finance development argue for a 125-year term on the basis that this would permit rebuilding halfway through the term. It might be logical to argue in that event that a 60- or 80-year term would be more appropriate.

The landlord will reserve the right to review the rent, thus ensuring that reviews will be upwards only. If the rental value has not risen, the landlord will not review. The frequency of rent reviews is a matter of negotiation. Review clauses were rarely written into ground leases until the mid-1950s, when 30-year review periods were often used, but fairly quickly the frequency of reviews dropped to 21 years and then 14 years and nowadays 10-year reviews are not uncommon. Attempts are being made to negotiate five-year reviews for sites for which there is a keen demand. The frequency of the ground-rent review affects the ground rent. Both are regarded together as one package. The more frequent the reviews, the lower will be the initial rent. This is a matter of common sense. Clearly neither party will expect the value of the buildings to be included in ground-rent reviews. The basis for the review should be simple, unambiguous, easily understood and easy to implement. The simplest is cleared-site value on the assumption that a 99-year lease will be granted at the time of the review with planning and all other statutory consents necessary for the erection of the buildings on the site: if the site is underdeveloped, the necessary permissions and consents for the erection of light-industrial (if that is the appropriate use) buildings up to the maximum plot ratio should be assumed. It is necessary to qualify what may be built on the site otherwise with the passage of time the site might become much more valuable for a completely different type of use, thus penalizing the gound lessee in a way not envisaged at the time the lease was granted. Some financial institutions prefer the revised rent to be calculated as a proportion of the rack rent of the buildings fixed at the time the ground lease is granted. Thus, if the initial ground rent is £3000 per annum and at the time the ground lease is granted the buildings erected are worth a rack rent of £24 000 per annum, the reviewed ground rent would be one-eighth of the then rack-rental value. In such arrangements ground- and rack-rent reviews are often made to coincide so the ground rent is more frequently reviewed than would otherwise be the case. From the viewpoint of the ground landlord the danger in linking the ground-rent reviews to rack-rent value is that after 60 or 70 years an industrial building might well be worn out and from that time onwards the rack-rental value would cease to raise and might indeed fall. It is for this reason that the institutions prefer the rack-rent link.

There are other difficulties. Highly specialized buildings do not have an easily ascertainable open-market value. Subsequent additions or alterations to the building might increase or decrease rack-rental values to the benefit or disadvantage of one of the parties. In the first instance the occupier might not wish to fully develop the site. It is possible to devise ways of overcoming such difficulties. For example, by linking to the rack-rental value of standard industrial buildings and providing that alterations or additions shall be ignored and assuming that the notional standard buildings fully develop the site. But this then takes the rent-review valuation into the realms of hypothetical assumptions.

There are arguments in favour of linking ground-rent reviews to rack rents. Evidence of rack-rental values might be more readily available — perhaps true in the case of small or medium-sized buildings but unlikely to be so when dealing with a very large building. In times of rapid inflation the value of the bricks and mortar might rise more swiftly than land values. The only certainty is that it is impossible to know which basis of review will turn out over the period of a long lease to be of greatest benefit to one party or the other. The landowner might be well advised to agree different rent-review bases for different sites. When rent reviews are linked to rack rents, ideally the term should be shortened to 60 or 80 years to overcome the danger of little or no increase in ground rent from the seventieth year onwards.

Not all ground leases will be granted for long terms. Regard will be had to the use of the site and to the capital invested in its development by the lessee. Sites for open-storage use and the like might well be let for a 20-year term with frequent rent reviews.

(d) Ground rents

The rents will be fixed by negotiation, having regard to the length of term, the frequency and the basis for rent reviews and other conditions of the lease. On the average employment area it is customary to fix ground rents in terms of so much per acre. However, when letting sites for a development which will have a considerably higher plot ratio than the average, for example, offices on an employment area, the ground rent is often fixed with reference to the floor space of the buildings or the site area whichever will give the greater rent.

The rent for smaller sites will be higher to reflect the proportionately greater road and service costs. It is commonly found that occupiers wish to take a site large enough to allow for about 50 per cent expansion in the future. In such circumstances the full rent should be charged for the site from the outset. If the occupier wishes to leave a margin for considerably larger expansion, it is advisable to make some special arrangements. Even if the full ground rent is payable, it will be unsatisfactory from a general planning and land-use viewpoint if a substantial proportion of the employment area remains permanently undeveloped. Substantial areas of land reserved for expansion should only be included in the lease subject to the right of the landlord to take back the expansion area with an appropriate adjustment in ground rent in the event of it not being developed within a given number of years. As an alternative the occupier might be granted a lease of the land which he proposes to develop and an option on the expansion area. The option fee will be calculated at the same rate as the ground rent to discourage frivolous requests for options.

The ground rent (or licence fee) should commence to run either on the signing of the building agreement or at the time development commences and when the formal lease is granted it should be back dated to run from the same date. This is beneficial to the landowner's cash flow and affects the date upon which the first rent review will fall due. Ground lessees will ask that the starting date for both rent and ground leases should be the date of completion of the development. A firm policy should be decided and adhered to.

(e) User covenants

Ground leases for warehouse research laboratories or office developments will normally have a user covenant which will limit the use to the particular use class. In the case of industrial developments it is usual to say that the premises may be used for the particular manufacturing activity in which the occupier is engaged or any other light-industrial use.

Beware of occupiers who will be troublesome to their neighbours. Covenants will usually be inserted in the ground lease to prevent nuisance to other occupiers and should be rigorously enforced. However, there are certain uses which by their nature are potentially troublesome and great care must be taken before letting a site for such a use. On occasions it might be better not to let a site rather than have a source of constant potential trouble. If noisy machinery is to be used, the necessary sound-reducing measures must be provided and the use of the particular machinery should be limited to certain specified hours. In light-industrial buildings near a residential area it might be advisable to prohibit the use of any machinery outside normal working hours.

(f) Employment policy

When disposing of land a local authority will be influenced by prevailing market conditions, also by its anxiety to attract employment. It must be recognized that on occasions an authority may dispose of land on terms less than ideal from an estate-management point of view because of overriding employment-policy considerations.

(g) Disposal of sites for speculative development

Although many industrialists will prefer to take a ground lease and build their own premises — particularly those able to benefit from generous capital investment allowances for tax purposes — not all will wish to do so. Many will prefer to rack-rent buildings erected by others. The local authority may meet this need by itself embarking on a building programme. In which event it will carry out the development function described elsewhere in this book along very similar lines to any other developer. Alternatively the local authority may decide to dispose of part of an employment area for development on a speculative basis.

A number of factors will influence the decision. Is the authority able to obtain the necessary finance either from public, or private sources? Is the authority prepared to accept the risk that is inherent in any speculative building programme? Does the authority have staff available with the necessary experience, or is the authority prepared to retain and rely on outside consultants? As a matter of general policy does the authority wish to see private enterprise developers helping to promote industrial growth? Will it be to the authority's financial advantage to let the land for private speculative development? Are developers willing to undertake speculative development in the locality? When in doubt as to the best course of action, perhaps the answer is to dispose of a small part of the employment area land for speculative development and decide in the light of experience whether to continue the policy.

Land disposals to speculative developers will be on a building agreement and lease basis along very similar lines described above, with the important addition of a provision for the local authority to share in the equity of the development. In other words, the authority will expect a share of the profit income retained by the developer after he has paid the basic ground rent and all financing charges. The precise terms upon which the equity-sharing agreement can be negotiated will depend very much upon the state of the speculative property-development market, which has fluctuated to such an extent in recent years that it is impossible to lay down any hard and fast guidelines. In some localities a local authority will find it difficult to persuade anyone to undertake a speculative building programme. In favoured localities, where there is a keen demand for industrial and warehouse accommodation and speculative developers are anxious to secure a site, competitive bids might be invited by tender from a selected list of developers able to demonstrate that they have the experience, ability and financial backing to carry out the development. On the basis that the development is to be carried out in accordance with an outline brief prepared by the local authority and the site taken at a basic ground rent subject to reviews, prospective developers might be asked to bid in terms of the amount of the equity of the development to go to the authority. If the authority is anxious to raise a capital sum, the developers might be asked to bid in terms of the payment of a premium for the lease.

In all cases where the ground landlord has a share in future rack-rent increases the frequency of the rack-rent reviews must be agreed. Reviews must be to the fair market rent in order to remove any possibility that a developer with the same tenant in a number of different development schemes will come to an arrangement whereunder the rack rent will be reviewed to something less than market rental value in those schemes where the landowner shares the equity, in return for the payment by the tenant of something over the market rental value in those schemes where the developer does not have to share the equity. Provision must be made for calculating the rental equivalent of any premiums for the purpose of the equity-sharing arrangement. Alternatively part of the premium should be paid to the landowner.

3.3.3 Sites for commercial development

Whereas it is relatively easy to lay down general guidelines relating to residential land or employment area development, it is a good deal more difficult to lay down general guidelines relating to the development of commercial sites which encompass such a wide range of different types of property the development of which is often governed largely by local circumstances.

Shops and offices are the two main categories of commercial development, which includes a miscellany of more specialized and speculative uses, such as licensed premises, hotels, garage and petrol filling stations, entertainment and leisure facilities, and the like. The following comments are made strictly subject to the proviso that local conditions and considerations peculiar to each individual site are likely to be of overriding importance.

(a) Shop sites

The value of a shop depends upon its economic viability which, in turn, is directly related to potential turnover. Location is of crucial importance as is the correct calculation of the right amount of floor space. Discuss matters with the local Chamber of Commerce, the various retail groups and some of the leading national retailers where the size of the prospective developments warrants it. A number of leading retailers are actively engaged as developers in the shop property field and are happy to co-operate with local authorities and offer valuable suggestions and advice based upon their own highly specialized knowledge even though there is no guarantee that they themselves will ultimately be represented in the particular developments. Over the last few decades substantial changes have taken place in the scale and methods of retailing and direct consultation with those actively engaged in the industry is highly beneficial.

Every new shopping development will inevitably influence trade elsewhere. The building of new shops does not result in any substantial increase in total retail expenditure, but does result in a shift of trade between the different retailing centres. Thus it is necessary to consider how any proposed shopping development will fit into the overall retailing pattern.

(b) Town centre

Consider the regional shopping hierarchy and the relationship of the town as a retailing centre to adjoining towns and to the main regional shopping centre. The economic and social characteristics of the population, the employment pattern and the prospects for economic and population growth, planning proposals and policies relating to shopping development throughout the region — redevelopment or enlargement of other town centres, out of town or edge of town shopping centres, the use of factories or warehouses as discount shopping centres — must be carefully evaluated as must the general planning and transportation policies throughout the region and of the town itself in order to judge their effect upon the overall pattern of retail trade. Are there other proposals for developments in the town centre or elsewhere in the town which will affect the estimated retail turnover in the proposed development? Are there any proposed traffic management schemes, such as the closure of roads to vehicles or the diversion of traffic or the rerouting of public transport vehicles, which will affect the development site? Is the site in a first-class location and likely to remain so. Overprovision of shopping facilities will adversely affect the secondary shopping positions to a much greater extent. Has the peak location in the town centre shifted over past years and, if so, for what reasons? In many towns particularly those which have expanded, it will be found that the peak shopping position has distinctly shifted over a period of years, perhaps because a

new bus station has been built or a new shopping development exerted a pull on the shopping public, or maybe the
road pattern in the former peak position prevented the expansion of major retailers, thus forcing them to move to
another location where they could build a new shop of the
requisite size. A thorough understanding of the history of
shopping development in a town centre will often provide
valuable pointers to likely changes in the future.

(c) Local shops

At the opposite end of the hierarchical shopping scale is the
individual, round the corner shop or group of small shops
found in residential areas. To provide the necessary economic
base, a certain minimum level of turnover is necessary which
limits the number of shops that can be provided in relation to
the population. The provision of shopping facilities in residential areas often represents a compromise between social
need and economic viability. The location of the site for the
local centre will be chosen with regard to the geographical
spread of the catchment population and the pedestrian and
vehicular routes in the area and the siting of other facilities
often associated with a shopping groups, such as a primary
school, public meeting hall, health centre and the local public
house. In new residential development areas these uses will be
frequently grouped together and can perhaps be thought of
as providing very much the same sort of facilities as are found
in small villages. The amount of total shopping floor space to
be built will depend upon the catchment population and the
proximity of other shopping. Much depends upon local circumstances but a typical basic local shopping group would
consist of a small food hall with a gross floor space of around
3000 sq ft (replacing the grocer, greengrocer, butcher and
baker), together with another shop unit around 1000 sq ft
for newsagent, tobacconist and confectioner, giving 4000 sq
ft in total. A basic local centre such as this would be supported by a minimum catchment-area population of 3500 people
living within twenty minutes' walking distance. Ideally the
catchment population should be around 5000. In the latter
case one or two additional shop units might be provided, for
example, a takeaway food shop and, if doctors' surgeries are
in close proximity, a dispensing chemist. Further units for

additional facilities requiring a much larger catchment-area population could be considered if those facilities were not provided in the nearby shopping centres: launderettes, hairdressers and banks, for example. Reasonable customer car-parking facilities are necessary and adequate road access and turning space for delivery vehicles. Very large vehicles frequently make deliveries to small shops. The grouping together of shops, public houses, meeting halls, and so on will often enable economies to be achieved in the provision of road access, turning space and customer parking facilities. Usually these small local shopping groups will be of single-storey construction each unit having its own individual yard space at the rear. It is rarely an economic proposition to provide residential accommodation over shops which will comply with all modern legislative requirements.

(d) District centres and superstores

In large towns there is scope for shopping development on a scale somewhere between the town centre and the local shopping group. These suburban shopping centres consisting of anything from 15 or 20 up to 100 or more shop units proliferated during the 1920s and 1930s alongside and often as part of the new speculative housing developments of that time. Many similar centres have been built during the last twenty years but the current tendency is towards the provision of one or more large supermarkets or superstores with far fewer individual shop units. Sites for district centres must be carefully located in relation to public transport routes and to the road network with very substantial car-parking provision. At least one car park space for every 200 sq ft of gross shopping floor space should be provided. Where the site permits and circumstances warrant, provision might possibly be at double that rate.

Many other facilities are often located at district centres. Doctors' and dentists' surgeries, public authority accommodation including maybe a local library and a public meeting hall, a sports hall and an indoor swimming pool, places of religious worship, office accommodation, car sales and servicing and a petrol filling station, a public house and other facilities, which will all help to make the district centre a focal point in the local community. The catchment area within the town of many district shopping centres will be found to include anything from 20 000 to 60 000 people. A district centre large enough to contain a superstore (commonly thought of in 1982 as a store with not less than 25 000 sq ft of selling space but often having selling space up to 50 000 sq ft or more) will attract people from a considerable distance, particularly if situated at the edge of the town. Twenty-five minutes' driving time is often taken as the outer limit of the catchment area of a superstore. Successful supermarkets and superstores might achieve turnovers in excess of £200 (1982 values) per sq ft of gross shopping floor space so that a store with selling floor space of 50 000 sq ft and gross floor space of 75 000 sq ft might achieve a turnover in excess of £15 million per annum. If for a rule of thumb calculation a turnover of £200 per annum per sq ft of gross shopping floor space is applied to the whole of a district centre shopping development, the potential total impact of the centre upon retail trade in the town and the region can be appreciated. This turnover figure is greatly in excess of the national average, but the latter is no doubt substantially reduced by the inclusion of a great deal of old-fashioned, outmoded, inconvenient and inefficient retail floor space in the calculation. Embarrassing surpluses of retail accommodation which appear in some localities in the wake of new shopping developments are undoubtedly due in part to failure to fully appreciate the impact of the new development on the existing pattern of retail trade.

(e) Out of town shopping

The difficulty of finding suitable sites of adequate size and high development costs in urban areas have led to attempts to find sites completely outside town boundaries. The theory is that the cost of site acquisition and development will be lower and in carefully selected locations the sites will be more easily accessible to customers travelling by car. In practice it is difficult to find sites suitable for development well placed with regard to major road networks and surrounding urban areas from which shopping population can be drawn and for which planning permission will be forthcoming. Planning authorities are generally opposed to this type of development not only because of the impact on the retail trading pattern in nearby towns, but also because such a development can change the character of the locality and impose undue strains on the road network at peak shopping hours. Interest in out of town shopping development in the UK has been encouraged by the success of similar developments in Europe, but the number of genuine out of town developments in this country is limited and it is probable that edge of town locations will more often than not prove to be the best practical compromise between a number of conflicting considerations.

(f) Site disposals

The foregoing remarks amount to no more than a simple summary of a very complex subject. It is not possible to slot every shopping development easily into one convenient category or another and local circumstances will often add new dimensions which will be peculiar to the particular development. It is impossible to overemphasize the importance of assessing the overall impact of a proposed development scheme when a local authority is preparing to dispose of a development site. The local authority and the developer and the retail occupiers will all have a common interest in ensuring the success of the development scheme, but it is upon the shoulders of the local authority that responsibility will usually rest for ensuring that the development will be a worthwhile gain to the community as a whole.

Usually competitive bids will be sought by tender not only to meet the requirements of public accountability, but because different developers might have differing views as to the development potential and development value of the site. The tender documents must be prepared with great care and clarity and make it absolutely clear on what basis competitive bids will be judged, whether financial, design, a combination of the two or some other basis.

The development brief will set out the requirements of the authority with regard to such matters as total floor space, pedestrian and vehicular access, car-parking provision, landscaping and any other facilities which the authority considers desirable. When dealing with large comprehensive developments, the authority might wish to stipulate that sites will be set aside or accommodation within the building be made available for public authority purposes. If so, the financial basis upon which this accommodation is to be made available must be specified: if it is to be for a nominal payment or something less than fair market value, this will be reflected in the amount of the financial bid made by the developer. There may be circumstances in which the authority will wish to supplement the design brief by a sketch layout or outline sketch drawings illustrating the development required, but in the great majority of cases it is best to prepare the brief with the greatest possible flexibility to enable prospective developers to put forward their own design contributions based upon their skill and experience which, in many cases, is substantial. While the development brief is still in draft form, the authority's intention to dispose of the site should be advertised and otherwise made known to all potential developers with whom meetings should be held to discuss the outline brief and the tender document generally. These discussions might well produce ideas which the authority will wish to adopt and the initial response from the developers will enable the authority to gauge the extent to which they are likely to be successful in disposing of the site.

When the development brief and tender document have been finalized, bids will be invited from a number of developers selected on the basis of the preliminary discussions. The amount of flexibility available to the developers must be made absolutely clear and developers should be asked only for outline sketch drawings to support their proposals, in the first instance, and not be required to produce detailed and expensive drawings. Tenders will normally be invited on the basis of a 99-year lease at a basic ground rent with equity sharing arrangements; but if the preliminary discussions with developers lead the authority to think that much better financial terms could be obtained on the basis of a longer lease, say 125 years, it might be advisable and would certainly be interesting for the authority to invite bids for both alternatives.

The invitation of competitive bids is, of course, only practicable when there is more than one bidder. This will not always be so, particularly in the case of sites for small developments in residential areas which are of no interest to the large property-development companies or the large retailers.

When an authority is anxious to see a particular development take place, it will sometimes be necessary to go out and search for a suitable developer and negotiate the best terms that can be obtained.

(g) Office sites

One reason for building offices is to meet the local needs of professional, business or industrial firms. Another reason is to attract new employment. The proportion of the total national labour force employed in offices is gradually increasing, whereas the proportion employed in manufacturing industry is gradually shrinking. Office development might play an important part in an authority's overall employment develop-ment policy. It is not possible to draw any hard and fast dividing line, there will be no difference in the basic principles underlying the design of offices for either purpose. In practice the scale of development will make an effective dividing line, because a prudent developer building a very large office block will in the absence of a known local demand look outside the local community for potential tenants. Certainly the neces-sary market-research programme for an employment-develop-ment policy will be of a very different scale and character from that undertaken to investigate the extent of local need.

Many of the comments relating to the development of sites on employment areas can with common sense be applied to the disposal of sites for office development and so need not be repeated again. If office development figures promin-ently in employment-development policy, an authority will wish to see as wide a choice as possible made available to potential office-occupiers. Sites should be available in town centre or edge of town locations and, perhaps, at district shopping centres, which are a compromise between the two. A certain amount of speculative office-building is desirable so that accommodation is readily available for those who prefer to rent, although care must be taken to ensure that speculative development is not carried to excess because a large surplus of office space will create a bad impression in the minds of those seeking a new location.

When dealing with sites within an existing urban setting, the character and scale of new office development is of great importance. The design brief should deal with the dimensions both vertically and horizontally with some degree of precision, in addition to fixing the maximum permitted floor space, so as to ensure that the development will fit happily into the urban scene. The authority will no doubt have a policy with regard to the provision of car parking for office development. In certain parts of a town centre it might be that only a handful of car-park spaces will be permitted for quite a large office development with the intention that office workers should use the public car parking which will otherwise be fully used only at peak shopping hours on Saturdays. If substantial amounts of car parking are allowed in office developments in or adjoining shopping centres, consideration should be given to the possibility of securing the use of the private office car parking for the shopping public on Saturdays. Speculative developers should be encouraged to produce buildings of good quality, and if air conditioning is not considered an economic possibility at the outset the dimensions of the buildings should be adequate to allow an installation at a later date. Many building owners find themselves having to spend large sums of money on upgrading the quality of office buildings: it is rare to find a developer who considers that he has provided a building of too high a quality in the first instance.

(h) Miscellaneous commercial uses

There are a number of highly specialized commercial uses the accommodation for which is built either by the operator himself, or by a developer who has an agreement with an operator who will take the premises on completion. Only in exceptional circumstances would any developer build accommodation for these specialized uses on an entirely speculative basis: the risks involved would be enormous as would the difficulty of raising finance.

There are various reasons why an authority might wish to make available sites for these purposes. Maybe a large, new, expanding residential area is short of amenities and a public house would be a useful facility. Perhaps a shortage of hotel accommodation is impeding efforts to attract new employment to the town, because the availability of good hotel accommodation for their business customers is an important consideration in the minds of many industrial and commercial firms. If a town is short of commercial entertainment facilities, a local authority might well endeavour to promote such development at any rate to the extent of making available a suitable site. The improvement of the quality of life in the community may well be the motivating force. On the other hand, an authority might find that it has land in its ownership surplus to requirements and that one of these specialized uses would be the most appropriate and profitable development.

There is no set of rules which is universally applicable to land disposals for these special uses. An intelligent application of basic principles, suitably modified to meet local circumstances and the peculiarities of each type of development, is necessary. The following comments might be of some help.

Site disposals will normally be on the basis of a building agreement and lease and competitive bids will normally be sought by the invitation of tenders wherever it is practicable to do so. It will often be possible and appropriate to relate the ground rent in some way to the business turnover on the site. This means that the ground landlord is to some extent relying upon the business ability of the operator so that it is highly desirable for the landlord to underpin such arrangements by reserving the right to call for basic groundrent reviews to cleared-site value at periodic intervals. When an authority decides as a matter of policy to offer a site for a use which is considered desirable, even though the land would be worth more for some other use on the open market, it is important to impose an absolute user covenant. Thus the land is limited to the desired use so that at any time in the future the ground landlord will have—subject to the overriding provisions of any relevant statutory legislation — complete discretion as to whether to agree to any change in the user covenant and in that event to require a payment in respect of such a change.

Generally the building of new hotels has for many decades been an uneconomic proposition. Very few new hotels were built between 1945 and 1968, when the availability of government grants under the Development of Tourism Act 1969 led to a surge in new hotel building which was no doubt also encouraged by the boom in the tourist industry. In the absence of government grants the local authority with a site available for hotel development will have to search for a developer, and a site may well be worth little more than a nominal value when good hotels are changing hands at market prices appreciably less than their rebuilding cost. In such circumstances it is important to relate the ground rent in some way to business turnover. There are various ways of doing this. For example, a site might be let on a 99-year lease, the landlord reserving the right to review the ground rent every 10 years by reference to cleared-site, open-market values at a basic rent per annum, or a certain percentage of the total takings in the hotel whichever is the greater. A variant on this arrangement would be to provide that the basic ground rent would automatically increase according to any increases in the room rate charges in the hotel. Percentage increases need not be constant, they can be calculated on an increasing scale or by reference to profit rather than turnover.

Although most existing communities are served by an adequate number of public houses, there is usually a good demand for a site in an expanding residential area where there are 3000—4000 people or more living in the catchment area, particularly if the site is at a focal point as mentioned in the commentary on local shopping development. The majority of sites are probably let on the basis of a straightforward ground rent, but it is not uncommon for the ground rent to be linked in some way to the trade turnover.

A site for a petrol filling station where only relatively little capital expenditure is involved might be let on a term of 40 years, and 25-year terms are not unknown. If the site is to be comprehensively developed for car sales showrooms, workshop servicing facilities, and the like, considerable capital expenditure may be involved and a lease for 60 years or longer will be necessary. A basic ground rent plus a payment in respect of the gallonage of petrol sold is a commonplace arrangement.

When disposing of a site for commercial entertainment or leisure facilities, the consideration uppermost in the mind of the authority will no doubt be the quality and extent of the facilities to be provided. This rather than the amount of the financial offer for the site might well be the deciding factor.

3.3.4 General comments

(a) Keep in mind the basic objectives underlying the land disposals. Will the disposal arrangements result in the achievement of those objectives? Will the development result in some overall gain to the community? If not, why is the development being carried out?

(b) For convenience of discussion the various land uses have been dealt with in their separate categories but, in practice, it will often be found that there will be a combination of uses in a proposed development. In this event it will be necessary to decide whether it is practicable and desirable to split up the land into various parcels for each use, or to deal with the whole of the land on a comprehensive basis — as will almost invariably be necessary when dealing with a comprehensive town centre development scheme.

(c) When making arrangements for land disposals and drawing up the development briefs, the possibility of achieving planning gains should be considered. For example, when disposing of a site for private housing development, would it be advantageous to arrange for the developer to level and seed an adjoining playing-field site in the possession of the authority, or maybe provide a sports pavilion, or perhaps the housing developer could provide a community hall within his development which would serve the neighbourhood generally? There are many other possibilities, particularly when dealing with large comprehensive schemes in town centres. The so-called 'planning gain' will invariably be reflected in the financial terms obtained for the site. No authority should ever delude itself into believing that by imposing planning gains it is able to obtain something for nothing. But if it is otherwise impossible to obtain money for desirable public authority development, the imposition of planning gains may be a very convenient way of achieving an objective, provided of course that the planning gain does not become so disproportionately large a burden on the development scheme that it outweighs the market value of the site.

(d) On occasions it will be necessary for an authority to strike a careful balance between a number of competing factors, such as architectural quality, planning gains and financial terms, when considering the disposal of a site. When making a choice between competing bids in such circumstances, there is a tendency to select the one which will produce the best financial return, because of fears concerning the ability to justify taking an alternative bid which while producing a more attractive scheme (that being a matter of subjective judgement) will be less advantageous financially. This problem should be frankly faced before the start of the land disposal process and, if necessary, procedures adopted which will not present the authority with such a difficult decision, for example, by fixing the financial terms for the site and then inviting competitive design bids.

(e) If an authority for its own good reasons is anxious to obtain capital receipts rather than annual income, and yet wishes to retain a ground landlord's interest, there is no reason why a long lease should not be granted at a nominal ground rent in return for the payment of a premium.

(f) When acting in its capacity as landowner, an authority should not rely upon planning powers or other statutory provisions. The legal documents relating to land disposals should be in themselves comprehensive and fully protect the local authority in its capacity as landowner.

(g) Do not confuse the cost of acquiring land with the value of that land for development purposes. There is not necessarily any relationship whatsoever between the two. When disposing of land for development, the relevant consideration is the market value of the land for that development. The market value at any particular time (and it must be remembered that market values do not remain constant but vary with the passage of time, changing circumstances and market conditions) can be established by inviting competitive bids either by tender, or auction. At a particular point in time a site may be worth no more than a purely nominal figure for the development which the authority wishes to see on the land, and in that event a decision will have to be made whether to dispose of the site for a nominal figure in order to see the development brought about, or retain the site in the hope that market conditions will improve when it will be disposed of at a later date on more advantageous terms. The cost of acquiring that very same site might have been considerable, because acquisition costs will normally have been based on the statutory code of compensation which in many cases will be in no way related to the value of the land for new development. This type of situation will frequently arise when acquiring land in inner-city areas for redevelopment purposes; it is obvious that it is bound to do so.

(h) Occasionally an authority might wish to dispose of a site for a development which is not commercially viable but which nevertheless would be of value to the community. Such disposals will often be to charitable or non-profit-making organizations who are not able to afford to pay a high price for the site. In such circumstances the use of stringent restrictive covenants will protect the interest of the authority and often reduce the value of the land to a figure acceptable to the potential developer. An authority is normally obliged to dispose of land for the best terms obtainable, but obviously the permitted development, the user covenant and restrictive covenant all have to be taken into account.

(i) The need for land and property to be adequately managed between the date of acquisition and the date of disposal for development should not be overlooked.

(j) The total property holdings of an authority should be regularly reviewed to ensure that all properties are efficiently and economically used and that any surplus property is either put to good use, or disposed of. If property is held for development which will not take place for some years, consideration should always be given to the advisability of disposing of that property with a view to making the necessary acquisitions for the development at a later date.

(k) All property dealings should be conducted in such a manner as to avoid the slightest suspicion of intrigue or corruption.

3.3.5 Acquistion of the land by the developer

We have examined at some length the various methods of land disposal. The landowner — whether local authority or private — will often regard the land disposal as the end of his involvement in the development process or, at any rate, the beginning of the end in those cases where the landowner retains ownership and reserves some financial interest in the development scheme. But the landowner's disposal also marks the acquisition by the developer who might well regard it as the end of the beginning. The developer will have begun by undertaking the necessary market research, preparing the evaluation and carrying out a certain amount of preliminary work and then deciding to acquire the particular site in the particular location at a particular time. The acquisition of the land is usually the developer's first major commitment to the development project.

It has been said that you can do anything with a building except move it and for all practical purposes that is true. The selection of the site, therefore, fundamentally affects the nature of the development. No amount of careful design or vigorous marketing can totally overcome the disadvantage of a poor location or a lack of demand for the accommodation at an economic price irrespective of location.

A competent local authority when disposing of land will have comprehensive particulars available and will often be willing to produce the results of its own market research. But some authorities are less competent than others and developers will often be acquiring land from private owners who will normally look to the developer to satisfy himself before entering into a commitment to acquire. A prudent developer will in any event wish to make his own investigations before entering into any commitment, because it is the developer who will suffer if the site acquisition arrangements are less than entirely satisfactory.

Many of the matters dealt with in the commentary on land disposals will be thoroughly investigated by the developer, albeit from the viewpoint of one who is on the receiving rather than the disposing end of the transaction. There is no point in examining all those matters yet again. but it will be useful to look from the viewpoint of the developer at the following points which are of vital importance.

(a) The site

Has a survey been made and do the boundaries agree with those shown on the title deed? If a site is being assembled by bringing together parcels of land in various ownerships, is it certain that the boundaries of all the parcels dovetail together and that the whole of the site is in fact being acquired? It is not unknown for a developer to find halfway through a development scheme that a small but vital part of the land has been inadvertently omitted. What are the boundaries — fences, walls and dtiches, for example — and who is responsible for their maintenance? Have boreholes been taken to ascertain the physical nature of the site and have any necessary tests for soil pollution (important when dealing with redevelopment areas) been carried out?

(b) Tenure

Is the developer acquiring a freehold or taking lease? If leasehold, what is the length of the term, the pattern of rent reviews and the main provisions of the lease such as the user covenant? Will the leasehold be acceptable to the financial institution from whom the development finance must be obtained?

Ideally the developer will endeavour to arrange that the term of the lease and the ground rent will start to run from a completion of the development. The developer may be able to take a building lease, in the first instance, which will immediately vest in him a legal estate no doubt subject to covenants relating to the satisfactory completion of the development. Otherwise the transaction might be arranged on the basis of a building agreement and lease, which in the first instance merely gives to the developer a licence to enter on to the site and construct the building with a commitment by the landowner to grant a lease when the building has been satisfactorily completed.

We have previously examined the length of ground leases and the frequency and basis of rent reviews when considering site disposals. These are matters where broadly the interest of the landowner and the ground lessee are diametrically opposed and whatever arrangement is to the greater benefit of one will probably be to the least benefit of the other.

(d) Possession

Is the whole of the property to be acquired with vacant possession? The existence of tenancies or licences or unauthorized occupancies will sometimes necessitate the expenditure of both time and money to obtain possession. The fact that a site or building appears to be derelict does not necessarily mean that no legal rights of occupancy exist.

(e) Easements and rights of way

Is the land subject to any private or public rights that will impede the development? If so, is it possible to negotiate their removal or modification in order to allow the development scheme to proceed? What will be the cost of doing so and how much time will it take?

Always check adjoining buildings to ascertain whether they have benefits of rights, such as light or air, which might conflict with the development scheme. Are there any party walls and, if so, is it necessary to agree schedules of condition or party-wall awards?

(f) Covenants and other restrictions

Are there any restrictive convenants? Will they adversely affect the development scheme? Is it possible to secure their removal by agreement or by reference to the lands tribunal?

Have any agreements been entered into under the Planning Acts or other legislation restricting the development of the land in any way? Are there any statutory restriction which will affect the development?

(g) Planning permission

Has the necessary outline or detailed planning permission been obtained? If not, is the land being acquired subject to planning permission being granted?

(h) Performance obligations

The vendor in a freehold transaction or the ground landlord might impose legal requirements, placing the developer under an obligation to fulfil certain conditions relating to the carrying out of the development. For example, the developer might have to obtain approval to the detailed designs or he might have to complete the development within a stipulated period of time. Are such conditions couched in reasonable terms and do they allow the developer whatever flexibility might be necessary?

(i) Finance

No sensible developer would consider entering into a commitment for the acquisition of a site without having first secured the necessary finance to cover the total costs of acquisition, including interest on the acquisition cost while the site is held pending development. But have all the detailed arrangements been made for financing the development project so that the developer is certain of being able to obtain the necessary finance as and when it is needed on acceptable terms?

(j) Taxation

The developer will obviously wish to arrange his affairs in a way which will put him in the most advantageous tax situation and specialist advice will no doubt be taken. For example, there are very substantial allowances in respect of expenditure on new industrial buildings. Certainly detailed records of all expenditure must be maintained in a form which will readily facilitate tax discussions.

(k) General

The risk inherent in any property development has already been referred to. The prudent developer will always endeavour to reduce the element of risk to a minimum, and this will be as true of site acquisition arrangements as of any other aspect of the development process. Ideally no acquisition will be made until all the relevant detailed information has been obtained and all problems resolved. In practice, however, it is virtually impossible to remove every element of uncertainty.

Unforeseen delays can add very substantially to the total interest charges incurred in holding land for development. Allowing for the effect of compounding and assuming a quarterly payment of interest, an acquisition at a total price, including costs of purchase, of £100 000 would on the basis of interest at 15 per cent per annum rise to £135 320 over two years, i.e. an addition of 35.32 per cent. It is, therefore, of the utmost importance that the acquisition of the land does not take place before the development is ready to proceed, or if it has to be bought before that time, then the price that is paid reflects the holding cost.

On occasions it might be necessary to acquire the land before all the necessary consents and approvals to the development scheme have been obtained, such as landlord's approval or planning permission, or approval under the building regulations or other relevant legislation. The precise details of the financing arrangements for the development scheme may not have been settled. The value of land acquired for development in stages over a period of years — a large housing site, for example — will almost certainly change with alterations in market conditions and will fluctuate to the developer's advantage or disadvantage.

The developer will on each occasion carefully weigh the degree of uncertainty and it will be a matter of judgement as to whether the risk involved is acceptable. To acquire land without any planning consent for a use which conflicts with the use shown on the approved town map would be hazardous, but if the land is already allocated on the town map for the type of development proposed and it is known that the planning authority wishes to encourage development as quickly as possible, the degree of hazard is thereby reduced. An outline planning consent will greatly reduce the risk and, of course, a detailed planning consent virtually removes the risk completely, at any rate as far as the statutory planning situation is concerned. A developer may feel that where a vendor or landlord approval to the development scheme is not to be unreasonably withheld, the risk involved, at any rate at the site-acquisition stage, is acceptable. Similarly if the precise details of the financing arrangements for the development have not been finalized, and when the developer knows that there are a number of institutions who would be agreeable in principle to providing the finance, he may feel sufficiently confident to proceed with the acquisition.

The degree of risk involved should be reflected in the price paid for the land. Occasionally a developer who would not proceed if he had to pay the equivalent of what the land would be worth with all risk element removed, might be tempted to acquire at a price very substantially below that amount. The distinction must always be drawn between a carefully calculated risk and an outright gamble. The business failure of so many property developers in the mid-1970s has resulted for the time being at least in a sharp contraction of the extent to which the average developer is prepared to take a risk. Recent taxation provisions, such as Development Land Tax, have also removed much of the incentive to take a risk on such matters as planning consent.

(l) Options

When it is possible to do so, a developer will often consider it advantageous to pay for an option to reserve the land for a sufficient period of time to enable the removal of, or substantial reduction in, the more serious risk elements.

CHAPTER 4

The statutory planning system

4.1 INTRODUCTION

The system of statutory planning control in the United Kingdom is one of the most sophisticated in the world. It is necessary to obtain a specific planning consent for virtually every development. The only exceptions, while large in number, are of a relatively trivial nature normally covered by General Development Orders. Although legally development carried out by the Crown — that includes all government departments — is not subject to the statutory planning process, in practice there is consultation with the appropriate local planning authority which is tantamount to the same process that is gone through when formal planning consent is applied for. It is beyond the scope of a general book on property development to deal in detail with all aspects of planning. Nevertheless those concerned with property development should have at least a general appreciation of the principles involved, and it is with this in mind that the following commentary is given.

Ultimate planning authority is vested in the Secretary of State for the Environment who, for example, must approve all County Structure Plans and who will decide the outcome of any planning appeal of importance. However, as far as day to day dealings with planning authorities are concerned, developers find themselves faced with the present two-tier planning system under which there are normally two local planning authorities concerned in any particular area. The two-tier planning system is inextricably bound up with the two main tiers of local government established when the radical reorganization of local government, throughout most of England and Wales, took place in 1974. The Local Government Planning and Land Act 1980 has since adjusted the balance of responsibility between the two tiers in regard to the administration of planning legislation to avoid problems due to differences of view that developed in some cases between the two tiers, and also to reduce the overlap of functions.

The metropolitan and shire county tier of authority is responsible for preparation of structure plans within its boundary. Structure plans might for example seek to encourage, or limit, population growth, or a policy might aim to restrict development in specified rural areas. This broad policy plan is developed in liaison with the districts in the county area. Counties and districts generally cooperate in seeking the same planning goals; counties monitor and advise on, and seek changes in the strategy in liaison with the districts; some counties might offer assistance to districts in preparing local plans for areas within a district. County authorities are also responsible for approval of their own county developments (e.g. roads, schools, etc.) and consult with the districts upon these developments. County planning authorities are responsible for deciding on applications for development that straddles the boundary of a National Park and for mineral workings and related development and waste disposal, although applications for these are registered initially with the district authority.

District planning authorities are responsible for local plans and for all development control functions other than those for which the county is responsible. In the first instance a planning application will be submitted to the district council. The district authority in coming to a decision on whether to approve or refuse an application for a development will be guided by the structure plan and any local plan in so far as it affects the application. When considering planning applications it is the duty of the local planning authority to 'seek the achievement of the general objectives of the structure plan'. In the absence of any agreement to the contrary district authorities must consult the county before deciding planning applications which have material implications for the structure plan and the county's role as local planning authority. A list of such 'county matters' is set out in Section 86 of the 1980 Act. Department of the Environment circular 2/81 contains a code of practice for such consultations. When district authorities receive planning applications which do not relate to county matters a copy must be sent to the local highway authority where there is no agreement between the authorities to the contrary.

The district tier of authority is now in effect the planning authority through which developers work except in a few very specialized cases. In Greater London planning control is divided between the GLC and the London Borough.

4.2 WHAT IS DEVELOPMENT?

The statutory definition of development is 'the carrying out of building, engineering, mining or other operations in, on, over or under land, or the making of any material change of use in any building or other land'. Thus in broad terms development might be thought of in two categories, one being the carrying out of physical operations, such as building or engineering works, and the second being the making of a material change of use. A publication concerned with property development naturally tends to concentrate on the physical activities, but the question of use is of vital importance. Indeed it is possible to argue that planning control is basically one of land use, because once the use of land has been determined the question of precisely what is built is a matter of detail albeit very important detail. In the final analysis it is the right to use land or buildings for particular purposes which determines their value.

For purposes of planning control the Secretary of State for the Environment publishes 'Use Classes Orders', which divide up the various land uses in various classes each separate class consisting of a group of very similar uses. Normally a change from one use to another within the same use class will not constitute development, whereas a change from a use which falls within one class to a use in a different class will constitute development for which planning consent will be necessary. In practice buildings are often suitable for a variety of different uses and a change from one use to another might involve a material change of use for which planning consent will be necessary. For example, a building might be suitable for use as a warehouse which will come within Class X or for a light-industrial use which might be carried out in a residential area without detriment to the residential amenities and would fall within use Class III. The same building might be suitable for use as a general industrial building within use Class IV and, having regard to current trends in the retailing trade, if the building is in a suitable location with reasonable road access and parking facilities, it might be suitable for a retail use. The value of such a building might be substantially affected by the possibility of being able to obtain the necessary planning consent to change from one use to another.

On the face of it the description of the physical works which need planning consent appears straightforward. But as is the case with virtually all legislation circumstances will arise in which there is room for argument about the interpretation of the statutory provisions and a considerable volume of case law has built up as to what constitutes building or civil-engineering operations for the purpose of planning control. Arguments are often concerned with the placing of mobile structures on land or the installation of plant and machinery on land. It is worth while noting that the installation of machinery in a building or physical works carried out inside a building which in no way affect the external appearance do not need planning consent, assuming that in both cases no material change of use results.

4.3   THE PLANNING APPLICATION

Anyone wishing to carry out a development for which planning consent is required must apply to the local planning authority for the necessary consent. At the outset it is prudent to check that a planning consent is necessary. There is currently (in 1982) a trend at government level towards some relaxation of the planning system in the sense that the provisions of the General Development Orders have been extended so as to remove a wider range of developments from planning control and the necessity for planning consent. In some cases where it is not immediately clear if a planning consent is required the planning authority can be approached for informal advice; in some cases it is necessary to apply to the local planning authority for a formal 'determination' as to whether the proposals would constitute development for which a planning consent is required. The local planning authority must give a formal decision within eight weeks and there is a right of appeal against the decision.

Anyone may apply for planning consent in respect of any property. It is not necessary for the applicant to have any legal or financial interest. However, if the applicant is not the owner of the property, he must serve notice on the free-holder and on any lessee with an unexpired term of at least seven years still to run and on any occupier of agricultural property advising them of his application for planning consent. In practice the planning authority has a set of forms upon which these notices must be served and the applicant must advise the planning authority of the names and addresses of the people on whom he has served the notices. Applications for planning consent for certain specialized types of development, for example, buildings for various types of public entertainment or buildings exceeding certain heights, must be publicized by putting a notice in the local press and the notice must make it clear where any member of the public might inspect the plans showing the proposed development. These specialized applications must be advertised, but in addition the planning authority might advertise others at its discretion by press advertisement or site notices and in those cases where the development might have a significant effect on neighbouring property the authority will normally draw the attention of neighbours to the application. Any owner or lessee or occupier of agricultural land upon whom notice is served or any member of the general public has the right to make respresentations to the local planning authority.

A developer wishing to carry out building or engineering works should consider the advisability of applying for an out-line consent. It is not possible to apply for outline planning consent for a change of use and such an application must always be made in detail. Preparation of the necessary design drawings for a large building project can be costly and the submission of an outline application may save a good deal of time and trouble ending abortively. An outline application must give sufficient information to describe adequately the type, size and form of development proposed. The local planning authority will reserve for subsequent approval all matters in respect of which it has not received adequate detailed information to enable a full consent to be given. A typical condition attached to an outline planning consent would be:

before any development is commenced detailed plans, drawings and particulars of the layout, siting, design and external appearance of the (proposed development) and the means of access thereto together with landscaping and screen walls and fences shall be submitted to and approved by the local planning authority and the development shall be carried out in accordance therewith.

Fees are now payable to the local planning authority in respect of applications and the appropriate fee calculated in accordance with scales prescribed by the Secretary of State under his powers derived from Section 87 of the Local Government Planning and Land Act 1980 must be paid at the time the application is submitted. The eight-week statutory period within which the planning authority should give a decision runs from the date the application is deposited, together with the correct fee. If no fee or an incorrect fee is deposited with the planning application the eight-week period will not start to run until the correct fee is paid.

Planning applications must be made on the form provided by the local planning authority. The forms are self-explanatory but many planning applications are delayed because applicants either do not complete the forms accurately or fail to provide all the information which is requested. When the application form is submitted, the planning officer should be asked to confirm that the form gives all the information he requires and that no additional information is needed from the applicant and also that no supporting documents are necessary. The application might be one of many received by the planning authority each week and will take its turn in the queue to be processed and checked; the site will be inspected by staff of the planning authority and they might need to consult with other organizations such as the highway authority or the water authority on site restrictions, or with amenity societies in areas of special environmental interest. During this process the staff of the planning authority might wish to discuss points that need clarification, or problems that are revealed, with the applicant or his agent. At this consultation stage it is often possible to make modest corrections or alterations in the application to avoid such problems, but more radical alterations might require another round of consultations, or a new application. Since applications now require a fee payment it is clearly advantageous to the applicant to research thoroughly and consider the requirements prior to submission of the application. At the time of submitting the application, it is useful to ascertain the date of the committee at which the matter will be considered and to check at the appropriate time that it has been placed on the committee agenda. If there is a particular urgency, the reasons should be explained to the planning officer who will usually do all that he can to help.

When considering planning applications, the local planning authority must have regard to the provisions of any approved development plan but is not inexorably bound thereby. However, if it is proposed to give a planning permission which will constitute a substantial departure from the development plan, the local planning authority must advertise the planning application and give opportunity for objections to be made. The Secretary of State must be advised of the proposals and he may issue directions concerning the granting of permission or requiring the application to be referred to him for consideration. In the absence of any such directions the local planning authority may grant permission.

4.4 CONSULTATION

It is useful to consult the local planning officer at the outset before any formal planning application is submitted. A great deal of time can often be saved by so doing and anything which saves time also saves money, particularly when interest rates are high and building costs steadily increasing. Through early consultations, it might be possible to agree the development proposals in principle with the planning officer. Some negotiation and compromise at this stage might overcome objections from the planning officer. Agreement reached in this way should ensure that the planning application will have a smooth and fairly quick passage through the necessary committees. Planning authorities have the power to delegate various powers of decision to their planning officer so applicants should always ascertain whether the planning officer himself is authorized to issue the necessary planning consent or whether he will be making recommendations to his authority. If it appears impossible to reach any agreement with the planning officer, or if negotiations are unduly protracted, then the applicant should submit a formal planning application. The planning authority must then give a formal decision within eight weeks of the receipt of the application or such longer period as the applicant may agree. If consent is then refused or granted subject to conditions to which the applicant has objection, he may then appeal to the Secretary of State. If no decision is given within the prescribed time limit the applicant may assume that planning consent has been refused and appeal to the Secretary of State accordingly.

Even though consultation with the planning officer does not result in agreement, the applicant should at least thoroughly understand the views of the planning authority and his attention will normally be drawn to all the relevant local policies and documents so that he is in a better position to consider the conduct of any appeal to the Secretary of State.

Some planning authorities appoint advisory committees to comment on certain types of development. Most commonly architectural advisory panels are set up to give advice on the architectural merits of proposed developments which are to take place in sensitive areas. Planning authorities must also consult parish councils in country areas and might also wish to consult the local residents' organizations or amenity committees of various kinds. Amenity societies are normally consulted when development is proposed within conservation areas and the local planning authority has a duty to advertise the receipt of planning applications for developments in those areas. A local 'conservation area' committee might exist and its comments will carry weight. The planning officer should be able to indicate whether it is possible or advisable to consult such committees or voluntary organizations at the informal preapplication stage.

If the development proposals entail the demolition or alteration of the character of buildings which are on the list of buildings of special architectural or historic interest prepared by central government, then special procedures are necessary. A specific consent for the demolition or alteration of the listed building must be obtained before any work can be carried out. Applications for the necessary consent must be made to the local planning authority and advertised so that any member of the public may make representations. There are a number of very reputable groups with a sincere interest in the protection of listed buildings and proposals for alterations or demolitions of listed buildings can become a very emotive matter. Developers should make every attempt to avoid the demolition or substantial alteration in the character of listed buildings, particularly when the buildings have considerable historic interest or architectural merit. Quite apart from the importance of preserving such buildings wherever possible in the national interest, it is very much in the developer's own interest to do so.

If there are any trees on the site protected by a Tree Preservation Order, it is necessary to obtain consent before felling or lopping them. Normally the necessary application is made to the local planning authority but in certain cases the consent of the forestry commission is necessary.

The Advertisement Control Regulations enable planning authorities to exercise a very tight control over all external advertising. This is frequently a matter in respect of which the planning authority will have a policy document. Normally the greatest weight is given to considerations of visual amenity and public safety in those cases where advertisements might possibly distract the attention of road-users.

4.5 THE DEMOCRATIC ASPECT

Some types of application might be decided by the planning officer using powers delegated to him by his authority. Lesser items such as house extensions or advertisements might be dealt with quickly in this way. More important or substantial applications will be decided by a committee of elected representatives of the authority, who will meet regularly and will normally have full powers to make a decision on the application on behalf of the council. The committee will be advised by the planning officer and his advice will be based upon his knowledge of the area and its problems and policies, and upon consultations he has had with such bodies at the high-way and water authorities. His professional advice will also be influenced by his knowledge of planning case law and the relationship of that to the council's policies and to the possible outcome of an appeal against a refusal. Authorities seldom wish to waste time with appeals they cannot expect to win.

The committee will listen to the advice of their professional officers and will also take note of any representations made by members of the public. Development is often highly contentious and public comment might come to the committee from individuals or groups, or in the form of petitions. The committee must consider the variety of advice and represen-tation it receives and make a decision to approve or refuse the application or perhaps, in some cases, to refer it back to the applicant to seek a modification.

Public interest in planning is often strong when existing values might be disturbed. These values might be financial or social or aesthetic. The planning committee is a com-mittee of elected representatives and works as a part of our democratic political machinery and must often make deci-sions in the face of contention.

An example of the difficulty that might be met is that of a commerical development (shops or public house) proposed on a residential estate. The committee might be faced with advice from their officers that the development appears to be an appropriate land use and at the same meeting have to consider a massive petition against the proposal from irate residents living within the vicinity of the site.

The statutory planning system has been devised as part of the democratic and legal machinery of society which has to attempt to try to overcome problems of conflict and produce a fair judgment within the terms of the planning legislation and the spirit of its intention. A decision must often leave one of the contending parties unsatisfied.

4.6 THE PLANNING CONSENT

Planning permissions may be qualified in various ways and it is proposed briefly to consider the more important of these.

Permissions may be granted subject to a variety of conditions, or for a limited duration of time, or for the personal benefit of certain people or organizations.

With regard to time limits, there are two separate aspects to be considered. Nowadays every planning permission will lapse unless the development is commenced within five years from the date permission is granted or such other time as the planning authority may specifically stipulate. In the case of outline permissions the necessary application for approval to the various reserved matters must be made within three years and the development itself commenced within five years of the date of the original outline permission, or within two years of the date on which detailed planning consent is granted, whichever is the longer subject to the imposition of any other specific time limit by the planning authority. Only a very limited amount of work on site is necessary to prove that development has commenced to meet the time-limit requirements. The digging of part of a foundation trench will probably suffice. To deal adequately with the evasion of the time-lapse provisions attached to planning permissions, local authorities have powers to serve a completion notice the effect of which is that planning permission will lapse unless the development is completed within a reasonable period of time. Completion notices must be approved by the Secretary of State and there are rights of objection for the people who are affected by them.

The second and quite different aspect of time limits is when the planning permission will only remain in force for a limited period and at the end of that period any buildings or works which have been erected must be removed and any use authorized by the permission must cease. Thus at the end of the limited period of planning permission, things will revert back to the state which existed before the permission was granted. On the expiration of a limited period planning permission, it is of course open to the applicant to make a new application for the retention of the buildings or the continuance of the planning use. Planning permissions for limited periods are obviously of limited value.

Conditions may be imposed limiting the occupation to a particular type of occupier. These fall into two broad classes. There is the condition which limits occupation of a building to someone engaged in some particular trade or vocation; perhaps the best known condition of this type is that limiting the occupation of agricultural cottages to those engaged in agriculture. The other and more restrictive type of condition is one which limits occupation to a particular occupier personally. An example of circumstances in which it might be appropriate to impose a personal condition of this type is when an industrial or commercial firm is badly short of office accommodation and wishes to use a large house at the edge of a nearby residential area temporarily for offices until such time as permanent office accommodation can be provided on its own site or elsewhere. Provided that the temporary use will not adversely affect the residential amenities of the area to any undue extent, the planning authority might be prepared to agree to such a temporary use with a condition limiting occupation to the particular company in question. The ability to impose limitations on the type of occupiers will sometimes enable a planning authority to grant a permission which otherwise it would not be prepared to consider.

Generally planning authorities are able to impose such conditions on the grant of planning permission as they think fit, provided that the conditions are not unreasonable and do have a planning context. Typical examples would be a condition imposed on a planning permission for a residential estate prohibiting the erection of walls or fences or other means of enclosure in front of the dwellings in order to preserve an 'open front' appearance, or planning permissions for an industrial development granted subject to a condition that no machinery would be operated before say 6 am or later than 8 pm, which might be appropriate if the industrial development were in close proximity to a residential area.

There is the same right of appeal against the imposition of a condition on a planning permission as there is against the refusal of planning consent.

4.7   PLANNING AGREEMENTS

The statutory planning system as traditionally administered by planning authorities is essentially negative in character in the sense that, while the planning authorities prepare the

necessary policies and plans to establish the planning framework, this in itself does not bring about the implementation
of the plan. Implementation depends upon the public and
private developers who choose to carry out development
within the plan area. Local authorities often undertake a
development role in their different capacities, for example,
as housing authority or roads authority or education authority,
but the amount of positive implementation by local planning
authorities acting as a promoter of development has been
relatively small. Having prepared the planning framework, the
local planning authority normally waits for developers to
appear and produce specific planning proposals and applications for permission to carry out the development. It would
be a mistake to underrate the powers of persuasion and
negotiation exercised by the local planning authorities, but
their legal ability to indulge in positive action when endeavouring to guide and control applications from developers
is limited. The system controls the development within the
plan framework by refusals of the unacceptable and only
rarely by investment by the planning authority acting under
its planning powers.

It is possible for developers and planning authorities to
enter into legally binding agreements which enable development proposals to be handled in a more positive manner than
would otherwise be the case if the authorities were relying
solely on their statutory powers of control. In some areas
planning agreements may be made under the aegis of Local
Acts but for the most part they will be made under the
provisions of Section 52 of the Town and Country Planning
Act 1971. Agreements might be made to phase the development of land to accord with the dates when various public
services will become available or improved road access will
be provided. Similarly, agreements might be made with
regard to the provision of a certain number of sites in a
comprehensive development area for public open space
or amenity purposes. Where there is inadequate infrastructure,
for example a lack of main sewers or adequate road access,
it might be possible for the developer to enter into a Section
52 agreement under which he will bind himself to make
financial contributions towards the cost of making available
the infrastructure so that development may proceed. With

regard to the provision of infrastructure it should be remembered that Section 52 agreements may be entered into with other public authorities as well as the local planning authority. Local planning authorities do not have a unanimity of approach to the use of Section 52 planning agreements. Some are a good deal more enthusiastic than others. If a developer feels that a local planning authority is attempting to exert undue pressure on him to enter into a Section 52 agreement which will impose unduly onerous burdens on him, his remedy is to make a formal planning application and take the matter to appeal if planning consent is not granted. However in many cases it will be to the advantage of the developer to propose a Section 52 agreement himself if some contribution from him will enable the development to take place at a very much earlier date than would otherwise be the case. High building and civil engineering costs coupled with high interest rates are making it so expensive for local authorities to provide new infrastructure that many are becoming reluctant to encourage some types of new development on any substantial scale involving new infrastructure because of worries about the burden on the local rates. Under the Local Government (Miscellaneous Provisions) Act 1982 Section 33 certain positive covenants in agreements under seal made by persons with an interest in land may be enforced against successors in title.

It may well be that a growing number of local authorities will discourage new developments requiring the provision of extensive infrastructure unless they are essential to meet some local need, if some way is not found to relieve the local authorities of the rate burden that would otherwise be created. In these circumstances an increasing use of planning agreements to help local authorities with the infrastructure burdens may become more widespread. Contributions towards the provision of infrastructure, whether they be given in cash or by way of sites for various public authority purposes, will obviously be reflected in the amount which a developer will be prepared to pay for the land needed for the development.

The extent to which a planning authority should, when considering a planning application, negotiate with a developer in order to obtain a 'planning gain' in the form of some material benefit for the community has always been a matter of some controversy. This has been highlighted by the publication of a report by the Property Advisory Group (*Planning Gain, Report by the Property Advisory Group*, HMSO, £2.20). Some feel that it is wrong for a planning authority to bargain to obtain a material benefit in return for a planning permission and that such a practice brings the whole system of planning control into disrepute. Others feel that developers should, and do, make their contribution to the community through the tax system (particularly development land tax) and should not be subjected to *ad hoc* demands from planning authorities which are regarded as potentially dangerous precedents in the nature of local taxes on development. There are many who argue that used in moderation and with common sense planning gains can often facilitate development in circumstances where the authority is not able to provide needed facilities and the planning gain makes a contribution to the welfare of the community in which the development takes place. It has been suggested that the government should issue a guidelines to codify the practice of negotiating planning gains. It is difficult to imagine how this could be done other than by a statement of broad principles which would be very much subject to individual circumstances. It must be remembered that the applicant has a right of appeal if planning consent is refused for any reason. It is, of course, important to remember that the controversy relates to planning gains obtained by planning authorities and not those obtained by local authorities in their capacity as landowners as part of the consideration at the time the land is sold as described in Chapter 3.

4.8 PLANNING APPEALS

The great majority of planning applications that are made receive an approval or an approval with conditions; a minority of applications are refused. The applicant has a right of appeal against that refusal and many, but not all, applicants exercise that right.

When considering a planning appeal, one of the first steps is to consult all the appropriate documents and consider their relevance to the proposed development. Many current statutory development plans were in preparation a quarter of a century ago and are often outmoded. A new statutory plan procedure was initiated to replace them and to provide an improved and more flexible system of strategic planning. The objective of this is that county councils should prepare structure plans for the approval of the Secretary of State, and the structure plans will then provide the broad planning framework within which a series of local plans will be prepared by the district councils. However, the length of time taken to prepare the structure plans — including the time needed to engage in the necessary processes of public consultation, submitting them to the Secretary of State and awaiting for the result of the public inquiry and the Secretary of State's decision with regard to the approval, with or without modification of the structure plan — is raising doubts in certain quarters about this procedure. Strategic planning must be related to the state of the national economy in which there can be substantial changes in relatively short periods of time and the adequacy and adaptability of the structure-plan system in times of rapid economic change are now being questioned. Some planning applicants will find that there is no approved structure plan, although if a plan has been submitted to the Secretary of State any matters in the draft plan which are relevant to the planning appeal will be of considerable importance. All other relevant documents must be carefully examined. These will include current development plans and town maps with their corresponding written statements, and it will often be found that planning authorities have produced policy statements or study documents which will have a bearing upon the proposed planning appeal. For example, planning authorities often have policy documents relating to the location of retail uses, including policies with regard to the establishment of out of town discount stores. In urban areas policy documents or statements often exist, expressing the views of the planning authority with regard to changes in the character or scale of the existing development. Residential planning policy documents may indicate the views of the planning authority with regard to pedestrian and vehicular segregation and the provision of public open spaces within the development, major landscaping, and the like.

The appellant must ascertain whether there are any Local Acts which might have some relevance to the development which is the subject of the appeal. Assiduously inquire as to whether any local organizations have at any time expressed views which might assist the planning appeal. For example, local organizations might have expressed concern about shortages of housing accommodation or lack of adequate shopping or entertainment facilities. Maybe these will have been reported in the local newspapers and can certainly be referred to at a public inquiry and perhaps suitable witnesses called.

Changing circumstances which have led to the existing planning policies becoming out of date must always be considered. Recent government policy statements must be studied to see whether they indicate that some change in local policies is appropriate. A good example of this is the Circular 71/77 from the Department of the Environment dated 11 July 1977 concerning local government and the industrial strategy in which it is made clear that local authorities should do everything reasonably possible to encourage and foster the growth of industry, and that local planning provisions and decisions on planning applications should have regard to the desirability of encouraging industrial development. An increase in local unemployment will often cause planning authorities to reconsider the question of relaxing any restrictive policies they might have with regard to developments which will result in new employment in the area.

The views of civic amenity groups and preservation societies and the like are worthy of serious consideration. If any of these bodies have objected to the proposed development and intend to appear at a planning inquiry, it is not unreasonable to ascertain their total membership and to make quite sure that the majority of the members are acquainted with the planning proposals and have been given an opportunity to express their views before the particular body has registered its objection to the planning authority. If the appellant and the planning authority agree, appeals can be decided on the basis of written representations submitted by the parties. In cases where there is a simple, straightforward difference of opinion between the parties and major policies are not involved, and there is no dispute about the relevant facts, written representations may save a great deal of time and expense. However, unless both parties are agreeable to written representations the Secretary of State appoints an inspector to hold a local inquiry and hear evidence from the appellant, the planning authority and other appropriate people. The Secretary of State has the power to direct that certain types of appeal shall be decided by the Inspector, but otherwise the Inspector must make a report including his own recommendations to the Secretary of State who will give his decision after having had due regard to the report and recommendations from the Inspector.

4.9 MISCELLANEOUS MATTERS

The planning authority will normally consult other appropriate authorities before giving planning permission. For example, the Highway Authority will be consulted on the deisgn of any new roads which are ultimately intended for adoption as public highways, or the local Environmental Health Officer might be consulted on potential noise or fume problems, or the Health and Safety Executive might be consulted on 'hazardous' or potentially explosive processes that might be proposed in the development.

There are various matters upon which it is important that the developer should satisfy himself by means of direct discussions with the appropriate authorities. The more important of these are the adoption of roads and footpaths by the Highway Authority where it is appropriate for them to be adopted; the acceptance by the local authority of public open space provided within any development; and the necessary approvals under the building regulations, fire regulations or any other statutory provisions which relate to the development in question, for example, the Factories Acts, the Shop Acts and Public Health Acts.

The developer will agree direct with the Highway Authority the design and specification for all new roads and footpaths and enter into the necessary adoption agreement. He will reach a similar agreement with the Water Authority in respect of sewers. A planning permission in no way constitutes an agreement for adoption.

Nowadays planning authorities commonly ask for public open space or amenity land to be provided in large-scale residential developments. It is reasonable that they should do so. However, it is important that the developer should make the necessary arrangements for the maintenance of the open spaces and amenity areas, and the best way to do this will be to ensure that the parks or open spaces committee of the local authority will be prepared to take over and maintain the areas as public open space. This means that the areas must be designed and laid out to the approval of the local authority. This will be a matter for negotiation. There may be circumstances in which the local authority will not accept responsibility for maintenance unless some capital payment is made by the developer. If the local authority is not prepared to take over responsibility for the open spaces and the developer requires a heavily planted scheme, it might be possible for the developer to arrange that occupiers of the buildings included in the development will enter into a management scheme for the maintenance of the open spaces. Such arrangements do not always work to everyone's satisfaction, and in residential areas it is far better to come to an agreement with the local authority. In commercial developments amenity planning will normally be maintained by the building occupant or his landlord. Situations should not be allowed to develop where public areas are provided within developments and no one is responsible for their maintenance.

Planning permissions in no way commit any other statutory authority. It is necessary for approval under the building regulations and any other relevant statutory provisions to be obtained. Therefore, at the time the planning application is made the developer should be confident that it will not be necessary to change the appearance or the design of any buildings in order to obtain the necessary approvals from other statutory bodies. Time and money will be wasted if a detailed planning permission is obtained and then the developer has to seek approval to amendments to the designs which have to be made in order to obtain the approval of other statutory bodies.

CHAPTER 5

Construction

5.1 INTRODUCTION

The developer's first major commitment is the acquisition of the land. The second is the placing of the building contract which finally commits the developer to a particular building design and content, and in this sense might be regarded as the ultimate commitment.

In this chapter we consider the various types of building contract, the necessary precontract procedures, the management of the building contract and what should be done on handover of the building and during the defects liability period. We also consider the various risks inherent in any building contract and how they may be reduced or shifted from the developer to the building contractor or vice versa. The successful outcome of any development will be greatly influenced by the efficiency with which the building arrangements are made and carried out.

The type of building contract to be adopted for any particular development must be decided at a very early stage. This decision will greatly influence the size and composition of the development team. As soon as the schedule of accommodation has been prepared and the broad design constraints decided, the decision on the type of building contract must be made. There are various possible arrangements and the extent to which the developer, albeit through his professional advisers, is responsible for the building design and the management of the building contract and the degree of risk to which he will be subject will vary according to the particular contract arrangement.

5.2 THE ALTERNATIVES

There is nothing sacrosanct about any particular form of building contract. It is open to the developer to devise a contract which suits his own particular requirements, provided that it is generally acceptable to building contractors. But there are advantages in using one of the forms of contract arrangement familiar to those in the building industry and in respect of which there is a good deal of practical experience so that the strengths and weaknesses of the particular type of contract are known. From the viewpoint of the developer, building contract arrangements may be broadly divided into two main categories albeit with many variations in each. The first is based on the use of the standard form of contract evolved by the building industry Joint Contracts Tribunal (JCT), which provides for the contractor to carry out the construction in accordance with the designs and specifications prepared by the developer's own team of professional advisers — upon whom he must rely for the quality of design, adequate supervision of construction and suitability of the building for the purpose for which it is designed. The second is the 'Design and Build' or 'Package Deal' contract, which is of a radically different nature. In essence the contractor is responsible not only for the construction, but also for the design and specification, and he takes full responsibility for ensuring that the building meets the requirements of the developer and is fit for the purpose for which it is designed.

5.3 THE JCT STANDARD FORM OF CONTRACT

This is commonly, although incorrectly, referred to by many laymen as the 'RIBA contract', although few architects wish to claim the credit for it. Although the contract has been subjected to a good deal of criticism, it nevertheless continues in widespread use and no generally accepted alternative which achieves the same results has yet been evolved. A number of variations and amendments are frequently used but the two basic forms of standard contract are 'With Quantities' and 'Without Quantities'. Generally quantities are used for contracts for work likely to exceed £50 000 in value.

The developer (referred to as the Employer in the contract

documents) appoints his own team of professional advisers who are responsible for the design of the building to meet his requirements, for supervising the carrying out of the works and generally administering the contract. The architect leads the professional team and calls in whatever specialist advisers he needs to deal with such matters as structural design problems and the provision of services which in large commercial buildings seem to become more and more complex. The quantity surveyor should be appointed at the outset in order that the full benefit of his cost-planning services are available. The roles of the various members of the professional team are more fully dealt with in Chapter 8.

Provided that the contractor executes the building work in a good and workmanlike manner and in accordance with the architect's drawings and specification in the Bills of Quantities, and with any instructions subsequently given to the contractor by the architect, the contractor will not normally have responsibility if the building is not suitable for the purpose for which it was designed. This is irrespective of whether the unsuitability is attributable to faulty design or to some physical inadequacy in the structure. The developer must turn to his architect and other professional advisers for a remedy. On occasions the respective responsibilities of the professional advisers for an inadequacy in the building are not clear-cut. In such circumstances the developer finds himself in a somewhat vexatious situation dependent upon the outcome of the arguments between professional advisers. Such situations may be avoided by the exercise of care in the selection of the team of professional advisers, and when a highly complicated or specialized or sophisticated building is involved, it is helpful if the professional advisers have had previous experience of dealing with that particular building type. The quality of the team has a significant influence upon the success of the development project.

Total mutal confidence between the developer and all the members of the team is vital. The developer has an important contribution to make at the design stage. He should establish at the outset positive and realistic cost limits. He should ensure that the architect thoroughly understands — preferably with the aid of a written brief — his requirements in respect of all the aspects of the building and its usage, the standard and type of finishes required, the services needed and date for completion. The developer should avoid changes of mind, which are expensive and wasteful of time and effort at any stage. Once the contractor has started work, changes necessitating revised instructions to the contractor can result in an alarming increase in costs.

5.3.1 The duration of the contract

The date for the completion of the building works contained in the contract is subject to extension for a number of reasons. Some of the reasons which justify an extension of the building contract time also entitle the contractor to recover any additional loss or expense he may have suffered as a result of the extension. Almost certainly any extension of time leads to an increase in the cost of what is known as 'preliminaries' (overheads such as insurance, cost of plant hire, etc.). Thus the developer might find that not only is the completion of the works delayed, which might have a very serious affect upon his cash flow, but also the cost of the work is increased because of the delay.

The main reasons for extension of the contract time which entitle the contractor to recover additional loss and expense are:

(a) Inadequacy in the contract documents, namely, the drawings and/or the Bills of Quantities. This may be attributable to the incompetence of those responsible for the preparation of the documents, or new legislation might be introduced during the progress of the contract which necessitates some amendment to the drawings, or some event may occur — a major fire elsewhere, for example — which leads those responsible for the implementation of the various statutory legislation to impose more stringent conditions which necessitates some design changes. It is sometimes found when the builder takes possession of the site that the physical conditions give rise to difficulties which require additional work of one sort or another. This underlines the necessity for a careful site survey and investigation before the drawings and Bills are prepared including not only the measurement of the boundaries of the site, but a detailed survey of its physical characteristics, and normally this necessitates taking a number of bore-hole samples. The site should also be tested for any form of chemical pollution. Measures to deal with this might necessitate the expenditure of considerable amounts of money.

(b)   Delay by the architect is issuing drawings or instructions.

(c)   Delays caused by artists and tradesmen directly employed by the developer.

Additional reasons which may entitle the contractor to an extension of time, but not to recover any additional loss or expense, include:

(a)   Failure of nominated subcontractors: on almost every building site some of the work is carried out by sub-contractors — the installation of services in buildings is one of the most commonplace examples. When the contractor finds and appoints his own subcontractors to carry out some of the work for him, the contractor is entirely responsible and has no redress against the developer if the subcontractors in some way fail to carry out their obligations. However, the architect often nominates particular subcontractors to carry out particular types of work. There are various reasons why the architect should wish to do this. In the case of certain finishing works the architect may wish to see a high standard achieved and for that reason wish to nominate a subcontractor in which he has every confidence. Sometimes a subcontractor is nominated to design and construct elements of the works, for example, structural steel work or a fire-alarm system.

(b)   Bad weather: the architect should ensure that careful note is kept of weather conditions on site.

(c)   Strikes and lockouts.

(d)   Shortage of labour or materials: sometimes this clause in the JCT contract is deleted, although the contractor in these circumstances normally inflates his tender price in various ways to make sure that he does not suffer as a result of the deletion.

(e)   Damage by fire when the contractor is responsible for insurance under the contract.

(f)   *Force majeure.*

The significance of the contractor's ability to claim an extension to the contract time is that, where the contract has a provision for the payment of liquidated damages by the contractor in respect of delays to the building works in order to compensate the developer for losses which he incurs, the delays in respect of which an extension of time is granted by the architect are not included in the delays in respect of which liquidated damages are payable.

It would be naive of any developer to assume that the building work will be completed within the time set out in the building contract and for the precise amount of the contract sum. A developer who fails to appreciate the various matters which can increase the contract time or cost might be in for a rude awakening.

5.3.2 Choosing the contractor

When using the JCT form of contract with its drawings and Bills of Quantities, the usual procedure is to invite contractors to submit tenders for carrying out of the contract work. But this is not essential: there is nothing to prevent one contractor being asked to price the Bills of Quantities. This might occur when the developer has been used to employing a particular contractor over a period of time and is entirely satisfied with the result of the contractor's work and for that reason prefers to employ that particular contractor. It may be that the contract contains a great deal of highly specialized work for which one contractor has an outstanding reputation and he might be chosen on that ground to carry out the work subject to a satisfactory pricing of the Bills of Quantities.

When choosing contractors to be invited to submit competitive tenders for carrying out the work, there are various considerations to be borne in mind. In practice it is necessary to limit severely the total number of contractors invited to submit competitive tenders. Six or eight contractors are often adequate for even the largest contract, because the pricing of Bills of Quantities for a large job can take a considerable amount of time (and therefore money) on the part of the contractors who are not keen on submitting competitive tenders when there is, in their opinion, an unreasonably large number of tenderers. If the work is of a specialized nature, contractors skilled in that particular type of work are obviously chosen. On some occasions it is thought advisable to employ a large national contractor, while on others local or regional contractors are preferred. Some contractors have a particular reputation for producing work of high quality, others for producing work quickly and on contract time, and this can be a matter of major importance to the developer's cash flow. Still other contractors have a reputation for submitting keen tender prices, and there are those who have a reputation for their considerable expertise in formulating claims for extra payments on any and every occasion during the contract. The architect or developer may feel that some contractors are entirely dependable, while others may have let them down on a job in the past. Unfortunately high-quality work and speed and low cost are a very rare combination. The developer is normally guided by the advice of his architect and quantity surveyor on the selection of the contractors for the tender list. Before any contractor is included, he should be asked whether he is willing to tender for the particular job. There are times when contractors are fully extended and are not keen to tender for extra work. Some contractors for a variety of reasons may not be interested in tendering for work in a particular locality. A good contractor is always perfectly frank with the architect in such cases. Unfortunately some contractors for reasons which they no doubt consider adequate appear to be reluctant to indicate that they do not wish to tender for any work — it may be that they are afraid of not being asked again on a future occasion — and often put in tender figures at a very high level, hoping that they will not be given the job. This can be a source of considerable irritation to architect and developer alike.

Reliability and financial stability are important considerations. The building industry is notorious for its financial ups and downs. Firms in this industry often head the yearly list of bankruptcy cases. Therefore, when the contractor has been chosen, it might be thought desirable for him to take out what is known as a 'performance bond'. The contractor usually takes out a performance bond with an insurance company which guarantees to reimburse the employer for any loss he might incur up to an agreed amount as a result of the contractor failing to complete the contract. The failure of a contractor can be reckoned as a major disaster from the developer's point of view. Very often there are long delays while the legal position is sorted out and another contractor found who is prepared to complete the work. The new contractor might ask a considerably higher price for completing the job than was contained in the original contract. If defects subsequently appear in the completed building, it might be very difficult to apportion responsibility as between the original contractor and the contractor who takes over and completes the job. Thus it is easy to understand why many employers ask for a performance bond even though the extent to which their losses are reimbursed is limited and the cost of the performance bond is normally added to the contract cost.

5.3.3 Paying the contractor

The method of payment for the building works has a considerable impact on the developer's cash-flow position. It also has considerable impact on the contractor's cash flow and he has regard to the method of payment when preparing his price for the work. For that reason the method of payment must be made clear at the time the contractor is invited to tender.

Under the JCT contract the architect commonly authorizes monthly payments based on the value of work certified by the quantity surveyor. Usually a certain percentage of the total value of the work carried out is retained until the end of the contract. The arrangement for regular payments is a happy one for the contractor who obtains payments for the work he carries out irrespective of when the building is ready for occupation. It is less so for the developer who, in the case of a large, complicated building, might have paid out very substantial sums of money over a considerable period of time without getting any benefit, because the building is not ready for occupation until handover at the end of the contract. To the developer the disadvantage of this situation is often highlighted in public authority housing contracts, where payment is made monthly on the basis of quantity surveyors' certificates, and perhaps in a contract for a large number of houses, when no particular handover schedule is linked to the matter of payments, it is sometimes found that the public authority has paid out 60 or 70 per cent of the total contract price before a single house is handed over. The developer, in consultation with his architect and quantity surveyor, should give careful thought to the arrangements for payment at the time the contract documents are being prepared.

On the face of it the ideal arrangement for the developer is for the whole of the contract price to be paid when the building is handed over so that the developer does not part with his money until the time when he should be receiving an income from the building, or have the benefit of occupation of the building. It must be remembered, however, that if it were possible to make such an arrangement, the contractor would increase his tender price by one means or another to take account of the payment arrangements. In the case of a large contract spread over a period of time, some contractors might not be able to finance the work easily without payments from the developer. In the case of a large, complicated single-building structure, some common-sense compromise might well be devised for payment to be made in certain set stages, the last payment on completion and handover of the building being heavily weighted so as to give the contractor an incentive to get the building finished. Where the contract is for the erection of a number of buildings — for example, a housing estate — it might well be possible to arrange for the total contract price to be split up so that payment is made for each building as it is handed over. The method of paying for the work obviously has to be related to the particular circumstances of each contract. But the developer must certainly bear in mind the disadvantages of paying the quantity surveyor's certificates as the work proceeds irrespective of when final handover takes place.

5.3.4 Calculating the cost

When using the JCT form of contract, it is customary for the contractor to submit his bid on either a firm price or a fluctuations basis. The firm price means that, although the cost of labour and materials used in carrying out the work may fluctuate with the market, the contract sum will not be varied to take account of these fluctuations. Whereas the fluctuations basis means that once the contract has been awarded to the contractor any increase or decrease in labour and materials will automatically be added to or subtracted from the contract sum, which will also be adjusted to take account of changes in insurance or other contractor's expenses affected by changes in the National Joint Council Rules. Under both types of contract adjustments are made to take account of alterations in cost due to government legislation.

Many laymen think 'firm price' means that the contract sum once fixed will not alter. This is not so. Quantity surveyors' remeasurement and architects' variation orders and instructions and extensions of time may affect the cost.

The developer and his professional advisers must decide on what basis they wish contractors to prepare their competitive bids in order that the contractors submit prices on the same basis. The developer does not always find it easy to decide which basis is likely to be to his advantage. The risk of fluctuations in the cost of labour and materials during the contract is a fact of life and cannot be avoided; the question to be decided is whether the risk is to be borne entirely by the contractor as in a firm price contract or whether the risk is to be borne by the developer as in a fluctuations contract. If the contractor has to prepare his bid on a firm price basis, he will clearly add something to his prices to cover himself against the risk of increased costs. Perhaps the best way of tackling the problem is to ask contractors to quote prices on both a firm and fluctuations basis and then decide in the light of the differing prices which basis is likely to prove most advantageous during the whole of the contract period. In matters of judgment of this kind there are no infallible rules to ensure that the developer always gets it right.

The hallmarks of the JCT form of contract are its flexibility with regard to the way the price for the job is to be fixed, and its elasticity, which enables the type and quantity of work within the contract to be varied and yet leave the quantity surveyor free to negotiate the final price for the job at the end of the day. But, of course, these advantages do introduce a note of uncertainty, so that the developer must ensure that at all times he is kept closely advised as to the likely financial outcome of the contract. The best arrangements for dealing with this are examined in Section 5.5 on project management.

5.3.5 Contractor-designed works

There is now a version of the JCT contract which provides for the situation where the whole or part of the work is designed by the contractor. There is a growing tendency for developers to use design and build contracts particularly for straightforward buildings although the traditional standard JCT contract still remains in widespread use.

5.4   THE DESIGN AND BUILD CONTRACT OR THE PACKAGE DEAL

This is of a radically different nature. The contract hinges upon the production of a performance specification by or on behalf of the developer.

The word 'performance' is of great importance and it is used in the sense of describing the various requirements which the building must meet. In no circumstances must the developer or his representatives attempt to instruct the contractor as to how he should prepare the design or what precautions he should take to ensure that the finished building meets with all the various statutory requirements and suitability for the purpose for which it is designed. The responsibility for these matters must rest fairly and squarely on the shoulders of the contractor.

By using a very simple form of performance specification, the building contract can become more in the nature of a property purchase. For example, a developer might wish to develop a site by putting up some very simple standard-design warehouse units. He could go to various contractors who specialize in 'package deals' and present them with a schedule of floor spaces for different sized units with an indication as to how much office accommodation is to be provided, the total amount of toilet accommodation, the services to be put into the building, the floor loadings and the clear floor heights, together with an indication of the total yard area, and on that simple performance specification ask the package-deal contractors to submit schemes for the erection of their own standard-design units to meet the requirements, together with the price they would need to carry out the contract. The complete responsibility for obtaining all the necessary statutory approvals, and for designing and erecting the buildings and ensuring that they will be suitable for the purpose for which they are required, rests upon the contractor. The performance specification can, of course, within reason be as detailed as the developer cares to make it. He might wish, for example, to specify that the warehouse units will have reinforced-concrete frames or steel frames, and he might wish to specify that the walls shall be built in brick or in concrete block or in some other material. However, the developer must be careful to remember that if he specifies a material which proves to be totally unsuitable for the purpose, it might be difficult to fasten responsibility for such a defect on the contractor.

It is quite possible to arrange for complicated buildings to be erected under a design and build contract. However, in these cases the performance specification has to be very carefully prepared, probably by a team of professional advisers. In a simple package deal where a standard type of building has already been erected by the contractor in a number of locations, examples of which can be inspected and the occupiers asked for their comments on the adequacy of the building, the developer may enter into a contract for such buildings to be erected on his own site with confidence. In the case of a complicated building the like of which has not been erected by the contractor elsewhere, the developer is entirely dependent upon the adequacy of his own performance specification to ensure that he gets a building which meets his requirements. Of course, in these design and build arrangements the contractor submits his drawings and specification to the developer, who can carefully check to see just what type of building he will be getting, what services will be provided, and so on. Perhaps the situation might be likened to the purchase of a house, where on the one hand it is possible to go on to a large speculative housing estate, inspect the various types of houses that have been built, decide upon the type which is suitable, find out the location of the next plot where that type of house will be built and decide to buy it. On the other hand it is possible to go to a builder, usually a small local builder who has a number of building plots, and ask him to build a house to meet the needs of the house-purchaser, who will no doubt indicate the number and sizes of the different rooms, the main materials which he would like to see used and then leave it to the builder to prepare designs for his approval and put up the house to meet his requirements.

The design and build contract is particularly advantageous where the buildings are of a simple, straightforward nature and can be built to a standard design which has been used by the contractor elsewhere. The advantages are that the design time and cost can be greatly reduced; the contractor is working to his own design with which he is thoroughly familiar; and the contractor may well use various standard types of components which he can buy advantageously and which he is used to using on site. The contractor's own designs undoubtedly reflect the contractor's practical experience of putting up buildings. The upshot should be that the contractor works more efficiently and speedily, and therefore more economically, so that the price of the building to the developer in theory at any rate ought to be somewhat lower.

The advantages from the viewpoint of the developer are that while it is possible to provide for fluctuations in the contract price, and there are various alternative ways of paying for the buildings as the contract proceeds, it is more usual in the case of the simple package deals to pay for the buildings on completion and to have a lump-sum fixed price so the contractor is committed to providing the buildings for a known cost and must take the risk involved in doing so. Obviously contractors allow for these risks when preparing their price, but the developer is greatly reassured to know that the price is fixed and that he will not have to pay until the building is handed over. The developer does not run any risk of becoming involved in vexatious professional arguments, if the design or construction of the building is defective — it will be entirely the responsibility of the contractor to see that matters are remedied. There are disadvantages. The developer does not have the same detailed control over the design (if that is required), and it is very dangerous for the developer to request any alterations during the construction of the buildings because the cost might be increased out of all proportion — the developer does not have the protection of the flexibility of the JCT type of contract. It might be argued that the final cost of the buildings under a fixed-price, lump-sum package deal might be higher in view of the risk which is carried by the contractor, but in practice this is often offset by the advantages to the contractor of using his own design and standard components, and so on.

There may be types of development for which the design and build type of contract is not suitable. Where the developer does have the choice, his decision as to which contract to use is obviously greatly influenced by his views as to what is an acceptable degree of risk for him to take and how much risk he would prefer to shift on to the contractor even at the cost of an increased price. A degree of risk which is acceptable to a developer when inflation is running at 7 per cent per annum and interest rates at 8 per cent per annum might be quite unacceptable with inflation at 17 per cent and interest rates 14 per cent per annum. So the choice of the type of contract is influenced not only by the circumstances relating to each particular development, but also by general economic and financial considerations.

5.5 PROJECT MANAGEMENT

The appointment of a project manager is not necessary for every project. A project manager is needed for the large and complicated rather than the small, simple projects. Only the largest multi-million-pound projects justify a full-time project manager. In many cases the developer acts as his own project manager or relies on 'in-house' staff or one of the professional advisers to exercise the management function.

Nowadays project management is becoming recognized as an occupation in its own right. The two questions to be considered initially are: What is a project? and What are the management objectives?

The answer to the first question must be that a project is whatever those responsible care to make it. Frequently a project is the construction of a single building which might be either very simple, or of great complexity, or a project might consist of the erection of many buildings. At the extreme end of the scale, 'project' might describe the whole of a new-town development scheme. Major developments have several distinct phases, ranging from the initial market research to design studies, preparation of contract documents, the construction of the building and the disposal of the building. Does the project cover all these stages, or only one or some of them? Perhaps the best piece of advice at the outset is, first, define your project.

This commentary is related to the building contract, and it is assumed that the initial market research has been carried out and evaluated and a decision made as to total floor space requirements. And in addition that the design constraints have been defined and a decision made to carry out the job on the basis of a JCT contract, so that the architect has been appointed and prepared the necessary drawings and a quantity surveyor, after giving the necessary cost planning advice, has prepared Bills of Quantities to be incorporated into the contract documents which form the basis for the invitation of tenders for the erection of the building.

When a project manager is needed, the first step at this stage is his appointment. Ideally he should be solely concerned with the overall management of the project and not be in any way involved in the work of actual carrying out any part of the project. The project manager needs plenty of common sense and administrative ability and a general working knowledge of what is entailed in dealing with the erection of a building. Although it is often suggested that project management should be regarded as a profession in its own right, at the moment this is not so and project managers might be drawn from any walk of life. Usually the project manager is one of the professional people who are normally found in a project team, but it is essential that the project manager should have no direct involvement in the particular project which he is appointed to manage. The project manager must be able to view things objectively and dispassionately without any personal involvement in any of the particular tasks concerned with the execution of the project for which he is responsible.

The management objectives must be clearly defined for and in consultation with the project manager and made known to all those working in the project team. Basically the objectives are to ensure that the finished project will be suitable for the purpose for which it is intended, that it is built to satisfactory standards, that completion takes place on time and that the whole job is carried out within the approved financial budget. Often the project manager is also responsible for ensuring that arrangements for the disposal of the building, either the letting or the sale, are also carried out efficiently and satisfactorily. The project manager has a team to help him control the project. The identities and duties of the various members of the team will become apparent as this commentary proceeds.

There are a number of essential preliminary steps which must be taken before the building contract can start.

5.5.1 The site

Has the necessary legal right over the site — freehold or lease-hold — been secured, and is vacant possession of the whole site available immediately? Have all the encumbrances on the site been carefully checked — such things as underground services, easements, and the like — and is it certain that the proposed building will in no way interfere with them? Are the site boundaries clearly defined, and has it been ascertained that the building will fit on to the site? It is the job of the surveyor (or valuer/agent) to ensure that these checks have been made and that the results are satisfactory. Has a schedule of condition of boundary fences, adjoining roads and foot-paths, etc., been prepared?

5.5.2 Statutory consents

Have all the required approvals under the building regulations been obtained? If the premises are covered by specialized legislative provisions, such as the Shops, Offices and Railway

Premises Acts, is it certain that the design meets all the necessary requirements? Has the fire office been consulted? The architect is responsible for assuring the project manager that all necessary statutory consents have been obtained. It is most important for the project manager to obtain unqualified assurances on these matters, because in practice many expensive delays are caused as a result of one or other of the statutory consents not being obtained before the contract starts. Sometimes there are circumstances which might persuade the project manager to allow a contract to start before the whole of the statutory consents have been obtained, but in so doing the project manager must realize the risk he is running.

5.5.3 The contract documents

A very great deal of aggravation and trouble can be caused by allowing a contract to start on the basis of inadequate documents. Incomplete drawings are probably the most common cause of contract delays and cost increases. If a contract is started before all the drawings are complete and the architect is unable to provide all the drawings in time to meet the contractor's required schedules, the consequences can be very serious indeed. So much so that the advisability of starting a contract before all the drawings have been completed must be called into question. The project manager must be absolutely satisfied that he knows the precise position with regard to the availability of the drawings. If he decides that a contract should be started before the drawings are 100 per cent complete, he must obtain from the architect a detailed schedule showing exactly when the outstanding drawings will be delivered to the contractor. Before the building contract is actually placed, the architect must obtain from the contractor a written statement confirming that — provided the drawings are supplied in accordance with the architect's schedule — there will be not claims for delays due to lack of drawings. The importance of getting this matter right at the outset cannot be overemphasized.

The project manager must also be satisfied about the state of the Bills of Quantities and in particular must know what proportion of the whole job is covered by Prime Cost (PC) and Provisional Sums. He must understand why the PC and Provisional Sums have been included in the Bills, in other words, be satisfied that it is not possible to make the necessary detailed provision at the outset. Prime cost items are used to allocate a sum of money for the purchase of materials or goods which usually can be precisely defined, such as sanitary equipment, fireplaces, and the like. Provisional Sums are usually allocations of money to cover specific work which it is not possible to detail properly and evaluate at the time the contract is entered into. The amount of the contingency provision in the Bills of Quantities must be known and careful arrangements made to account for how it is spent, and the quantity surveyor should be closely questioned to ensure that he has received adequate information from the architect to enable him to prepare his Bills with complete confidence in their accuracy.

5.5.4 The contractor

If it is proposed to invite competitive bids from a selected list of contractors, the project manager should agree with the architect the names of the contractors who are going to be invited to submit tenders. When the competitive tenders have been received and evaluated, the job is normally awarded to the lowest tenderer. The project manager decides whether a performance guarantee bond has to be obtained by the contractor. If he is entirely satisfied on all matters, the project manager then authorizes the placing of the building contract. All the contract documents should be ready so that the contract may be signed before work actually starts on site. Although in practice work often starts before the documents are signed, it is difficult to justify this procedure. With an efficient administrative arrangement, it should be perfectly possible to have all the necessary documents signed before work starts. Circumstances might arise during construction which might create considerable difficulties in the absence of legally binding documents and, although such circumstances may be rare, there is no excuse for running any avoidable risk.

The project manager also discusses with the architect his reasons for wishing to appoint any nominated subcontractors and authorize their appointment. The sooner these arrangements can be finalized, the better.

5.5.5 Site supervision

The project manager should be continually satisfied about the arrangements made by the architect for site supervision during construction. On a sizable job a Clerk of Works is usually appointed. The architect should also arrange for progress photographs to be taken periodically on the site, so that a clear visual record of the state of the job at any particular time is always available to supplement the Clerk of Works' weekly reports and the architect's own reports on the progress generally. No matter how good the reputation of the contractor, the work on site is only as good as the workmen and staff employed by the contractor and the competence, alertness and awareness of the developer's professional team.

5.5.6 The construction period

Once the contractor has taken possession of the site, the project manager is responsible for ensuring that the works are carried out on schedule and that the overall cost is kept within the budgetary provision.

To enable him to carry out his duties effectively, he organizes regular meetings of the project team. The frequency and composition of the meetings depends upon the size of the particular job and might vary at different stages of the job. The project management meetings are often arranged on a monthly or fortnightly basis, although the project manager should not hesitate to call special meetings whenever they are necessary. The project manager, the architect and the quantity surveyor form the nucleus of the project management team. If the project manager is also controlling the letting or sale of the project, then the surveyor/valuer/agent is normally a member of the team, particularly in those cases where the purchasers or tenants might wish to have special works carried out. The contractor should always be invited to attend the part of the project management meeting at which the progress on site is discussed. Very often this idea is resisted by architects on the ground that the architects themselves hold their own site meetings with the contractor and are able to keep the project management team advised of the building progress. Unfortunately there is always the risk of misunderstandings, and if difficulties arise between the architect and the contractor, commonly because of the delay in supplying necessary drawings and information, or because of dislocation caused by site instructions from the architect, these difficulties may not be made absolutely clear to the project management meetings. It would be inappropriate for the contractor to remain during the whole of the meeting, because many matters will be discussed which do not directly concern the contractor and indeed some matters are best discussed in his absence. But a project manager who is determined to exercise a firm control over the job insists on the contractor appearing while the progress of work on site is discussed. Unless he acts in a way which suggests otherwise, the contractor should be regarded as part of the team and as a friend rather than an enemy. The contractor can often make a useful contribution to any discussion as to how best to overcome any difficulties which might arise. All project management meetings should be carefully minuted.

The project manager has his own style of conducting the meeting. Typically at the beginning of the meeting the minutes of the previous meeting are considered and any matters arising dealt with. The contractor is then called into the meeting and in his presence the architect presents a report on the progress of the work, indicating what parts of the work are ahead of or behind schedule and whether the overall progress of the job appears to be satisfactory. The architect should indicate any difficulties which have arisen and should at every meeting state whether or not the contractor is in any way delayed as a result of any lack of information from the architect. The architect should also report as to whether any variation orders or architect's instructions have been given to the contractor and if so their likely effect on the progress of the work. The contractor should then be invited to give his own view as to his progress and indicate any reasons which might possibly have an adverse effect upon the progress of the job. The contractor should confirm that he has all the necessary information to enable the job to proceed smoothly, that all the necessary materials have been ordered and that there appears to be no difficulty in getting hold of them, and he should also confirm that the labour position on the job is adequate. At this point a general discussion on progress takes place with all those present making their contribution. The contractor then normally leaves the meeting.

The quantity surveyor then presents his report on the financial situation, indicating that his work of measurement on site is well up to building progress and whether to his knowledge any variation orders or architect's instructions have been given which affect the cost of the job. He should also indicate the position with regard to PC and Provisional Sums and present an overall summary as to how the cost of the job so far compares with the contract sum. The quantity surveyor should also indicate any factors which in his opinion might increase or decrease the cost of a job at a future date.

When appropriate, the surveyor reports on the progress he is making with regard to the disposal of the property and on any requests for special or extra work which he has received from prospective purchasers or tenants. The practicability and advisability of carrying out those special works are then discussed. Ideally purchasers or tenants should take over the completed building in accordance with the original design and specification and then carry out any special works they require at their own expense once the building has been handed over to them. However, it is not always possible to insist on such an arrangement, particularly when sales or lettings are difficult, and it may be essential to carry out works in order to dispose of the property satisfactorily. Given a reasonable amount of common sense and a realistic approach, these problems should not be insuperable.

The project manager then summarizes the overall financial situation, particularly with regard to the payments to the contractor, compares them with the budgetary provisions, checks on dates of handover and compares the estimated date for the receipt of income or capital payments with the budgetary expectation. These are matters of vital importance to the developer's cash flow. If at any stage it appears that the project is running behind schedule, then methods of speeding up the work to recover the position have to be considered, together with their cost implications. Usually there is a liquidated damages provision in the building contract and the question of its enforcement has also to be considered. In practice liquidated damages are often quite inadequate to compensate the developer for the losses which he incurs as a result of the delays, because if the true cost is written into the contract documents at the time of the invitation of tenders, contractors feel obliged to inflate their tender prices out of all proportion in order to safeguard themselves against a very heavy liquidated damages clause which might in fact never be enforced.

This very simple summary of project management arrangements where a JCT contract is being used is intended to illustrate the basic principles involved. Frequently building projects are of a very complicated nature and the project management is that much more intricate. On the other hand, where simple contract methods are used, problems of project management are simplified accordingly. For example, in the case of a lump-sum, fixed-price contract for the contractor's proprietary standard buildings, the project manager is essentially concerned with quality control and progress. He may inspect the buildings himself during construction or arrange for a professional adviser to do so. Periodic meetings with the contractor to discuss building progress and the achievement of the handover dates should enable him to keep control of this aspect of the job.

5.5.7 Handover

A short time before the date for completion and handover of the building from the contractor to the developer, the Clerk of Works prepares a snagging list indicating all the minor defects that must be remedied before handover takes place. At that time it is useful for the developer's surveyor and the representative of the intending occupier — assuming that the building is to be let or sold — to accompany the Clerk of Works to ensure that they are both satisfied with the snagging list which is prepared. It is irritating if the architect accepts the building from the contractor and then the developer's representative or the intending occupier's representative is not entirely satisfied on one or more minor points.

At the outset of the job the project manager will have confirmed that the building works are adequately protected by the contractor's own insurance arrangements. The contractor's insurance will no longer protect the building once it is handed over, so one of the most important things is for the project manager to ensure that the developer has adequate insurance cover from handover until such time as the insurance cover provided by the occupier takes effect.

Occasionally the occupier wishes to have access to the building before the formal handover by the contractor. Maybe he wishes to install special machinery in a factory production area or perhaps arrange for the installation of special services to be started in the areas which have been cleared by the contractor or he might simply wish to store furniture or equipment until the formal handover date. Contractors are quite often prepared to co-operate in such cases and, in these circumstances, the project manager should make the necessary arrangements in respect of two very important matters. First, he should insist that the occupier takes out adequate insurance cover on the property so that if one of the occupier's employees or one of the occupier's own contractors causes damage — maybe sets fire to the building and burns it to the ground — there is no worry as to whether the contractor's insurance covers such an eventuality, because the damage is covered whether it be by the contractor's or the occupier's insurer. Similarly the contractor and the occupier should both agree in writing that if there is any argument as to the responsibility for any damage as between the contractor and the occupier the decision of the architect shall be final and binding on both sides. Such an arrangement can save a great deal of vexatious argument in respect of relatively minor matters, such as broken windows or damage to decoration or floor surfaces, when there might otherwise be an argument as to whether the contractor or the occupier's men were to blame. More serious argument can arise in respect of work carried out by the occupier's builder which affects the work of the main contractor: for example, a flue through the roof. In practice it is usually found that both the contractor and the occupier are quite happy to agree that the architect shall be the arbiter before any damage has occurred, but once damage has occurred it can be very difficult to get both parties to agree to accept the decision of an independent arbiter such as the architect. Attention to small details such as this can save a great deal of time and trouble and ill-feeling later. If a requirement for early access or occupation of part is known at the outset, arrangements are written into the contract documents.

The quantity surveyor should be asked when he expects to complete any outstanding remeasurement work and be in a position to agree his final account with the contractor so that the architect may issue a final certificate. The JCT contract will have provided for a certain percentage of the total cost to be retained by the building owner until the end of the defects liability period, which is very often six months from the date of practical completion. Special maintenance periods may be agreed for particular parts of the work (e.g. landscaping). The contractor is responsible for remedying any defects (other than design) which have occurred during the defects liability period, provided of course that they have not been causes by the occupier. It is most important that the buildings should be carefully inspected at the end of the liability period, because if there are any obvious defects at that time which the architect does not identify it may well be assumed that the architect was prepared to accept the building subject to those defects.

The importance of inspecting the site and its immediate environs on the handover date should not be overlooked. If any damage has been caused to adjoining property — damage to boundary walls and fences is not unusual — during the building contract, then the contractor must be required to remedy it. Do not forget to inspect the roads, footpaths, curbs, grass verges, and the like immediately adjoining the site and see that the contractor remedies any damage otherwise the highway authority might subsequently ask the developer to bear the cost of any remedial works.

The architect should produce a building manual and maintenance schedule to assist the occupier by giving a comprehensive schedule and description of all components (taps, locks, fastenings, sanitary ware, and the like) which might need replacing at some future date, together with recommendations for regular maintenance work to preserve the fabric.

Ideally the occupier should be ready to take possession of the property immediately it is handed over by the contractor and every effort should be made to arrange this. Where it is not possible and the developer is responsible for vacant buildings, the insurance policy should be checked to ensure that it does give protection against vandalism. Whatever physical arrangements are reasonably necessary to protect the property against vandalism, should be made. An obvious example is in the case of a shopping development, where any unlet shop units will have a neat hoarding put across the frontage immediately before the handover date. Consideration is often given to the advisability of employing security patrols. Owners of empty properties have onerous legal obligations to anyone who might be injured on the property, particularly children. Recent legal decisions have made it clear that if an owner of an empty property knows or ought to have known that children were in the habit of entering the property, then the owner might be held absolutely responsible if a child is injured. Insurance cover should not only give protection against loss due to the damage of property, but also against claims from injured third parties.

5.5.8 Local rates

If buildings are being erected on a speculative basis in an area where the local authority has a policy of levying rates on vacant buildings, the project manager must know whether the buildings are to be completed so that they are handed over by the contractor in a state ready for occupation, or whether the building work should stop short of that point if no tenant appears to be in prospect at the time completion is drawing near. Local rates might be an onerous burden on vacant property.

5.5.9 The management team

At the outset, we made it clear that there are no hard and fast rules for defining a project. For the purpose of commenting on the building contract, we assumed that a project was the work entailed in the erection of the buildings. It is easy to see how the project manager responsible for that particular project could himself be a member of a development team responsible for a very much wider range of operations. For example, in the case of a comprehensive commercial property development involving shops and offices, perhaps with entertainment facilities and maybe residential accommodation, the development team would regard the project as starting with the initial market research operations leading to an economic feasibility study. The project would cover the acquisition of the site and no doubt a great deal of discussion about the precise design of the buildings, the appointment of the architect, quantity surveyor and other professional people. All this would have taken place before our own project manager assumed his responsibilities for the erection of the buildings, although clearly it would be advantageous for him to have been sitting in as a member of the development team from the outset. The composition and work of such a development team is examined in Chapter 8.

Whatever the arrangements and however the project may be defined, the essential requirement is that at all times the members of the project team should clearly understand their own responsibilities and ensure that they are properly carried out. In particular it should be clearly understood who is able to authorize the expenditure of money. Careful administrative arrangements must be devised and followed by every member of the team to ensure that financial expenditure is not only properly authorized, but properly recorded and where appropriate recovered from other people. Every member of the project team must know whether he is able to spend money and if so what authorities he must obtain and what reports he must render to the appropriate people to ensure that the financial controls are adequate.

5.5.10 Monitoring construction progress

Finally we need to draw attention to some of the methods that can be used to monitor the progress of construction. The importance of such an exercise is clear. First, a longer construction period adds to the cost of borrowing short-term building finance. Second, a delay in completion may mean that the letting or selling programme is unable to start at the optimum time of the year. This is particularly so in the residential market which has two buying peaks — one in the spring and one in the early autumn.

Monitoring progress is the responsibility of whoever is leading the development team. It may be a project manager or it may be the developer himself. All methods used are based upon testing actual progress against a model of estimated progress. There are many methods, but we are going to look at three: the bar chart; the development timetable; and the cash-flow table.

(a) The bar chart

The bar chart is in effect a calendar marked to show the contractor's programme of work. The programme is divided into various tasks and the period during which each of these is to be carried out is shown on the chart.

Such a chart is shown in Fig. 5.1. The chart clearly indicates when each task is to start and when it is to finish. It shows how the various tasks overlap and the work that should be in hand at any particular time. From time to time the contractor's programme, and therefore the bar chart, may need to be changed but by comparing what has actually been achieved with what the chart shows gives the developer, or his project manager, a simple test of progress.

The bar chart can also be used to indicate when information or decisions are needed by the contractor. This again is of great importance, for one of the principal causes of delay is lack of information or instruction.

(b) The development timetable

Another method of monitoring progress and highlighting the importance of providing information and decisions is to prepare a chronological timetable of events. Such a timetable, which is produced by studying the contractor's bar chart, is shown in Fig. 5.2. The advantage of the timetable is that at each project meeting the developer or project manager can establish what has been achieved and compare it with what should have been achieved. Any revision in programme can be reflected in a revised timetable.

(c) Cash-flow table

Where a JCT building contract is being used and the contractor is being paid throughout the building period against

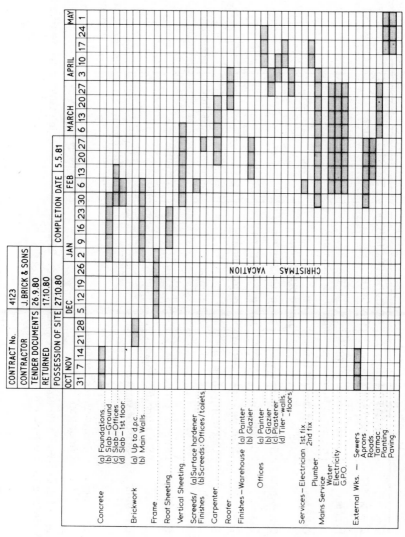

Fig. 5.1 **Contractor's bar chart.**

DATE	ELEMENT	ESTIMATED PROGRAMME	ACTUAL POSITION ON SITE	REVISED PROGRAMME	COMMENT
28th Dec	Frame	Continuing erection or portal framework	up to programme	—	—
2nd Jan	Concrete	Start of ground floor slab	up to programme	—	—
2nd Jan	Brickwork	Start of main walls	up to programme	—	—
6th Jan	Frame	Completion of frame	up to programme		
9th Jan	Roof	Start on roof sheeting	up to programme		
27th Jan	Roof	Completion of roof sheeting	2/3 complete	Completed 3rd Feb.	delay due to bad weather
30th Jan	Concrete	Start of office slab		no change	
30th Jan	Concrete	Start first floor slab		no change	
30th Jan	Cladding	Start of vertical sheeting		start 6th Feb	follows delay to roof sheeting
3rd Feb	Concrete	Completion of ground floor slab		no change	

Fig. 5.2 Detail of development timetable being considered on 27th January. A new timetable would be prepared for the next project meeting to incorporate revisions.

MONTH	1981									1982						TOTAL
	1(APRIL)	2(MAY)	3(JUNE)	4(JULY)	5(AUG)	6(SEPT)	7(OCT)	8(NOV)	9(DEC)	10(JAN)	11(FEB)	12(MAR)	13(APRIL)	14(MAY)	15(JUNE)	
INCOME	–	–	–	–	–	–	–	–	–	–	–	2660	9820	–	15120	27590
EXPENDITURE																
Civil Contract	–	15845	23455	34480	41870	28540	46160	29330	5520	19635	20450	16000	–	–	–	281435
Building Contract	29000	–	10150	7775	36175	21895	29630	33820	25170	46135	69885	34000	–	–	–	343635
Fees	6000	12000	1500	1000	1000	1500	6400	3160	3660	3160	3160	4720	6090	–	1080	54430
Marketing	2000	–	–	–	–	–	–	–	1100	–	–	–	–	–	–	3100
Monthly Payment	37000	27845	35105	43205	79145	52035	82190	66310	35450	68930	93495	52070	(3730)	–	(14040)	–
Total	37000	64845	99950	143155	222300	274335	356525	422835	458285	527215	620710	672780	669050	–	655010	655010
Interest**	415	730	1125	1610	1500	3430	5050	5990	6490	7030	8225	8970	8920	8920	8735	77190
Running Total	37415	65990	102220	147035	227680	283145	370385	442685	484625	560585	662355	723395	728505	737505	732200	732200

*The figures in months 1 to 9 are actual and in months 10 to 15 estimated.

**Interest rate charged between April 1981 and August 1981 13%, September 1981 15%, October to December 1981 17%. Estimated rate of interest January 1982 to June 1982 16%.

Fig. 5.3 Cash Flow Table, £'s (as at January 1982*)

the quantity surveyor's valuations of work done, a cash-flow table should be prepared. The purpose of the table, an example of which is shown in Fig. 5.3, is to estimate the developer's flow of cash payments and cash receipts throughout the building period. The table, thus prepared, tells the developer what his financial liabilities will be and therefore enables him to plan his borrowing accordingly. In so far as the table reflects an estimate of how the building contract will progress, it also provides another means of checking progress by comparing actual payments with estimated payments. It is, however, a much less sensitive barometer of progress than either the bar chart or the development timetable.

Furthermore such estimates of cash flow have often to be revised and there is a danger that they do not really highlight problems of delay until the last months of the contract. In order to determine more exactly the cash flow, it is sometimes possible to agree with the contractor either fixed periodic payments irrespective of the quantity surveyor's valuations, or a fixed tolerance of fluctuation around an agreed estimate of cash flow. If such arrangements are made, it is all the more important that the progress of construction is monitored in some other way.

The cash flow shows both expenditure and income. In a project during which some buildings are sold or let, the developer will be receiving income and the effect of this on his net cash flow should be shown.

5.5.11 Revisions

We have referred to the fact that the bar chart, the development timetable and the cash flow may need to be revised during the course of the construction period. No revision, however, should be made without a justification. The developer or his project manager must know why the estimate has had to be revised. If they fail to do so, their controls are meaningless. They must, therefore, maintain a tireless scrutiny of events and of the advice they are given.

CHAPTER 6

Promotion and selling

6.1 INTRODUCTION

Promotion is an essential and integral part of the development process. Vigorous promotion enhances and accelerates regional growth prospects, helps to convert planning proposals into reality, transforms efforts to dispose of individual properties.

A clear understanding of the potential market and the needs, perceptions and prejudices of the intended audience is essential. Without this it is all too easy to waste time and money on misdirected effort. When dealing with extensive promotions and selling campaigns, market research at the outset and possibly at intervals during an extended campaign will help to gauge the effectiveness of the impact on potential customers. It is important to obtain maximum value for money and a careful analysis of all enquiries in terms of both numbers and 'quality' will help to identify the most effective methods of promotion. Careful recording and analysis of results will provide a useful data base for the planning and direction of future promotional activities. Of course ultimate success depends on dealing with enquiries in such a way as to convert them into business transactions.

The same basic principles underlie the work of both public authorities and private developers. However, the scale and size of their respective operations are frequently very different. The public authority will often be dealing with the promotion of a town or a large region, and the scale of such an operation will clearly be much larger and likely to extend over a longer period of time than the promotion of an individual development with which the private developer is normally concerned. Thus public authorities will often think in terms of a continuous, ongoing promotional programme extending over several years to promote economic growth generally, whereas the developer will usually be concerned with a much shorter promotional programme concentrated on a particular development.

Let us, first, consider large-scale promotional activities relating to a town or region which will usually be undertaken by a public authority. The basic matters to be decided at the outset are the size and scope of the campaign, particularly in monetary terms, the objectives of the campaign and the length of time over which the campaign will run.

The objectives of any public authority campaign will clearly be determined by the circumstances prevailing in the authority's own particular area. Leaving aside the special cases, such as the coastal towns anxious to promote their image as holiday resorts, it will usually be found that the basic objective is to attract employment into an area. Indeed employment is normally the lifeblood of any economic expansion.

The first step will be an assessment of the facilities in the area and this will form the basis for a general-purpose brochure. Describe the geographical location and the communications facilities available — road, rail, air and water. Prepare a brief history and summary of the growth of the area up to the present time and an indication of future growth prospects. Include a note about the total population and the total working population — men and women — with an analysis of the total employment into the different categories — those used by the Department of Employment will be the most useful. Indicate whether any pool of labour is available or any special facilities for the recruitment of labour into the area. Educational facilities are important and should be carefully described, together with a note of the total number of school leavers each year and their educational attainments. A comment should be made about the attitude of the educational authority with regard to the provision of special courses to suit the needs of employers moving into the area. Housing is always a topic of great interest to everyone. Describe the situation concerning the availability of housing both for those interested in purchasing their house privately and those interested in renting accommodation. In connection with the latter, clearly indicate what provision if any is made for housing to rent for workpeople moving into the area — most employers will expect that at least their key-workers will be offered housing to rent, if they need it. Give an indication of the annual rate of housing development and of the potential growth in housing production to cater for the needs of people moving into the area. Are plots of land available for those who would prefer to design and build their own houses? Shopping, leisure and recreational facilities should be described in detail, including those within reasonable travelling distance.

Having given the general background picture, next deal with the availability of accommodation. What sites and buildings are available or can be made available, and on what terms? Indicate whether the supplies of electricity, gas and water and the sewerage systems are adequate to cope with any new development. If any sources of raw materials are available in the immediate vicinity which might influence the type of employment moving into the area, indicate them. Nowadays employers are particularly interested in good labour relations, and where it is possible to say with complete honesty that good labour relations do generally prevail in an area, then emphasize that fact.

What financial assistance is made available to employers moving into the area either from government, or local authority sources? The availability of accommodation at low rents, substantial grants towards the provision of new plant and machinery can be powerful inducements to any employer. It cannot be emphasized too strongly that any promotional campaign to be really successful must bring out every point of advantage. Be careful to ensure the honesty of a promotional campaign by describing all the advantages objectively and accurately. The slightest suspicion that given information is not to be entirely relied upon can to a large extent negate the time, trouble and expense taken in preparing a promotional campaign.

6.2 PROMOTIONAL EXPENDITURE

Total expenditure by different public authorities and private-enterprise developers on promotion will vary enormously.

Local authorities anxious to attract development in order to deal with substantial unemployment problems or other economic difficulties will perhaps spend many tens of thousands of pounds every year, even though they are not themselves to any considerable extent engaged in development which will bring them a direct return on the expenditure. If local authorities are taking an entrepreneurial role and providing sites or buildings for employment or other industrial or commercial activities, the expenditure will be substantially justified as part of the commercial operation. There are no rules, no infallible methods of calculation to determine the correct amount that should be spent on promotion. Expenditure will be a matter of judgement, and subjective judgement at that. Once a decision has been taken as to the total expenditure in any given period of time, the next decision will be the apportionment of that expenditure. Decisions as to where to spend money are always choices between alternatives; money spent on one form of promotion means that there will be that much less to spend on others. Ensure that promotional activities take account of the work of other authorities which might also help to promote the area. For example, a local authority should take careful note of the activity of government departments or of private developers so that all the different activities will be complementary rather than competitive. Bear in mind that some of the most effective means of promotion (which are referred to below) do not have to be paid for, at least not directly.

6.3 THE PRESS

Prospective advertisers are faced with an almost bewildering range of choice: from quality newspapers to the most sensational popular papers; learned journals and business publications to magazines catering for any and every aspect of human activity. Some are very expensive to buy; at the other end of the scale they are given away free of charge.

When dealing with the promotion of a town or region, the range of possible publications in which to place advertisements is almost unlimited. Indeed it is possible to argue that almost any publication might well be read by someone interested in moving to or developing business in the town or region in question. However, it will usually be found that the quality daily newspapers provide the best backbone for any advertising campaign. Have regard to the audited circulations of each publication and to their class of readership. The advertising managers will all have convincing explanations as to why their publication would make a good vehicle for your own advertising campaign. Indeed on some occasions advertisers will find that the majority of inquiries relating to their advertisements are from other advertising managers endeavouring to sell advertising space.

When using daily newspapers, ascertain what is their best property day because some people will buy that particular issue simply to read the property advertisements. If there is a special property page, that will probably be as good as any location in the paper. Alternatively choose one of the special positions, such as those on front or back pages, or at any rate ensure that as far as possible the advertisement is opposite interesting editorial matter. The 'earpieces' in the top corners of front and back pages are good value. Do not place an advertisement where it will be lost in a mass of other advertisements dealing with different and quite unrelated subject matter.

Certain broad guidelines may be drawn up to assist in the difficult decision as to where to spend the money available to the best advantage. What is being sold and what type of people is the advertising aimed at? To attract estate agents or property developers, the property papers will be an obvious choice. For specialized properties, such as shops, the use of appropriate trade journals can produce results. When advertisements are aimed at potential occupiers of buildings or sites with a wide range of possible business or industrial users — this applies to most offices and factories — the choice becomes more difficult. The quality daily papers are often the safest and most reliable. When advertising in these newspapers, be careful to ensure that any additional advertising in other publications is simply not going to be read by the very same people. The wide range of business and specialized industrial magazines can sometimes be used to advantage, but here the danger of overlapping with the same readership as the quality papers is considerable.

People do not spend the whole of their time reading newspapers or business or trade journals. Some of them are, for example, interested in a variety of sports, gardening and countryside pursuits. An occasional advertisement in a magazine devoted to such matters might bring results, but the danger of overlapping readerships must always be borne in mind.

Advertising costs vary greatly between one publication and another and according to different positions in the same publication. There are a number of special locations for which the charge for advertising is considerably higher because they are the most prominent positions. It will often be worthwhile paying the extra charge, particularly when there is no special property page. Today many publications offer the opportunity of placing advertisements in colour, albeit at a substantially higher cost. Normally only important advertisements will be placed in colour and the question of whether the extra expense is worth while or the money better spent elsewhere is very much a matter of opinion. There is always a limit to size of an advertising budget. Once the publications into which the advertisements are to be placed have been selected, it will then have to be decided whether a small number of large advertisements are to be used or a large number of small advertisements or some combination of both. A limited number of large advertisements, each followed up by a number of small advertisements reminding readers of the advantages outlined in the first advertisement, is often a good combination.

It is always difficult to judge the effectiveness and worth of any advertising campaign. In so far as press advertisements generally are concerned, an attempt should be made to enable the advertiser to identify the source of any inquiry. This is sometimes done by including a coupon in the advertisement for readers to send to the advertiser, although not all readers will do this and inquiries are often made by telephone. Another method which is usually quite effective is to include some code letter or number in the advertiser's address. Of course, it must be remembered that some readers might see an advertisement and take no immediate action but the information will stick in their memory and, subsequently looking for accommodation, they recall the advertisement and make inquiries, so the response to any advertising campaign can be spread out over a considerable period. This particularly applies to advertising campaigns to promote towns or regions where no specific properties are mentioned in the advertisement. Certainly the style and advertising media should be varied from time to time in a constant attempt at improved results.

When dealing with inquiries, it is always helpful to ascertain how the first contact was made with the inquirer. Over a period of time it is possible to develop a sixth sense as to which publications produce results even though this is difficult to justify by hard facts and figures.

6.4 DESIGN AND AGENCY

It is a matter of common observation that some advertisements are more noticeable and attract more attention than others. The content of an advertisement obviously has a bearing on its interest but unquestionably the design and layout of an advertisement has an important effect. Good design and layout undoubtedly increase the impact of the advertisement, whereas poor design is not only wasteful of money, but can sometimes create an adverse impression.

Some advertisers endeavour to develop a house style for their advertisements or at any rate for a particular series. Many nowadays include a logo or symbol so that their identity can be easily recognized. Providing that a particular house style is not too restrictive on the design and layout, it can often be distinctive and in that respect worth while.

The design, style and layout of advertising material is so important that it should always be placed in the hands of those with specialist skills. Unless the advertising budget is large, the business will usually be placed in the hands of advertising agents. The advertising agents will be carefully chosen in the light of the work they have carried out for other clients in addition to discussions with them concerning the contribution which they consider they can make to the campaign and the services which they can give to the advertiser and of course their charges. Often advertising agents placing a substantial amount of advertising matter will be able to work for little or nothing, because they are able to negotiate with the various publications percentage reductions in the advertising charges which will cover their agency fees.

Where the volume of advertising is substantial and perhaps includes other work such as exhibitions and the like, then consideration should be given to the desirability of employing an 'in-house' design team. The relative advantages and disadvantages are much the same as those to be found with the employment of any other in-house professional team. It is important that the team should be large enough to encompass all the skills, for example, commercial artist, copywriter, design and layout specialist and typographic designer, and the team must be capable of creative and original thought. Although the majority of publications are reluctant to give advertising discounts to anyone other than a recognized advertising practitioner, nevertheless when an in-house team is employed the possibility of negotiating some discount should always be investigated. The cost effectiveness of an in-house team should always be carefully compared with that of an agency.

Media buying agencies are sometimes employed to deal with the placing of substantial advertising. They specialize in advising on the best combination of advertising to reach most effectively the target audience and usually operate on a percentage of discounts negotiated with Press, Radio and TV — the discounts can vary quite considerably. On this basis the creative content is left in the hands of the in-house team or the advertising agents.

6.5 RADIO AND TV

Until recently Radio and TV have been generally considered too expensive for development advertising. These media are now being used to a limited extent by, for example, some public authorities for regional promotion and by national house builders. The growth in local commercial radio covering 'drive time' and the coming of TV channel 4 will allow business and commercial audiences to be reached cost effectively.

The use of the TV screen for videotext — the generic term for information accessed through telephone lines (Prestel) or direct TV transmission (Ceefax on BBC or Oracle on ITV)

— although growing slowly will undoubtedly become of increasing importance.

6.6 POSTER ADVERTISING

The term is used generally to describe any form of advertisement displayed on a noticeboard or billboard even though it may not necessarily be of the traditional poster type.

When dealing with individual properties, poster advertising is normally restricted to the property or site itself perhaps together with prominent locations around the town in which the property is situated — for example, at the railway station, the bus station, hoardings on prominent road corners, and so on. Poster advertising will usually be considered on a more widespread basis only in the case of very extensive properties or for the promotion of particular towns or regions. Posters displayed on railway stations, in the Underground, outside and inside buses, and perhaps in taxis in the centre of London can be an effective means of advertising to those who are forced to travel in crowded, uncomfortable conditions in the capital, the benefits of decentralized office accommodation.

Poster-style advertising at main airports and railway stations and any main travel termini can effectively promote particular towns or regions, although to be worth while in such locations advertisements must be displayed very prominently and will therefore be expensive. People busily engaged in travelling from one place to another will only have time to glance at an advertisement and rarely have time to study it carefully. Also remember that advertisements which are approached by people walking past are often seen for the greater part of the time at an oblique angle, reducing their impact.

Poster advertising at trade fairs and exhibitions can be worth while. There are many trade fairs and exhibitions at which the advertiser will not consider it worth while having his own stand. In that case the possibility of poster advertising should automatically be thought about. Position is again of crucial importance and unless a good prominent position can be obtained it will often be best not to bother.

Any good advertisement should convey its message at a glance. This is particularly important when dealing with poster advertisements, which are frequently seen by the readers for only a few seconds.

6.7 EXHIBITIONS

Exhibitions can be time-consuming and expensive. They are not seen by as many people who will read an advertisement in one of the quality daily papers. They are of widely differing types and are held in many different locations. Different exhibitions will seek to attract quite different types of people. Money spent on exhibitions is that much less available for other forms of promotion, so it is important to ensure that it is no less productive of business than that spent elsewhere.

The exhibitor must decide whether he is going to put on his own independent exhibition or take stands in exhibitions organized by others. He must decide whether he is going to attempt to attract his customers to his exhibition or whether he will take the exhibition to the customers. He might decide to do all these things.

An individual property development would have to be on an exceptionally large scale to justify the holding of special exhibitions in other cities or taking stands in trade fairs and specialist exhibitions. These activities are normally confined to public authorities anxious to promote their towns or regions, or to developers or estate agents with a very wide range of property to offer on a national basis.

An independent exhibition must have sufficient content to make it attractive and will have to be held in a convenient location. Few people will be prepared to spend a great deal of time travelling to an exhibition which is bound to be fairly small and specialized. The exhibition will be publicized by advertising in the local newspapers, maybe by asking the Chamber of Commerce to notify all its members in its next newsletter and by sending letters of invitation to those likely to be interested. The exhibition should be open throughout the lunch hours and at least on one evening so as to give an opportunity to those who are not able to attend during normal working hours. Where appropriate, others may be invited to take part: if, for example, a local authority is staging an exhibition to invite people in general to move to its area, so that most of the visitors to the exhibition will be potential house-buyers or people looking for jobs, the local authority might well invite local estate agents, local house-builders and some of the larger employers to have a stand. Care should be taken to exclude the type of exhibitor whose presence is more likely to be an irritant than an asset — certain types of salesmen would come into this category. On the other hand, where an authority is seeking to attract factories or offices, the exhibition will be aimed at a selective group of people who might well wish to discuss their inquiries in confidence. In these circumstances it will perhaps be best for the local authority to go it alone. At an exhibition aimed at industrial and commercial firms the number of visitors will be considerably smaller, and it might be thought appropriate to make available a light buffet lunch and refreshments to help to create a friendly atmosphere. The staff at exhibitions must be unfailingly cheerful, efficient, helpful and adequate in number to enable them to deal promptly with all inquiries. If in doubt about the duration of an exhibition, choose the shorter time. An exhibition which is staged for too long so that it is very thinly attended can be a rather depressing affair for both visitors and staff.

Press announcements, advertisements or letters of invitation should make it clear that anyone not able to attend, but who would like to have more information, can be visited on an individual basis. If the exhibition happens to coincide with any larger-scale advertising campaign, always put a small flash in the national advertisements mentioning the fact that the exhibition is on. Typically exhibitions of this type are staged in convenient locations in large cities by public authorities attempting to persuade industrial and commercial firms to decentralize the whole or part of their activities into surrounding small towns; or to draw to the attention of people living in the cities, particularly those in inadequate housing, the advantages of moving to a town where homes and jobs are readily available.

Alternatively a stand might be taken in an organized exhibition containing many exhibitors. There is a very wide variety of such exhibitions. Some specialize in property development and the opportunities for those seeking factory or office accommodation or developers seeking sites; the visitors attending such a specialized exhibition will be smaller in number but will already have an interest in the subject matter, so that a much higher proportion are likely to be interested in the stands of those offering development opportunities. The very large trade exhibitions, on the other hand, will often attract huge attendances but the numbers interested in property development will be very small. People who attend trade exhibitions are not often those who make decisions about factory or office or other accommodation. When considering exhibition attendances, therefore, have regard to the quality of the visitors, i.e. in the sense of the likelihood of their being interested in property matters. Study the type of visitor to an exhibition in the same way as the readership classification of newspapers. Ascertain whether in the past public or private organizations interested in development have taken stands and, if so, try to learn from them what their experience has been. People are quite often happy to swap experiences of this type, if it is on a reciprocal basis. It is often difficult to judge the potential business that might be obtained by taking a stand at any particular exhibition; the only way to find out is to take a stand and experiment.

The question of future participation in that or any other exhibition in forthcoming years can then be carefully considered in the light of experience. Always compare the results obtained at an exhibition with the results likely to be obtained by spending the same amount of money on press advertising. Remember that it is often possible to take a prominent poster at an exhibition at a very much lower cost.

Another possibility is to stage an independent exhibition at a convenient locaton in a town or city where a conference is being held, and the people attending the conference are likely to be interested in the subject matter of the exhibition. Obvious examples of this form of activity are exhibitions by public authorities in the cities which are the locations for the annual FIABCI conference. At the conference property people from all over the world might well be interested to see the facilities for investment and for setting up manufacturing operations in the towns putting on the exhibition. If it is possible to obtain a list of the names and addresses of the delegates who will be attenting such conferences, a personal invitation to each delegate to visit the exhibition would obviously be helpful.

6.8 MAIL SHOTS

Direct mail shots are effective and relatively economic. They are aimed at a very carefully selected list of people and the success of a direct mail shot will depend very much on the compilation of the mailing list. There are a number of specialist direct mail organizations who can provide a first-rate service and are capable of producing mailing lists with a remarkable degree of specialization and accuracy. They maintain general lists of industrial or commercial firms which can then be broken down into particular categories, such as company size, trade and location. There is a limit to the frequency with which direct mail shots can be used and the employment of one of the specialist firms on the occasions when the mail shot is required will often be found advantageous. Ensure that the firm selected frequently updates its mailing lists. Nothing is more irritating than to have large numbers of envelopes returned because the identity or the address of the original addressee has altered. To overcome the almost automatic tendency of the recipient to throw the contents of the direct mail shot into the wastepaper basket, make sure that the message can be seen at a glance; a very long letter which has to be read through to the end before the message is fully understood, or a brochure or leaflet without any covering message, will often fail, whereas a short sharp covering message attached to a brochure or leaflet will often be absorbed by the recipient before he has time to throw it away. The letters should be prepared in such a way that each one appears to be an original with an original signature.

6.9 GENERAL ACTIVITIES

A great deal of the normal negotiating and promotional activity is taken for granted. It is none the less important because of that. Those concerned with the disposal of property must keep themselves closely in touch with the property market generally. They must have a knowledge of local property values and of the demand and supply situation in the locality. They must keep themselves advised of national trends and changes in fashion and outlook. The current views of developers, the financial institutions and the estate agents are of considerable importance. In other words, it is essential to keep a finger firmly on the pulse of the market.

There are a number of organizations with whom it is valuable to maintain contact. The various management consultants and national firms of surveyors and estate agents frequently advise industrial and commercial clients who are seeking new locations. The joint stock banks and merchant banks, insurance companies and pension funds are often consulted at a very preliminary stage in the planning of major industrial and commercial projects and it is useful if they are aware of opportunities in various locations. The CBI and the various employers' federations are sometimes called upon to give advice on new locations. Managements are usually anxious for the majority of their employees to accompany them to any new building or new location so that employees are usually consulted at a reasonably early stage — therefore, no harm can be done by making sure that the trade unions are also aware of the advantages offered by any particular location. Keep in touch with the local authorities in areas from which business might be drawn. Even though nowadays the authorities in the large cities and conurbations are usually anxious to retain all forms of employment within their own areas, it is sometimes impossible for them to do so. For example, if the acquisition of an extensive area of land providing very low employment is necessary, the acquiring authority may not be able to make available a suitable alternative site within its own boundaries and will perhaps advise the occupier in those circumstances about other opportunities, where the receiving authority is able happily to contemplate making available a large site area for a development which will produce relatively little employment.

The local Chambers of Commerce and Trade will perhaps be able to make contact with their counterparts in areas from which business might be drawn and play a useful part in attempting to attract the business to their own locality. These, then, are some of the more important organizations with whom it is useful to maintain contact. A vigorous estates department will also establish its own network of contacts by the personal activities of the members of the department. Over a period of years a considerable amount of friendly goodwill should be built up.

Monitor the financial, business and company news which appears in the press. Useful pointers can be gained to companies to whom a letter or telephone call concerning the possibility of moving into a new location might bring results. Information about changes in the general level of activity in the various industries will often suggest where promotional activity might best be concentrated at a particular point in time.

Some of the best advertising material does not have to be paid for. Ensure that all information about interesting developments is passed promptly to appropriate press contacts and from time to time invite representatives from the press to visit the area to learn of recent developments. Editorial comment about the development of a locality is much more interesting and readable than advertising matter. When the promotional activities are on a sufficiently large scale, sporting and social events might be arranged which will serve the dual function of increasing the entertainment facilities in the area and also provide a vehicle for the promotion of the area.

6.10 ADVERTISING MATERIAL

The phrase covers a whole miscellany of brochures, leaflets, exhibition material, give-away gimmicks, and the like. Most time and money will probably be spent preparing brochures and leaflets. These are expensive to produce and are quickly out of date. First impressions count and often it is the brochure or leaflet which gives a prospective customer his first impression of a particular authority and its area. Thus ensure that the design and production standards are of the best. If a general brochure might be in use for some time, always consider whether certain facts and figures which would normally be in the brochure can be taken out and put on a loose sheet of paper, perhaps in a pocket at the back of the brochure, thus enabling the loose sheet to be brought up to date periodically without the expense and waste of having to reprint the whole brochure. A good general-purpose brochure will often form the backbone of the advertising material, but no one brochure will be suitable for every occasion. Those engaged in large-scale promotion will probably have a range of brochures and leaflets; for example, a first-rate town guide together with a brochure dealing with industrial and associated development in the area and in addition, if the amount of development justifies it, a brochure on offices. A comprehensive housing brochure will be necessary. When deciding upon the total number and type of brochures to be produced, it is necessary to have regard, first, to the subject matter to be covered by each brochure and then, second, the type of readership. For instance, a brochure describing the opportunities available for industrialists wishing to take sites or buildings in an area will be written in a somewhat different style from a brochure describing general housing opportunities. The first will be read by businessmen interested in the facilities for establishing their business, whereas the second will be read by employees and their wives interested in moving into the area to live; while there is a good deal of common ground between both types of reader, nevertheless the emphasis on various aspects will be different in each case. The decision as to whether this type of advertising material should be produced in-house or by an independent advertising agency will be influenced by much the same considerations as is the decision with regard to press advertisements, although the volume of work involved will perhaps figure more prominently.

Most authorities with a large promotional campaign will at one time or another consider making a film. This is quite an expensive business — in 1982 a relatively modest film cost around £20 000 — and films like brochures can very quickly become out of date, particularly in an area where a good deal of development is taking place. Subject to the obsolescence factor a good film can have its uses, although it must be borne in mind that representatives from a business or industrial organization thinking of moving to an area will usually wish to see the area for themselves at the outset. The film will also have a limited impact on the minds of employees or others who are to be taken to the area cn guided tours. Certainly a film can be very effective when it is shown to people who would not normally visit the area. For example, an authority wishing to attract people from a large city or conurbation will perhaps arrange for a film to be shown on a number of occasions in different locations in the city, when it will be seen by many people who would not otherwise consider moving. Promotion work can be helped by the showing of a film to people abroad, who will not visit the area unless their preliminary negotiations and contacts lead them to think the area might be suitable for their new location. In view of the cost and the obsolescence factor a film will probably be made only when it is certain that it can be shown to many people during the first year or two of its life. In a rapidly developing area the film will probably be out of date after that time.

A very good alternative to a film is automatic slide-projection equipment with a recorded commentary. For a much smaller financial outlay a comprehensive picture can be given of a locality or of a particular development and it is a relatively easy matter to keep the subject material up to date. It is quite simple to operate this type of visual aid in an ordinary office with portable equipment and there is considerable flexibility in running back over the sequence of slides to facilitate business discussions. It is likely that there will be a considerable growth in the use of this particular promotional aid.

Rapid development in video and its increasing use makes possible the production of low cost but effective cassettes which can be used for selective mail shots.

Recent years have seen an increase in give-away gimmickry. A ballpoint pen and a notepad can have a useful function. A very small giftpack containing samples of things traditionally produced in the area might be a useful memento of a visit. Beyond these things the queston of the extent to which one should engage in give-away gimmickry is to a large extent a matter of common sense and good taste.

6.11 PROMOTIONAL ACTIVITIES OUTSIDE THE UK

As a result of the slow growth in the UK economy many authorities now carry out promotional activities abroad with a view to attracting foreign investment. The fall in the value of the pound sterling which has led to UK exports becoming more competitive, and entry into the EEC, which has reinforced the attractions of the UK as a manufacturing base for those outside the community, have led to a substantial increase in promotional activities in the last few years.

Foreign investment in any locality can provide not only additional jobs, but also help to widen the economic base and provide useful international contacts. Success in attracting investment on an international scale can greatly improve the image of a locality generally. British businessmen looking for new locations will often regard a local authority's foreign promotional activities as a sign of breadth of vision, liveliness of mind and a willingness to abandon the bureaucratic straitjacket. Thus foreign promotional activities can have a very valuable spinoff in improving the ability to attract British businessmen at home.

Promotion abroad will not be attractive to those anxious for quick results or those who are only able to think in terms of relatively short-term time scales. To avoid disappointment, activities abroad ought to be regarded in a sense as a long-term investment. Patience and persistence are essential virtues. However, the first results will give an enormous sense of satisfaction and once a breakthrough has been made the going seems to become progressively easier.

Where does one start? The European countries are on the doorstep and a selling campaign can be mounted with relatively less travelling time and expenditure than in any other continent.

If time and money were unlimited, then ideally a campaign could be mounted in almost every European country. But with limited resources a decision has to be made as to where the efforts are to be concentrated. West Germany has a remarkably strong economy. France, Belgium and Holland are close and there is already a good deal of trade between those countries and the UK. Businessmen in Sweden and Denmark are often looking for manufacturing or distribution facilities in the UK. These, then, are perhaps countries where the best results are most likely to be obtained.

The USA and Canada have been the source of much investment in this country for many years. Although language difficulties abroad are not generally a major problem, the common language nevertheless makes campaigns in North

America just that little bit easier. Although to achieve results, the time and money involved will usually have to be considerably greater. It is virtually impossible for any one authority to run an effective promotional campaign throughout the whole of North America and, therefore, a decision will have to be made as to the regions in which activities are to be concentrated. The Eastern seaboard, the manufacturing cities to the south of the Great Lakes and California, which is the home of so many of the space-age industries, are obvious areas to consider. There are other areas of interest and the final choice as to where activities should be concentrated will depend not only upon the outcome of investigation, but also upon whether there are any existing links between the authority running the campaign and any particular location in America.

The countries mentioned above by no means exhaust the list of possibilities. Japanese businessmen have made substantial investments in facilities in the UK and promotional campaigns aimed at attracting investment from Japan have not been without success. However, for those who are making their first ventures abroad Europe and North America are probably the best places in which to make a start.

What are the first steps to take on this journey? A good deal of groundwork can be done and, indeed, should be done at home. Talk to the people who can be helpful. The commercial attachés at the foreign embassies and the UK branches of the foreign banks can often provide much useful information. The Departments of Trade and Industry and other government departments can be of assistance. In European countries Chambers of Commerce play a vigorous part in business life. There are usually joint Chambers of Commerce to deal with matters affecting the UK and many of the European countries; for example, the Netherlands British Chamber of Commerce, German Chamber of Industry and Commerce, Chamber of Commerce Francaise De GrandeBretagne, Belgian Chamber of Commerce in Great Britain, Norwegian Chamber of Commerce and the British—Swedish Chamber of Commerce. The representatives of these chambers in the UK are unfailingly helpful. The various export councils and trade organizations, while not established for the purpose of attracting foreign investment into this country, nevertheless

have a great deal of information at their disposal. Useful
people are to be found at the Headquarters of the European
Economic Commission in Brussels. Foreign departments of
British banks can sometimes provide valuable contacts.

Look carefully at the people already established in the
locality: are there any overseas firms and, if so, can they
provide introductions? Have the old-established firms in the
locality customers or business contacts abroad whom it might
be worthwhile to cultivate? Are there any historical or other
links — town twinning, for example — between the UK and
the continental countries? Do continental businessmen visit
the locality, and can meetings be arranged with them to obtain their views on the best way of promoting the locality in
their own country?

It is possible to increase the number of continental visitors
by making contacts with professional institutions, trade
organizations, foreign embassies, Chambers of Commerce and
others who might be concerned in organizing such visits? In
short, to obtain the maximum benefit from the time and
money spent on promotional activities abroad, every possible
preparatory action should be taken first within the UK.

When after completion of all the preparatory work an
itinerary has been decided and appointments made with the
people whom the representative wishes to meet, he will set
out on his journey. To those who speak only English the
realization that language is rarely a problem when abroad will
come as a welcome relief. Have the courtesy to inquire
whether the people on the continent are able to converse in
English. Almost invariably those interested in business location and property matters will be able to do so, and on the
rare occasions when it is necessary, they will have a business
colleague who is able to interpret for them. Obviously it is
advantageous to be able to converse in the language of the
particular continental country, but it is not essential. Time
spent in learning a few elementary phrases sufficient to
enable one to exchange the time of day in the way of preliminary remarks at a meeting is always well spent. Foreign
language brochures of a high standard should be prepared,
explaining the facilities available in the UK. It is particularly
important to list all the continental firms already established
in the locality and to emphasize any contacts which already

exist. Traditional tenurial arrangements for land and buildings in many of the continental countries are somewhat different from those in this country. A flexible policy with regard to these and other matters will help business negotiations and where the UK authority is prepared to be flexible this should be emphasized.

The personal contacts should be strengthened by direct mail shots and a certain amount of advertising on the continent. The appointment of agents in continental countries can be of great help when buildings and sites in the UK are to be sold or let. When choosing an agent, the first decision is whether to appoint a foreign national or a British agent established in the particular continental country. At first sight the appointment of a foreign national as an agent might appear to be most advantageous. However, a good British agent will have established many contacts, will have no difficulty in communicating with people in the continental country and will have the advantage of an intimate knowledge of business customs and practices in the UK — this is a matter of some importance when dealing with property, which is not as simple as dealing with any normal commodity. There is little or no risk of misunderstanding between a principal and his British agent abroad, whereas there is some risk of misunderstanding between a UK principal and a continental agent when dealing with property matters. Once an agent has been appointed, it is vitally important to keep him advised about all matters, including all contacts with people from the country in which the agent is working. The agent will be able to give valuable advice as to how best to spend the amount of money allocated for promotional activities and there is a great deal to be said for having a man on the spot. Representatives from the UK must always be prepared to travel abroad at very short notice to take part in negotiations whenever necessary.

6.12 DISPOSAL OF INDIVIDUAL PROPERTIES

Many of the comments concerning large-scale promotion apply with equal force to the disposal of individual properties, which is, however, a more concentrated process requiring a detailed understanding of a specific market and a knowledge of the ways of informing and attracting potential tenants and purchasers. There are two parts to the disposal process: communication and negotiation. First, the potential purchaser or tenant must be made aware of the availability of the property, and second, he must be persuaded to purchase at the right price and on the right terms.

6.12.1 The use of estate agents

Traditionally the estate agent is responsible for selling. But if the developer — private enterprise or public authority — has an in-house selling team, what are the advantages to be gained by appointing agents to help sell or let the property? Why appoint agents? And what type of agents? What should be the basis of appointment? Much will depend upon the particular circumstances.

When there is a vigorous in-house team responsible for promoting a town or region, it will be natural for the team to handle the sale or letting of property. In many cases the publicity for property disposals can be combined with the general promotional activities and the team will function at least as effectively as an agent. In any event the team will usually handle all the detailed negotiations and occupancy arrangements, such as the handover of property, insurances, special works for tenants, instructing solicitors, etc. Where the in-house team is able to handle the sale and letting of properties competently and efficiently at whatever rate of development is required, there may be no necessity to appoint agents. However, it is not always possible to rely solely on in-house efforts. Agents are able to offer certain advantages.

Agents are often in a better location for attracting business. If a developer is trying to attract industrial or commercial firms from a large city to a new development in another location, it will frequently be advantageous to employ agents with offices in the city.

A good agent should have detailed knowledge of the particular market in which he operates, being thoroughly familiar with current and future levels of demand and supply. He may also have additional special knowledge and experience. He may, for example, specialize in selling houses within a certain price range or concentrate upon certain types of property, such as factories and warehouses. In order to be effective, he must be continuously involved in the marketplace so that he may be aware of changes in market conditions.

An agent can be retained on a 'sole agency' or 'joint agency' basis. As a sole agent he alone is responsible for disposing of the property and is entitled to a fee on each letting or sale. A normal range of fees might be 10 per cent of one year's rent for a letting and between 1½ and 3 per cent of the sale price for a sale. A joint agency arises where two or more agents are instructed to sell the same property. This can often happen where a national and a local firm of agents are instructed together. In such a case, on each letter or sale, the developer will have to pay a larger fee, perhaps 1½ times the normal amount, the agents sharing the fee between themselves on some agreed basis.

The selling of houses and flats is most often handled by local agents, although some of these may be local branches of a regional or national firm. In the commercial and industrial sectors, however, it is usual to employ a national or regional firm of agents operating with or without the help of a local firm. There is no general rule to apply; each case must be looked at on its own merits, but a national agent normally has a greater understanding of the larger and more complex schemes and has more direct and more frequent contacts with the larger companies and multiple traders attracted to them. On the other hand, the local agent normally has a better understanding of the particular characteristics of the local market and of local occupiers and traders.

Whichever type of agent or combination of agents is used, it is important that they are appointed at an early stage of the development so that they can have the opportunity of contributing to the planning, design and evaluation of the project. They should be able to draw attention to features of the design that add to or detract from the marketability of the property and be able to comment on prices or levels of rent, the nature of competitive development and the most effective time for letting or selling. By being brought in at an early stage, they become thoroughly familiar with the product that they are going to sell. Nothing is more annoying to a potential purchaser or tenant than to find that the selling agent cannot provide full details of the property that he is offering.

To summarize, the main advantages of employing a good firm of outside agents are:

(a) They bring to the project additional knowledge and experience.
(b) They provide selling expertise.
(c) They have well-located offices.

It is necessary to distinguish between the appointment of agents and offers to simply pay commission to an estate agent introducing purchasers or tenants.

There is a contractual relationship with an agent as such the terms of which, both expressed and implied, need careful consideration. The agency agreement should make clear the length of time the agency will remain in existence and how it may be terminated, specifying any retainer payable and setting out the rate of commission and in what circumstances and when it will be payable. In addition, it will specify whether the agreement is for a sole or joint agency and what are the principal's rights concerning his discretion to employ additional agents. It should be made clear whether agents are entitled to expenses, whether or not they succeed in disposing of the property. A little time and care spent in precisely defining the relationship can save a good deal of misunderstanding and ill-feeling later. For example, a sole agent might be entitled to a commission on the disposal of the property even if the sole agent played no part: if this is not the wish of the principal, he must ensure that the agency agreement clearly sets out the conditions which entitle the agent to a payment.

On occasions offers will be made to pay commission to estate agents on the signing of legal agreements for sales or lettings with purchasers or tenants introduced by the estate agent with whom the developer is not in active negotiation. No formal agency appointment is made in these circumstances and this type of arrangement is significantly different from the formal appointment of agents to act for the developer. Sometimes the offer is open to anyone introducing a purchaser or tenant, sometimes the offer is made to a limited number of estate agents.

On the face of it, a developer might think that an offer to pay introductory commission to anyone and everyone would be likely to result in most business. This is not necessarily so. If too many agents are handling a property, there is a danger that it will be 'peddled around the market', thus creating an unfavourable impression on the ground that, if so many agents are handling the property, it must be difficult to shift because there is something wrong with it. After an initial flush of enthusiasm agents tend to lose interest if they know that the property is in a large number of hands and some of the best agents might be reluctant to be involved with properties widely and indiscriminately offered in such a way. Sole or joint agents or perhaps three or four working on an agency basis are much more likely to have a sense of involvement. Whatever the arrangements, it is important to keep all agents informed of them at all times.

Meticulous records must be kept so that it can be seen at a glance which prospective purchasers or tenants have been introduced by which agents and precisely when. The question of nomenclature is important. If an agent is already retained to find accommodation for the prospective purchaser or tenant, he will not be able to accept an introductory commission from the developer. When agents refer to 'clients' they are normally retained and will not seek a commission, but when they refer to 'applicants' they will normally expect a commission because they are not retained by applicants. In all cases the position should be explicitly clarified at the outset.

A word of caution might be useful in conclusion on one particular aspect of the appointment of agents. It is quite commonplace for developers to advertise for sites, asking agents to send the particulars to them and offering to retain the services of the agents for the disposal of the completed property development. Whereas the activities of reputable developers and professional firms of agents are above suspicion, it nevertheless behoves the people concerned in such transactions to ensure that it is absolutely clear beyond any doubt that the agent has obtained the best possible terms for the vendor and has not been influenced in any way by the prospect of being retained by one particular developer in order to dispose of the development. This is important when the commission earned by the disposal of the development is likely to be considerably greater than the commission earned on the sale on behalf of the original vendor of the site to the developer.

6.13 COMMUNICATION

6.13.1 General

The traditional means of attracting purchasers and tenants are:

(a) Advertising
(b) Mail shots
(c) Particulars and brochures
(d) Siteboards
(e) Launching ceremonies

The extent to which each of these is used depends in part upon the character of the development, and in part upon the amount of money that is allocated to the selling campaign.

6.13.2 Advertisements

Advertisements are aimed directly at the potential occupiers or indirectly at occupiers through their agents. The advertisements are placed in national or local newspapers, in various property journals, such as *Estates Gazette* and *Estates Times*, or where appropriate special trade journals.

Great care needs to be taken over the way in which the advertisement is worded and presented and in nearly all cases it is worth employing an experienced advertising agency to ensure the maximum impact. Some large firms of estate agents have such an amount of advertising work that they have their own in-house advertising department. The advertisement should contain sufficient information to attract the potential occupier, but should not be so cluttered that it is difficult to read (see Fig. 6.1), and it should show:

(a) The type of property
(b) Approximate size
(c) Location
(d) Whether the property is for sale or to be let
(e) Price

Designed and Produced by Humphrey Lloyd Publicity Ltd.

Fig. 6.1

The telephone number of the agent or the developer, or both, should be given so that the potential occupier can make a direct contact. Figure 6.1 shows a bad and a good example of a simple advert. When the property justifies it, a much more elaborate advert might be used, perhaps including photographs and colour. Examples of such advertisements can be seen in any copy of the *Estates Gazette*.

Newspaper and magazine advertising is by far and away the most common form of advertising that is used. Very little use has, so far, been made of television and radio for individual properties.

6.13.3 Mail shots

A mail shot is used on its own or to support an advertising campaign. It comprises the sending of a letter describing the property to a selected group of potential occupiers. The group can be selected either by the developer or his agent, or by a specialist outside agency. Rather more information can be given in the letter than the advertisement, but the letter should be written in a direct style without too much 'padding'. It is often helpful if photographs of the property are included. It must be remembered that the people to whom the letter is sent will have a tendency to throw the letter into the waste-paper basket without looking at it on the basis that it is 'just another circular'.

6.13.4 Particulars and brochures

Particulars are either sent to potential occupiers, or to estate agents. The nature of the particulars will depend upon the nature of the property. In some cases ,they are set out on a single sheet of paper and are sent out with other properties as part of a general circularization. In other cases, the property is of such a nature and importance that more detailed information is needed and particulars are sent out on their own.

The particulars, which may be supported by photographs or illustrations should contain:

(a) A description of the location of the property.
(b) A description of the accommodation, giving areas, heights and a brief specification.
(c) A description of the services supplied to the property, such as gas and electricity.
(d) The nature of the interest that is being sold. If it is freehold, the nature of any leases or restrictions to which it is subject; and if it is leasehold, the length and terms of the lease.
(e) The price or rent that is being asked.

The particulars should give the name, address and telephone number of the estate agent and developer and the name of the person in the agent's office or on the developer's staff who is dealing with the property, so that a direct contact can be made by the potential occupier.

It is usual to include a 'saving clause'. These vary in content but a typical one might be as follows:

'Messrs —— for themselves and for the vendors or lessors of this property whose agents they are give notice that:

(1) Those particulars do not constitute, nor constitute any part of, an offer or a contract.

(2) All statements contained in these particulars as to this property are made without responsibility on the part of Messrs —— or the vendors or lessors.

(3) None of the statements contained in these particulars as to this property is to be relied on as a statement or representation of fact.

(4) Any intending purchasers or tenants must satisfy themselves by inspection or otherwise as to the correctness of each of the statements contained in these particulars.

(5) The vendors or lessors do not make or give, and neither Messrs —— nor any person in their employment has any authority to make or give, any representation or warranty whatever in relation to this property.

In most cases it is necessary to prepare a brochure describing the property and giving more details than the brief particulars referred to above. The brochure is sent to the people who reply to the initial advertising, mail shots or particulars, or may be sent directly to people who are known to be interested. The appearance is of great importance as it reflects the quality of the development that it describes. Unless the developer or his agents have in-house specialist staff, it is best to employ an outside designer to ensure the most effective use of typography, colour, shape, and so on. The brochure should include maps, plans, photographs and a brief specificaton. It should also provide information about the locality which will be helpful to a potential occupier. In the case of an office development, this may be the relationship of the building to the shopping centre. In the case of an industrial or warehousing complex, it includes information about roads, ports and airports. In the case of a residential development, it includes details of schools, leisure facilities and local shops. In a lengthy marketing campaign it may well be necessary to produce more than one brochure at different stages of the development.

6.13.5 Consult the solicitor

A solicitor is invariably employed to deal with the sale or lease of a property. It is useful to send the draft particulars or brochures to him so that he may not only familiarize himself with the property, but also cast a friendly eye on the documents for statements which might otherwise have unforeseen legal consequences. Close collaboration between solicitor and those dealing with property disposals is highly desirable. If where possible the solicitor prepares a 'blank' contract (i.e. requiring only the insertion of the names of the parties and the price or rent) beforehand, transactions may be dealt with that much more expeditiously. Once a bargain has been made, the faster it is enshrined in a legally binding contract the better.

6.13.6 Siteboards

Most development sites will have a board giving details of the development, both during the course of construction and after the building has been completed until sales or lettings have been effected. Great care should be given to the positioning of the board and the way in which it is worded in order to extract the maximum advertisement value. The board should be well maintained and cleaned. A shoddy board casts doubt upon the quality of the development itself.

6.13.7 Launching ceremony

In some cases it may be appropriate to launch the development by a topping-out ceremony during the course of construction or by an opening ceremoney when the building is completed. It is normal to invite to such functions local or national press, local or national agents and potential occupiers. The local councillors or their officers may be invited, and in the case of a residential development the managers of the local offices of the building societies and banks should also be invited to attend. The type of ceremony varies enormously but it normally involves some kind of refreshment, perhaps a buffet lunch, and centres around a short speech by the developer himself or maybe the mayor or local Member of Parliament. It may be possible to give some demonstration of the way in which the building can be used and all those who attend should be given the opportunity of a thorough inspection of the development. Where an estate of warehouses has been completed it may be possible to arrange for a local firm to give a demonstration of, say, forklift trucks, or if it is an office building a local office furnisher may be prepared to lay out a typical half-floor with desks, chairs, filing cabinets, and so on. The opening of a shopping centre may be quite a grand affair with elaborate decorations, music and a 'celebrity' to perform the opening ceremony.

Whatever form of launching ceremony is devised, it is of the utmost importance that at the time of the ceremony the development is in very good order. At an opening ceremony the buildings must really be ready for occupation with all services working. In the case of a shopping centre, the major units may be let and occupied and the opening of the development may be linked to the opening of those units.

6.14 SPECIAL POINTS

6.14.1 Offices

In some cases, the buildings will be let before the development starts. Where the development is carried out speculatively, however, the marketing process will start during the period of construction and the selling will be supported by the use of plans, elevations, models, and the like. Once the building has been completed, its appearance is of vital importance, and it will often be advisable to fit out a floor or a part of a floor with partitions and furniture so that a potential occupier can see clearly how the office will look when it is occupied. It may also be advisable to fit out the main entrance hall and reception area and it is important to ensure that the common parts and lavatories are kept clean. In nearly all cases nowadays carpeting is provided by the developer throughout the building, and it may be that this practice will be extended by the developer offering to fit out or furnish an office for a particular tenant if lettings prove difficult.

A particular building may only be suitable for a small number of occupiers. It may be that because of its location it it is suitable for one type of insurance company, or it may be that it has a particular advantage to a local authority or a central government department. The good agent, and indeed the good developer, should be aware of these possibilities and make his contacts accordingly.

6.14.2 Shops

Larger schemes will be based upon prelettings to particular occupiers, such as department stores and superstores. The standard shop units, however, will not normally be offered until the scheme is nearing completion, although selected traders may be invited at an earlier stage to reserve space in order to ensure the correct mix of tenants. Whereas the covenant of an occupier is important to all developers, in shopping developments the actual use to which the trader is to put the building will fundamentally affect the success of the scheme and careful thought must be given to this. Furthermore it will be important that the opening of the scheme is successful. It will, therefore, be necessary to ensure so far as it is possible that all the shops in the scheme open at the same time.

Depending upon the size of the shopping development, a straightforward advertising campaign may well be replaced by a series of direct approaches by the agent or developer to particular occupiers.

6.14.3 Industrial and warehousing

Unless the industrial development has been pre-let it is unlikely that much interest will be shown by potential occupiers until the development is substantially complete. This will also be true of warehousing development. Most companies seeking space are aiming to move within a matter of three or four months and are not particularly attracted to a scheme that has only just started and will not be available for a much longer time. Most industrial and warehousing occupiers are attracted to a building not only by its general appearance, but even more so by its workmanlike qualities, the eaves-height, the loading facilities and the access to the site. Some companies may need special services.

6.14.4 Residential

In the residential sector, the general forms of advertising referred to above are also used, although the media for advertising is different, greater reliance being given to local newspapers. Particulars are sent to those people on the agents' register who are looking for the type of accommodation being offered and to other local and national agents. Whereas the brochure on an industrial property is normally sent to a company secretary or a company property manager, the brochure on a residential property is sent to a lay person and must be prepared accordingly. Great care must be taken to ensure that the important features of the development are clearly described in language that is not too technical. While the brochure should be supported by plans, it must be remembered that many lay people find it difficult to understand plans and where possible, therefore, photographs and other visual aids should be included.

The board that identifies the site should not only describe the accommodation that is offered in terms of size and price, but also by its general appearance give an indication of the quality of the development. It should show quite clearly to whom potential purchasers should speak if they are interested and give details of the times of the opening of the showhouse and site office.

Whether or not a local agent is used, it may be necessary to have a site office to serve the people coming to see the houses. It is not sufficient merely to use one of the contractor's huts. The first impression the potential purchaser obtains is of great importance. The purchase of a house is the largest single purchase made during a person's lifetime and it is not, therefore, a matter to be taken lightly. The entrance to the development must be properly landscaped and cleared of builder's debris, and indeed the site should not be open to the public until this is possible. Where the development is still continuing, the houses that are completed need to be separated from the construction area by some form of fencing and the roads that serve the houses that have been built should be kept clean and free from mud and rubble. The site office must be easily identifiable and, therefore, encourage people to come into it. Brochures and plans for the development should be available, giving details of prices, fittings and fixtures and other information that the purchasers will need. The office should be staffed by people who are well informed of the details of the houses and have a knowledge of the area in which the houses are being built.

The best way to demonstrate the advantages of the houses is to complete and fit out a show-house. This should be done thoroughly, with attention being given to the details of pictures, furniture, towels in the bathroom, and so on and so forth. The land surrounding the show-house is carefully prepared with trees planted and lawns laid down and kept in good order. The garden should be planted and maintained. If necessary, the heating in the house is kept running to keep the property warm and inviting, and the services, such as water and electricity, should be working. The way in which people are shown over the show-house is also of great importance. Care must be taken to bring to their attention the particular advantages of the propety and, if possible, visits should be ordered in such a way that the attractive features of the property are dealt with towards the end of the inspection.

It should also be remembered that house-purchasers are often without knowledge of house-buying procedure and the agent, whether he be an external or internal agent, must be able to explain the buying process, the amount of the reservation fee and deposit and which building societies are likely to be able to offer mortgages. He should also be able to advise on the arrangements to be made for moving into the house. Where the house is being sold to a family, the husband, wife, and children all share in choosing the house and their attention should be drawn to those particular parts of the house which are likely to interest them most.

6.14.5 Strategy and control

The agent should be involved in the development process from the start and play his part in setting the selling strategy, and once the strategy has been set be fully but firmly briefed. He should report to the developer throughout the development process, keeping him up to date with the latest changes in the local marketplace, monitoring the selling campaign and the progress of competitive developments. The developer should at all times keep control of the campaign. This involves meetings at regular intervals, both on and off the site, with the agent and other advisers.

The developer needs to monitor, through his agent, the effectiveness of the advertising campaign not only for what it tells him about the present project, but what he will be able to learn for future developments.

CHAPTER 7

Finance

7.1 THE PRIVATE SECTOR

Within the private sector, two forms of finance are required
for property development: short-term finance to pay for the
costs of production, that is, the purchase of land, building
costs, professional fees and marketing costs; and long-term
finance to enable the developer to repay his short-term
borrowing and retain or realize his profit. Because their
requirements are so different, we deal separately with residential development and commercial/industrial development.

7.1.1 Residential development

(a) Short-term finance

Short-term building finance is normally provided by the clearing
and merchant banks. Small firms of builders tend to operate
on the basis of a bank overdraft or short-term loan secured
against the value of the land upon which the houses are being
built.

Larger firms, with more financial 'muscle' are, in addition,
able to raise loans against the security of their overall business
reputation. The interest rate charged varies with the strength
of the covenant of the builder/developer and the quality of
the development which he is carrying out.

Currently, a small builder might expect to pay a rate of
interest 3 to 4 percentage points above the clearing bank base
lending rate. If the base rate is say 12%, he has to pay 15 to
16%, depending upon the nature of the scheme and his own

reputation. Such loans are normally related to a specific site and project and repayment is likely to be linked to sales.

A larger builder might have to pay a rate of interest 1 to 2 percentage points above the clearing bank base rate. If the base rate is 12%, he has to pay 13 to 14%. Alternatively the rate of interest might be related to the six-month inter-bank rate. Once again the actual rate of interest charged depends upon the project and the company's reputation. He may well have to pay, in addition, a separate 'commitment' fee of 1% of the total loan. His borrowings are likely to be a mixture of overdraft and separate-scheme finance.

Very large companies are likely to arrange their development finance on a mixture of overdraft and medium-term loans. The medium-term loan may well be unrelated to a specific project and may be available for land banking. There is normally some condition restricting the amount of money allocated to a particular site and a plan which provides for the loan to be reduced by an agreed annual amount. Such a medium-term loan, say, five years, could currently be available for land banking. Such a medium-term loan could currently be available at 1 to 3 percentage points above the London one-year inter-banking lending rate. If that rate were 11% the rate charged would vary between 12 and 14%, depending upon the company's status and the purposes for which it was made available.

Although the facility to borrow the total development cost may need to be arranged at the outset of the development (dependent in part upon the extent to which the builder/developer is providing some of the money himself), it is not borrowed all at once. Initially money is required to purchase land and then to prepare the site. As the development proceeds, further amounts are required. Figure 7.1 shows a typical breakdown of total cost and gives an indication of the way in which finance is required over the period of development. In this example, almost 20% is needed at the outset to purchase the land, a further 22% being required to prepare the site and provide foundations. Almost one third of the cost is taken up by the superstructure, whereas the finishes only take up 11%.

Unlike most forms of commercial and industrial develop-

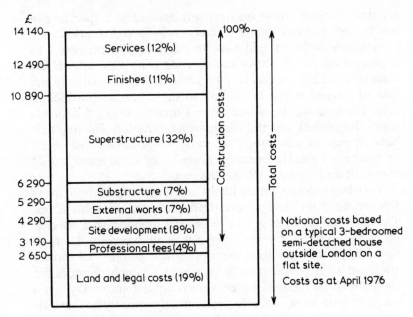

Fig. 7.1 Housebuilding: total cost breakdown

This chart gives an elemental cost breakdown of a typical private-sector house outside London as at April 1976. Construction costs are shown to be 77% of total costs, the remainder being professional fees and land and legal costs. The superstructure constitutes less than a third of the total cost of a house.

(Source: *Trends in Housing and Construction*, National Building Agency, August 1976)

ment, housing development is produced in units, i.e. houses, that can be sold during the course of the development project. The profitability of the development is very much affected by the rate at which sales take place compared with the rate at which they are constructed, as the receipts from sales reduce the total amount of money that otherwise has to be borrowed. Tables 7.1 and 7.2 make a comparison between a development in which the houses are sold during the last six months of the construction period, and a development in which no houses are sold until the development is completed. Although this is a deliberately extreme example, it shows that the delay in sales and the increase in interest charges reduces the profit by some two-thirds (i.e. from 17.1 to 6.3%).

Table 7.1 Cash flow and estimate of profit (for development comprising twenty houses each selling for £50 000 and sales being spread evenly over last six months of development)

Item	1st quarter £	2nd quarter £	3rd quarter £	4th quarter £	5th quarter £	Total £
Receipts:						
Sales receipts				500 000	500 000	980 000
Less sale costs				10 000	10 000	
Net receipts				490 000	490 000	980 000
Cost:						
Land (including costs of purchase)	110 000					
Building (including fees)[a]		168 000	168 000	168 000	168 000	
Marketing			4 000	2 000	2 000	
Total cost	110 000	168 000	172 000	170 000	170 000	790 000
Interest:						
Per quarter @ 16% per annum on capital outstanding[b]	4 400	11 295	18 630	6 575	5 965	46 865
Profit on total cost incl. interest:						
£						143 135
%						17.1

For the purpose of this example, it is assumed:
(a) That building cost is spread evenly over a period of twelve months.
(b) The total cost of development is borrowed and that interest is 'rolled up' until the end, although sales receipts are used to reduce borrowing.

Table 7.2 Cash flow and estimate of profit (for development comprising twenty houses each selling for £50 000 and all sales taking place in the period of three months following the completion of the development)

Item	1st quarter £	2nd quarter £	3rd quarter £	4th quarter £	5th quarter £	6th quarter £	Total £
Receipts:							
Sales						1 000 000	980 000
Less sale costs						20 000	
Net receipts						980 000	980 000
Cost:							
Land (including costs of purchase)	110 000						
Building (including fees)[a]		168 000	168 000	168 000	168 000		792 000
Marketing[b]			4 000	2 000	2 000	2 000	
Total cost	110 000	168 000	172 000	170 000	170 000	2 000	
Interest:							
Per quarter @ 16% per annum on capital outstanding[c]	4 400	11 295	18 630	26 175	34 020	35 460	129 980
Profit on total cost incl. interest:							
£							58 020
%							6.3

For the purpose of this example, it is assumed:
(a) That building cost is spread evenly over a period of 12 months.
(b) That it will be necessary to spend a further £2 000 on marketing because of slow sales performance.
(c) The total cost of development is borrowed and that interest is 'rolled up' until the end, although sales receipts are used to reduce borrowing.

(b) Long-term finance

The vast proportion of dwellings built by the private-sector builder/developer are built for owner-occupation. They are, therefore, built for sale and the builder/developer has only to arrange for the provision of short-term development finance. It is the individual owner-occupier who seeks long-term finance and in most cases this comes from one of the building societies.

Table 7.3 shows the dominance of the building societies over all other forms of lending. In the early 1970s local authority lending grew quite rapidly only to be cut back from 1976—8, leaving building societies responsible for 92% of all lending in 1978. More recently the clearing banks have entered into competition with the building societies and in 1981 accounted for over 23% of all lending, the proportion for the building societies having fallen to some two-thirds.

Table 7.4 shows the allocation of building society advances between new and existing dwellings. Two points are of interest. First, the figures highlight the dominance of second-hand housing in the housing market. Second, the allocation alters with the activity of residential development. From 1970—4,* a period of relatively high development activity, the percentage of advances for new dwellings varied between 23.6 and 26.1%. From 1975—7, a period of relatively less activity, the percentage of such advances fell to between 18.0 and 18.6%.

Although the developer does not have to seek long-term finance for his own use, he is fundamentally affected by the availability of mortgage funds and the rate of interest charged. Restrictions on the amount of funds available or increases in mortgage rates, tend to restrain demand. Figures 7.2 and 7.3, for example, show a decline in the increase of house prices at a time when loans for house purchase fell. It should be noted that the National Building Agency who prepared these figures state that 'the supply of loans for house ownership is a crucial factor affecting the demand for private housing. During 1971 and 1972 the value of loans made increased

*The decline in activity in terms of 'housing starts' in fact began in 1974, but no doubt the figures of advances reflect the fact that during 1974 houses started earlier were completed and advances negotiated earlier were made.

Table 7.3 Loans for house purchase (net advances £m)

Period	Building societies	Local authorities	Insurance companies and pension funds	Banks	TSBs	Other public sector	Total
1973	1999	355	183	310		46	2893
1974	1490	557	189	90		113	2439
1975	2768	619	150	60		133	3730
1976	3618	67	103	80		60	3928
1977	4100	4	119	120	1	18	4362
1978	5115	−43	166	270	5	17	5530
1979	5271	293	357	590	7	74	6592
1980	5722	461	376	490	93	247	7389
1981	6207	250	239	2200	182	348	9426

(Source: *Building Societies Association Bulletin*, No. 31, July, 1982)

Table 7.4 Building Society advances: new and existing dwellings

Period	New dwellings		Existing dwellings		All dwellings	
	Number 000s	Amount* £m	Number 000s	Amount* £m	Number 000s	Amount* £m
1970	133	510	407	1 492	540	2 002
1971	165	713	488	2 016	653	2 729
1972	164	862	517	2 752	681	3 614
1973	142	903	403	2 601	545	3 504
1974	102	700	331	2 220	433	2 920
1975	121	946	529	4 003	650	4 949
1976	129	1 125	586	4 972	715	6 117
1977	122	1 174	615	5 699	737	6 889
1978	134	1 504	668	7 204	802	8 734
1979	117	1 519	598	7 562	715	9 103
1980	94	1 406	584	8 183	675	9 614
1981	87	1 446	649	9 346	736	11 915

*Includes further advances to borrowers and second and subsequent advances of instalment mortgages.

(Source: *Facts and Figures — a Quarterly Bulletin of Statistics and Background Commentary on Housing and Housing Finance*, by Building Societies Association, July 1977 and *Building Societies Association Bulletin*)

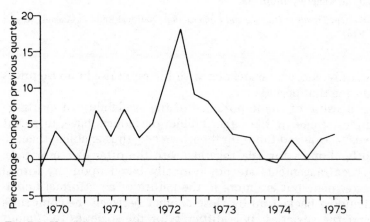

Fig. 7.2 Housing: movement of house prices

This chart shows the rate of increase of house prices over the previous quarter. This illustrates very well the exact point of take off of house prices, i.e. the first quarter of 1972 and lasting for about 12 months thereafter. Since that date the rate of increase has reduced to a level below the general rate of inflation, allowing the normal relationship between incomes and house prices to be restored.

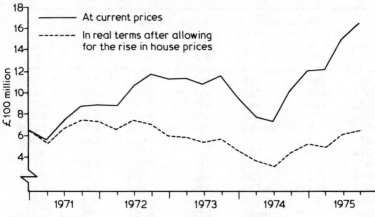

Fig. 7.3 Housing: loans for house purchase — all sources

The supply of loans for house ownership is a crucial factor affecting the demand for private housing. During 1971 and 1972 the value of loans made increased sharply and was associated with the rapid rise in house prices during that period. Loans declined during 1973 and 1974 when building societies were short of funds, but surged ahead again from mid-1974 onwards with the help of government loans and as the cash flow to the societies improved.

(Source: *Trends in Housing and Construction*, National Building Agency, August 1976)

sharply and was associated with the rapid rise in house prices during that period'.

Because of the importance of the availability of mortgage funds, some of the larger builder/developers have, in recent years, arranged funds for their own use, thus enabling them to offer houses for sale together with the offer of a mortgage. The arrangements are not normally based upon any formal agreement but are more in the nature of an informal understanding backed up by close contact between the companies and the societies. It is difficult for the societies to commit themselves to precise allocations as they can never forecast the particular requirements of the purchasers of the companies' houses. Furthermore such arrangements must always be subject to the society being able to refuse a particular application on the ground that the applicant does not meet their normal criteria.

7.1.2 Commercial and industrial development

In the last thirty years, the way in which commercial and industrial development has been financed has changed as the impact of inflation has been recognized. Until the early 1960s the roles of the developer, the short-term financier and the long-term financier were quite distinct. The developer acted as a promoter, creating and often holding the long-term asset. Short-term finance was provided by clearing or merchant banks against a prearranged mortgage commitment by an insurance company. As security, the banks took a charge against the site and sometimes the buildings. With the exception of some of the merchant banks, they rarely participated in the equity or the risk of the development. Some building contractors also provided short-term finance by 'rolling up' the building cost during the period of construction.

Long-term funding was usually provided by insurance companies by way of a fixed-interest mortgage. Typically the amount of the mortgage was approximately two-thirds of the value of the completed development and the developer's target was:

(a) To ensure that two-thirds of the value was not less that 100% of the development cost, and
(b) That the income from the completed development was not less than the interest and capital repayments of the mortgage agreement.

Occasionally the development would not be retained by the developer but would be sold, as an investment, to an insurance company or sold directly to an occupier. This would be so particularly where the developer could not arrange for a suitable mortgage, perhaps because the development cost was in excess of two-thirds of the value of the completed development. Where an insurance company agreed to acquire a development, they rarely took any part of the development risk and would only be bound to acquire once the development was fully let.

In the period 1947—59, the period of the first post-war property boom,* insurance companies became more and

---

*See Oliver Mariott, *The Property Boom*, Hamish Hamilton, 1967.

more involved in the property market. In the period 1947–53 their total acquisition of property rose from £149 to £303 millions, and in the same period the money that they lent to developers by way of mortgage rose from £158 to £417 millions.*

As inflation became recognized as a permanent feature, the insurance companies became aware of the dangers of granting fixed-interest mortgages and equally of the advantages that could be obtained by participating in rental growth. At the same time long-term interest rates rose and developers were faced with an initial shortfall of income over mortgage interest and capital repayments. Thus, as insurance companies became less inclined to grant mortgages and developers were forced to give away some share of future rental growth in order to close the 'reverse yield gap', the insurance companies began to become more directly involved in the ownership of property investments. As Tables 7.5 and 7.6 show, they gradually increased the amounts of money allocated to property investment and were joined by pension funds and, in time, by specially formed property unit trusts and property bonds in an increasingly active investment market.

As more and more institutional funds were attracted to property, traditional roles began to blur. At first, in order to attract the best investments, long-term investors began to compete with and take on the additional role of the short-term financier. At the same time some of the traditionally short-term financiers, the clearing banks and the merchant banks, began to seek a share in the equity of the development itself. As the competition for the best, the 'prime' investments, increased some of the insurance companies, pension funds and property bonds — either on a project basis or by the acquisition of properties companies — began to take on the role of the developer, accepting the additional element of risk in return for a marginally better long-term yield.

This level of activity increased to the height of the second post-war boom of 1971–3. Then in late 1973 and early 1974 as a result of the rise in short-term interest rates, the rent freeze and the proposals for a first-letting tax, the property boom collapsed and for a time, throughout 1974 and part of

* Ibid.

Table 7.5   Investment by insurance companies and pension funds, 1962—81

Year	Insurance companies (£m)	(%)	Pension funds (£m)	(%)
1962	50.9	9.1		
1963	62.8	10.2	26.0	6.1
1964	58.7	8.6	30.0	6.7
1965	89.1	13.5	39.0	8.0
1966	117.0	18.0	48.0	9.0
1967	95.3	12.5	79.0	15.3
1968*	119.4	13.4	93.0	15.8
1969	185.9	22.8	112.0	18.7
1970	197.5	19.8	97.0	13.2
1971	198.1	16.0	91.0	10.4
1972	131.1	8.0	121.0	11.2
1973	306.8	18.5	248.0	18.0
1974†	405.1	21.2	305.0	18.3
1975	406.3	16.1	342.0	13.6
1976	449.7	16.0	513.0	16.4
1977	370.0	12.4	670.0	17.9
1978	490.0	12.5	610.0	16.7
1979	580.0	12.8	550.0	10.1
1980	700.0	14.1	800.0	13.2
1981	970.0	16.4	840.0	12.2

*Including for the first time net acquisitions by Commonwealth companies life funds.
†1974 is the first year which includes non-members of BIA.

(Source: 1962—76 Michael Cunnane, The Property Sector, Panmure Gordon & Co., November 1976; 1978—81, The Henley Centre for Forecasting, Investment Markets, July 1982)

1975, the market was in complete disarray.* Although Table 7.5 shows that money continued to be invested by the institutions during that period, this was largely as a result of prior commitments. A more accurate reflection of the market conditions at that time is shown by the change in investment yields in Table 7.7. During this period virtually no new funds were made available for development. Indeed as developers licked their wounds, very few of them were anxious to take on new schemes.

In 1976 the market began to re-establish itself and a pattern

* See David Cadman and Alejandra Catalans, Property Development in the UK —Evolution and Change (Property Development Library), College of Estate Management, Summer 1983.

Table 7.6   Property Growth Assurance Company Ltd: ownership of commercial property, 1970—82 (January)

	Commercial property owned (£m)	Offices	Shops (%)	Industrials
1970	1.2	64.0	4.0	32.0
1971	2.7	72.6	5.9	21.5
1972	11.7	57.3	11.5	31.2
1973	23.0	43.7	17.3	39.0
1974	38.5	64.8	14.2	21.0
1975	24.8	56.5	22.2	21.3
1976	27.9	56.8	22.6	20.6
1977	27.1	54.7	23.8	21.5
1978*	29.8	44.6	26.5	25.4
1979*	33.5	46.5	30.0	20.9
1980	33.8	49.3	24.6	26.1
1981	36.1	50.3	25.0	24.8
1982	—	53.9	25.6	20.5

*During these years a small percentage was invested in overseas properties.

(Source: *Property Growth Assurance Company Limited*, September 1977 and April 1982)

of yields began to appear for completed and let property investments. Some new developments were started but the level was still much reduced and the general economic uncertainties of 1976 and 1977 kept the level of activity low. However, during 1976—7 the market for completed and let investment re-established itself firmly with yields returning to levels of 1971—2. By 1981, prime investments yields had fallen to an historic low. At the time of writing (August 1982) the institutional investors have come to dominate an increasingly selective prime market in which the supply of suitable properties does not meet investment demand. Direct development is now an established form of investment for the larger pension funds and insurance companies.

(a) Sale and leaseback

The sale and leaseback was devised to enable the developer to obtain long-term finance for a project while retaining, as an

Table 7.7   Prime property yields

Year	Offices(%)	Shops(%)	Industrials(%)
1960	7	6½	10
1961	7	7	10
1962	6	6¾	9
1963	6	6¾	9
1964	6½	6¾	9
1965	6½	7	8¾
1966	6¾	7	9
1967	6¼	6½	9
1968	6	6¼	8¾
1969	5¾	6	8
1970	6	6¼	9
1971	6½	5½	8½
1972	5	5¼	8
1973	4½	4½	7½
1974	7	7¼	10½
1975	7¼	8¼	10
1976	6	6¼	8¾
1977	6½	6	8¼
1978	5	4½	6½
1979	4¾	4¼	6½
1980	4½	4	6¼
1981	4½	4	6¼
1982	4½	3½	6¼

(Source: Michael Cunnane, *The Property Sector*, Panmure Gordon & Co., November 1976; The Healey & Baker Yield Graph, 1st June 1982)

investment, a share in its future rental growth. Perhaps the best way to describe such a transaction is by an example. Consider the following financial analysis of a development of 20 000 sq ft of warehousing let at £50 000 per annum:

Purchase price of land (including costs of
purchase) acquired by developer with his
own capital   £75 000

Opportunity cost to developer of
investing his capital in the purchase of
the land for the period of the
development, say   £10 000

Developer's total investment   £85 000

Building and marketing costs provided by short-term borrowing from bank	£550 000
Interest on bank-borrowing for building and letting period, say	£ 60 000
Total of short-term borrowing	£610 000

From this example it will be seen that the developer has invested £85 000 in the project and has borrowed a further £610 000 (including interest). At the end of the project the short-term borrowing, £610 000, has to be repaid and the sale and leaseback enables the developer to do so while retaining, as an investment, a share in future rental growth. If in this case the current investment yield required by an institution is 7%, the developer can sell his freehold interest to the institution for £610 000 and take back from them a long lease at 7%, that is, say, £42 700 per annum. He is thus enabled to repay his short-term borrowing and retain an initial profit rent of £7300 per annum. The lease will provide for periodic rent reviews related to those in the occupational lease and the formula for calculating the institution's share will probably be as follows:

$$\frac{\text{Initial rent paid by developer}}{\text{Initial full rental value}} \times 100$$

$$\text{i.e.} \ \frac{£42\,700}{£50\,000} \times 100 = 85.4\%$$

The developer's initial return on his capital investment would be:

$$\text{i.e.} \ \frac{£7\,300}{£85\,000} \times 100 = 8.6\%$$

At the time of the first review the developer will be entitled to 14.6% of the new rental so that if, at that time, the occupational rent has risen to £100 000 per annum he will be entitled to a profit rent of £14 600 per annum and his return on his investment will be as follows:

$$\frac{\pounds 14\,600}{\pounds 85\,000} \times 100 = 17.2\%$$

The developer's share or profit rent has become known as the 'top slice'. The first sale and leasebacks were arranged on the basis that the rent payable to the fundings institution at the time of each review was 'upwards only'. That is, that at each review the new rent paid to the institution would not be less than the previous rent. In our example it would mean that, at the first rent review, the rent paid by the developer to the institution could not be less than £42 700 per annum. Such a condition was perfectly acceptable where the 'top slice' was say 30—40% of the occupational rent, and as long as rents continued to rise and the property remained let. But when, as in our example, the developer was left with a much smaller 'top slice', he found that it was almost impossible to sell his interest to anyone other than the original funding institution, for potential purchasers saw a time when the property might be unlet or rents would fall, so that the developer's profit rent would be substantially or entirely eroded.

In order to overcome this problem, a variation of the basic form of sale and leaseback was created which became known as the 'vertical slice method'. In this case the institution and the developer shared the income at reviews in accordance with the initially agreed proportion and the developer was not burdened with an 'upwards only' condition. This made the developer's investment more marketable as potential purchasers could value a given proportion of the future income stream. In some cases there was no reference to the review date at all, the income being shared throughout the length of the lease in accordance with the initial proportions. This gave the institution the added advantage of enjoying inter-review increases in income where, for example, in an office building let to a number of tenants, one tenant surrendered his lease before the date of the next review and a new tenant was found at a higher rent.

Since the late 1960s the sale and leaseback method of financing has also been adopted by commercial and industrial occupiers, as a means of releasing capital tied up in existing land and buildings or as a means of providing additional buildings with limited or no capital investment on their part. An industrial company owning and occupying a modern freehold factory of say 50 000 sq ft with a current rental value of £100 000 per annum could sell the freehold interest to an institution for say £1.4 million and take back an occupational lease at a rent of £100 000 per annum with periodic rent reviews of say five years. Subject to the incidence of capital gains tax the sum released would then be used for financing the company's industrial activity.

Another example might be that of an industrial company that has constructed, on land that it has owned for several years, a new factory building of 15 000 sq ft at a total cost including interest and fees but excluding any land 'cost' of £350 000. The factory has a rental value on completion of £40000 per annum. When the building is finished, the company might wish to repay the capital it has borrowed in order to erect the building. It, therefore, agrees to sell the freehold interest of the property to an insurance company and take back a lease. If it only wishes to release the £350 000 of borrowed money, it can sell the freehold interest for that sum and take back a lease at a yield to the insurance company of say 7%, that is an initial rent of £24 500 per annum, rent reviews being geared to a proportion of the full rental value at the time of the review based upon the following:

$$\frac{\text{Initial rent paid}}{\text{Initial rental value}} \times 100$$

that is, in this example:

$$\frac{\text{£24 500 per annum}}{\text{£40 000 per annum}} \text{ or } 61.25\%$$

By this method the industrial company has released the capital it has invested and acquired a share in the future equity of the investment by virtue of the occupational profit rent. The insurance company has achieved an acceptable investment return, a share in rental growth and a relatively secure income as the rental paid will always be less than the full rental value.

The traditional division of financial roles is as follows:

Short-term development finance:	Long-term investment finance:
Clearing banks	Insurance companies
Merchant banks	Pension funds
	Property unit trusts
	Property bonds
	Charities

However, in the past, some of the long-term financiers have taken on, in addition to their traditional role, the role of the short-term financier providing interim development finance either at a commercial banking rate, or at a lower rate in exchange for a higher long-term investment yield. In the example on pages 36—38 we assumed that the short-term finance had been provided by bank-borrowing. It is possible, however, that prior to development taking place the developer could agree, with say a pension fund, that they provide the short-term development finance and the long-term investment funding. In such cases, where the finance is provided without a preletting, the developer will normally have to agree to guarantee the investor's return at the end of the development period.

An alternative method is a reduced rate of interest on short-term finance in return for a higher long-term investment yield. The example below shows a comparison in which this alternative method gives the developer a marginally better return and the pension fund a higher initial yield.

Example

Assume a developer owns a freehold interest of a site with planning permission for 10 000 sq ft of offices. The total building and marketing cost is £580 000. The current market rental value is £60 000 per annum:

Alternative 1

Short-term development finance at 15% and long-term investment yield of 6%:

Total development cost	£580 000
Interest over development and marketing period at 15% say	£ 44 000

Total investment by pension fund £624 000

Rent required by pension fund to
show a return of 6%, say   £ 37 400 per annum
Current rental value   £ 60 000 per annum
Developer's profit return   £ 22 600 per annum
Developer's proportion of rent   37.7%

Alternative 2
Short-term development finance at 10% and long-term investment yield of 6½%:

Total development cost   £580 000
Interest over development and
marketing period at 10% say   £ 30 000

Total investment by pension fund £610 000

Rent required by pension fund to
show a return of 6½%, say   £ 39 650 per annum
Current rental value   £ 60 000 per annum
Developer's profit rent   £ 20 350 per annum
Developer's proportion of rent   33.9%

One further variation needs to be described. Where a
developer arranges his short- and long-term funding prior
to the start of development and without a preletting, calcula-
tions have to be based upon a level of rent which may rise
during the period of construction. The institutions claim
that they should share in this rental growth. In such cases,
therefore, the leaseback must be arranged so that the institution receives its basic investment yield on the capital that
it invests and a proportion of the amount by which the actual
initial rent exceeds an agreed estimated initial rent.

If we take, as an example, Alternative 2 above and assume
that the actual initial rent paid by the tenant at the completion
of the scheme is £70 000 per annum instead of the estimated
initial rent of £60 000 per annum, the initial rent received by
the institution might be calculated as follows:

Rent required to show a return
of 6½%   £ 39 650

Plus 50% of the amount by which the actual initial rent paid exceeds the estimated initial rent, i.e. (£70 000 — £60 000) divided by 2	£ 5 000
Initial rent received by institution	£ 44 650 per annum

The institution's yield has risen from 6½ to just over 7¼% but their share in future rents has fallen from 66.1 to 63.8%. The developer's initial profit rent has increased by £5000 per annum and his share in future rents has risen from 33.9 to 36.2%. Whilst the institutional investors are eager to achieve higher initial yields, they are conscious of the dangers of overletting and normally exercise some control over the terms upon which tenancies are agreed.

(b) Debentures, mortgages and loan stock

Property companies can raise finance for development from the financial institutions by enabling them to participate in the equity of the company itself. By acquiring debentures or granting mortgages, the institutions effectively lend money at a rate of interest below the current market level in return for a share in the company's potential growth. The money is typically lent for a long term, perhaps fifteen years, at a fixed rate of interest and is secured upon the company's property assets. Normally the security is specifically related to named properties but sometimes provision is made to allow the company to substitute one property for another, subject to agreement on valuation.

In addition or as an alternative, property companies may issue to the institutions unsecured loan stock which may within a specified period be converted, at the option of the institution, into the ordinary shares of the company.*

---

*Michael Cunnane, *The Property Sector*, Panmure Gordon & Co, November 1976.

(c) Ownership of property company shares

A further way in which an institution can invest in property
development is through the ownership of property company
shares. Several insurance companies have taken a substantial
or in some cases a controlling interest in property companies.
Table 7.9 shows the holdings of various institutions at
September 1982.

Table 7.9   Institutional holdings of property company shares

Company	Institution	Property held (%)
Allied London Properties	Eagle Star	7.6
Allnatt London Properties	Kuwait Investment Office	5.6
Anglo Metropolitan	Britannia Arrow	15.6
	M & G	9.7
Apex Properties	Courtaulds Pension	7.7
Aquis Securities	Guardian Royal Exchange	64.5
Bilton (Percy)	National Coal Board	12.4
Bridgewater Estates	Largs	21.1
Brixton Estate	Clerical Medical and General	23.4
	Royal Insurance	7.7
Capital and Counties	Liberty Life	29.6
	Kuwait Investment Office	6.0
Centrovincial	General Accident	18.3
	Barclays Nominees	6.4
Chesterfield	Prudential	16.2
Churchbury Estates	Courtaulds Pension Fund	5.2
	Royal Insurance	6.7
Clarke Nicholls Coombs	London Overseas Land	17.4
	Barclays Nominees (M & G Group)	7.8
Country and New Town	British and Commonwealth	40.5
Estates and General	Guardian Royal Exchange	6.1
Evans of Leeds	Scottish Amicable	5.8
Great Portland Estates	Kuwait Investment Office	5.6
Greencoat Properties	Canada Life Assurance	5.1
	Guinness Peat	7.7
R. Green Properties	Throgmorton Street Nominees	11.3
	Pearl Assurance	10.7
Hales Properties	Wesleyan and General Assurance Society	24.8
Hammerson ('A' Shares)	Standard Life	28.5
	Royal London Mutual	9.3
Imry Property	Norwich Union	30.2
	Rothschild	27.8
Land Investors	Norwich Union	10.1

Table 7.9 (*continued*)

Company	Institution	Property held (%)
Land Securities	Prudential	7.6
London and Provincial	Legal and General	16.0
McKay Securities	General Accident	25.8
MEPC	Eagle Star	5.4
Municipal Properties	Equitable Life Assurance	8.0
	Western Heritable	7.4
North British Properties	Sun Life	24.1
Peachey Property	ICI Pension Fund	5.0
	Sun Alliance	5.2
PHIT	Pearl Assurance	19.1
	Kuwait Investment Office	8.9
Property Partnership	BBC Pension Scheme	7.0
Property and Reversionary	General Accident	19.0
Property Security		
Investment Trust	Royal Insurance	7.8
	Brown Shipley	6.1
Raglan Property	Kleinwort Benson	5.2
Regional Properties	Friends Provident	29.9
Scottish Metropolitan	Royal Insurance	20.4
	Guardian Royal Exchange	18.3
	Scottish Equitable	8.7
	Unilever Pension Fund	5.7
Second City Properties	Scottish Amicable	14.5
Slough Estates	Kuwait Investment Office	5.1
Stock Conversion	Kuwait Investment Office	7.8
Town Centre Securities	General Accident	7.4
	Barclays Bank	7.1
Town and City	Hambros	10.5
	Prudential	5.7
Trafford Park	Britannic Assurance	10.3
	Outwich Investment Trust	8.9
	Largs	6.3
United Real	Co-op Insurance	10.0
Warnford Investments	Co-op Insurance	10.0
	Kuwait Investment Office	5.2

(Source: Michael Cunnane, Panmure Gordon & Co., September 1982.)

(d) The future

Following the debacle of the collapse of the property market in 1974—5, the institutional investors have emerged as the dominant force in prime commercial and industrial property markets. The criteria that they adopt have become increasingly narrow leading to a widening of the gap between the 'prime' or 'institutionally acceptable' properties and the rest. Despite a faltering economy the 'weight' of institutional money has moved prime yields to historically low levels. Typical yields for prime properties are currently (August 1982)* as follows:

Offices	4½%
Shops	3½%
Industrial/Warehouse	6¼%

and the removal of Exchange Control has encouraged many institutions to look for investments abroad, particularly in North America. Nevertheless, with growing awareness of the power and importance of the financial institutions, questions are beginning to be raised about their behaviour and performance. In the meantime the institutions themselves are becoming increasingly experienced in both direct and indirect investment. Many of the larger insurance companies and pension funds now carry out their own development schemes and some of the most experienced are beginning to demand from their advisers a much more extensive and detailed form of appraisal, including data on the performance of property markets in the context of the local and regional economy. The property companies continue to have an important role to play although most of the small companies operating in the prime market are forced by institutional competition to trade, selling or preleasing their developments to the insurance companies and pension funds.

7.2 THE PUBLIC SECTOR

Although a very substantial proportion of the work of the construction industry is carried out for public authorities, the great bulk of the work is to enable them to carry out their statutory functions as distinct from undertaking the role of property developer in the generally understood sense of that term. Various different types of public authorities are from time to time in varying degrees engaged in speculative property development. The New Town Development Corporations, the Scottish and Welsh Development Agencies and the English Industrial Estates Corporation are obvious

---

* Since preparing this book 'prime' yields have risen to: Offices 4¾%; Shops 3¾%; Industrial/Warehouse 6¾% (April 1983).

examples. However, the widest area of general interest will be in the financial activities of local authorities related to their involvement in and with property development and their responsibilities for providing a great deal of the infrastructure which is essential to enable development to proceed. It is that area to which these comments are directed.

7.2.1 The local authority developer

The role of the local authority in making land available has been examined in Chapter 3. But the ultimate objective is not necessarily limited to making land available. The authority might decide to proceed to carry out the development itself.

A local authority will often raise development finance in precisely the same way as a private developer. The lease and leaseback is one of the arrangements used to obtain development finance even though its attraction has been reduced by the provisions in the Local Government Planning and Land Act 1980 to the effect that the capital value of an authority's leasehold interest has to count as prescribed expenditure and rank against any capital allocations. Although a local authority is not able to offer its own corporate shares for sale, it is nevertheless quite possible to establish a development company for the purpose of carrying out a particular development scheme and authorities do raise money on the stock market, as we shall see later.

7.2.2 The provision of infrastructure

There are three basic questions. What is infrastructure? Who provides what? Who pays for it?

There is a good deal of elasticity in the definition of infrastructure. Often the term is used in a limited sense to encompass roads and sewerage and statutory undertakers' services. Frequently the term is enlarged so as to include all the amenities and services provided by local authorities, such as open space, education and welfare, libraries and social service facilities and the like, which have such an important effect upon the life of a community. The ultimate definition sometimes used when planning on a regional or national scale will include facilities which are planned on a national basis, such as motorways, inland waterways, ports, airports and railways.

The functions of principal local authorities in England are set out in the table in the Appendix (taken from *Local Government in England and Wales: a Guide to the New System*, HMSO, 1974). This clearly shows 'Who provides what'. Precisely who pays for what is a more difficult question.

7.2.3 Local authority finance

In an attempt to give a simple summary of a complicated subject, it is proposed to examine two questions. From what sources are local authorities able to obtain money for capital expenditure? How do authorities raise the necessary revenue to service capital and to meet their current expenditures?

(a) Capital expenditure

Local authority capital expenditure is controlled by central government in various ways. Part 8 of the Local Government Planning and Land Act 1980 introduced new arrangements for the control of local authority capital expenditure. From 1 April 1981 a single block borrowing approval is given for all capital expenditure on all services except police, probation and magistrates' courts, where loan sanctions are to be sought from the Home Office. The block borrowing approval is divided between housing, education, transport, personal social services and 'other services'. These service block allocations are capable of aggregation and thus there is flexibility for local authorities to utilize capital resources according to their individual priorities. For certain services, in particular education, central government still requires scheme by scheme approval. An authority may also increase its capital resources by applying certain types of net capital receipts and profits arising from trading undertakings towards capital expenditure.

Local authorities may to a limited extent finance capital expenditure from revenue. But generally capital expenditure will be financed by borrowing.

General powers to borrow money are contained in the Local Government Act 1972. In addition to borrowing money from the Public Works Loan Board, authorities may raise money by mortgage, the issue of stock, debentures or annuities, bonds and bills and by any other means such as syndicated loans approved by the Secretary of State with the consent of the Treasury. Local authorities may also with the appropriate consent raise money outside the UK. For certain specific purposes loans might be made available from the EEC, often on advantageous terms, although by and large these are restricted to loans for schemes of regional importance. From 1 April 1977 local authorities have operated a Voluntary Borrowing Code. This was introduced as a result of pressure from central government on local authorities to lengthen the average life of their outstanding loans to a period of seven years by the financial year of 1981–2. It was thought that too many authorities were relying on relatively short-term loans to finance their expenditure and hence ran the risk of suffering significant fluctuations in their average borrowing costs at a time of public expenditure restraint.

Temporary loans (for not more than one year) may be raised, although their amount is restricted so that the total amount borrowed in this way does not exceed 20% of the total loan debt. Within certain very restricted limits bank overdrafts may also be sought. The advantage of temporary money is that it is usually much cheaper than money raised on a longer-term basis and if long-term interest rates were to be expected to fall in the near future it would be to an authority's advantage to borrow short term in the intermediate period. The maximum period for which money might be borrowed is normally sixty years, although the greater bulk of local authority loan debt is still relatively short term in nature. Replacing maturity loans and funding capital expenditure is a continuing process. Local authorities, within the general constraints to which they are subject, seek to borrow from sources which offer the most advantageous terms. Conditions in the money market vary from time to time as in any other market. Public Works Loan Board interest rates will not always be the most attractive, but each authority has a borrowing quota from the PWLB which is fixed by formula. Once the quota has been exhausted, an authority will have to look elsewhere to borrow long term money. An authority which finds itself in difficulties could return to the PWLB from whom in the last resort, it might be allowed to borrow above its quota, albeit at a penal interest rate. Following the introduction of the Voluntary

Borrowing Code the London money markets have initiated medium term syndicated loans which in many respects are particularly attractive to local authorities not wishing to borrow for a period of say 60 years.

The rates of interest paid by an authority will vary according to the sources from which the money is borrowed and the duration of the loan. Most authorities operate a loans pool into which all money borrowed is put and from which it is allocated at an average or 'pool' rate of interest.

Whilst capital expenditure is predominantly financed by borrowing, there are other possibilities. Local authorities have powers to establish capital funds and repairs and renewals funds as well as financing capital expenditure from revenue. Capital receipts may also be obtained from the disposal of land and property and these can be applied towards financing further capital expenditure. Local authorities may also receive contributions from developers towards the provision of essential infrastructure. Leasing arrangements, particularly those in relation to plant and equipment, offer an attractive alternative to capital expenditure.

(b) Revenue

The total estimated gross expenditure (£30 000 million) of local authorities in Great Britain in 1981—2 was derived from the following sources (consultative document *Alternatives to Domestic Rates*, CMND 8449, December 1981): rates 36%; government grants 48%; other income 16%.

Local rates are levied by the district councils, although the greater proportion will be paid over to the county councils who serve precepts on the districts which have to be taken into account when the district is deciding the amount of the local rate. Regional water authorities levy a lump sum in respect of their services to cover the cost of sewerage and environmental health functions and water supply and these are collected by the water authority levying charges direct.

Government grants may be in respect of capital schemes (for example: 75% of the net annual loss on slum clearance, 50% of the net annual deficiency on comprehensive development schemes under the Town and Country Planning Acts) or in aid of revenue expenditure. There are a limited number of specific revenue grants (for example that in respect of the Police Force) but the majority have been combined into one or other of the two main general grants, namely, the Rate Support Grant (RSG) and the Transport Supplementary Grant (TSG).

The TSG is a government grant in respect of local authority revenue expenditure on roads and passenger transport. The RSG is in respect of revenue expenditure on other services provided by the local authority which are not covered by specific revenue grants. The Local Government Planning and Land Act 1980 combined two of the three previous elements of the RSG, namely the resources and needs element into one single Block grant. The domestic element is still given in pursuance of the current government policy to subsidize the domestic ratepayer and the rate in the pound levied on domestic premises is reduced accordingly. The Block grant is intended to average out the position of authorities with disparate resources in terms of rateable value per head of population in providing a common standard of service for a uniform rate burden.

The RSG is calculated afresh each year. Joint discussions take place between the government and local authority representatives. The main topics are the agreement of total relevant expenditure in the forthcoming year and the percentage of that expenditure which will be met by government grant.

Other income is derived from a miscellany of sources. These include rents and charges in respect of certain services, income from the collection of licence fees and possible profits from trading activities.

7.2.4 Who pays

This brief résumé of local authority financial arrangements demonstrates the difficulty of deciding the precise incidence of the burden of payment for the infrastructure and services provided by local authorities. Developers, taxpayers, rate-payers and users are all involved.

7.2.5 **The statutory undertakers**

No discussion on the provision of infrastructure would be complete without reference to the essential services, namely, electricity, water and sewerage, gas and telephones. The different undertakers have their own systems of charges the essential objective of which is normally to ensure that the charge, together with the expected revenue derived from payments for the service, will provide the undertaker with a reasonable return on expenditure.

The availability of the statutory services, particularly water, sewerage and electricity is of major importance in the consideration of development proposals. In some circumstances substantial payments might have to be made to secure the availability of services for a particular development, for example, one which is to take place some distance from existing water mains or sewers. On occasions — if, for example, the sewers or the sewerage works are working at full capacity — inability to provide essential services at an economially viable cost will effectively prevent development from taking place.

CHAPTER 8

The development team

8.1 THE DEVELOPMENT TEAM

In describing the development process, we have drawn attention to the necessity of combining a number of different skills and disciplines. Some of these are required throughout the process and others are only required from time to time. In this chapter we select and describe some of the more important roles and consider how they are combined within the development team.

8.2 THE PLANNER

Any discussion of the role of the planner in the development industry seems to involve an argument as to whether his role should be restricted or extended. On the one hand, the exponent of the free market points to the costs of delay within the planning system and raises doubts as to its effectiveness*. On the other hand, the exponent of a planned economy argues that if planning has failed in the past, it is because planners have not had enough control and that what is needed is more, rather than less, planning. In the paper that he gave to the Town and Country Planning Association Conference in December 1976, the Rt Hon. Reginald Freeson, then Minister for Housing and Construction, said: 'The trouble is not that Town and Country Planning has been tried and found wanting but that it has been wanted and has not been tried.' Somewhere in the middle stand many people conscious

---

* Slough Estates Limited, *Industrial Investment: a case study in factory building*, April 1979.

of the need to work within some framework and trying to improve the dialogue between the various interested groups, so that development can proceed in such a way that it benefits the local community and is at the same time economically viable.

8.2.1 The public sector

Since the Second World War, and more particularly since the Town and Country Planning Act 1947, the role of the land-use planner within the public sector has been to set a framework for development and land use by the preparation of development plans, and to scrutinize and control the planning applications of the private sector to ensure that their proposals fit into predetermined planning policy. In a period of general growth this has been a largely negative role, limiting and containing development and land use. It is not surprising, therefore, that the relationship between the public and private sector has been largely one of confrontation with greatest emphasis being placed by local authorities on development control.

It may be that future economic conditions will require the planner to take on a more positive role in order to stimulate development. It may be that far from being overwhelmed by planning applications to carry out development, the planners may find themselves more concerned with devising methods of encouraging development to take place.

8.2.2 The private sector

Planners working within the private sector tend to work in private-practice consultancy teams, rather than be employed directly by development or financing companies. As such, they are able to advise both the public and private sectors on the formulation of major strategic policy or on the consideration of the development potential of a particular site. They require a sound knowledge of planning law and procedure. They may be required to obtain planning permission or help prepare a case for a planning appeal, giving the evidence at any subsequent inquiry. They need to have a thorough understanding of national and local planning policies.

8.2.3 Social factors

Increasingly, planners are being asked to take account of the social as well as the economic and physical factors of a community in determining future land use and development. It has been argued* that in the past insufficient attention has been given to the social impact of new development upon a local community, too much emphasis being placed upon the physical or 'architectural' aspects or even upon the potential increase in rateable income. Whether or not this is so, pressure from local ratepayers' associations and other local groups, combined with a feeling among some professional advisers and socio-political commentators that some of the major urban redevelopments have not been an unmitigated success, has lead to an attempt to reflect with more sympathy the needs of the people in whose community new development takes place. This has already been shown by a tendency to favour the refurbishment of some existing areas of housing, rather than wholesale demolition and redevelopment, in the hope that the maintenance of the fabric of an old community will prevent the sense of dislocation that has been described in such studies as Young and Willmott's *Family and Kinship in East London*.†

8.3 THE ARCHITECT

Traditionally the architect has performed three main roles in the development process:

(a) The acquisition of planning permission
(b) The design of buildings
(c) The control of the building contract.

8.3.1 Planning permission

Although it may be necessary in larger and more complex schemes to employ a specialist planning consultant to prepare a planning application and negotiate with the planning auth-

---

*Peter Ambrose and Bob Colenutt, *The Property Machine*, Penguin Books, 1975.
†Pelican Books, 1962.

orities, in most projects which are modest in size and straightforward in concept, this task is undertaken by the project architect possibly assisted by other members of the development team. Most practising architects are familiar with the planning system and the generality of planning law. They prepare the application form and the drawings that support it and, usually after discussion with the officers of the planning authority, submit the application and monitor its progress to a decision.

This last aspect is of great importance. Despite the statutory timetable for the consideration of planning applications, decisions are often delayed and it is essential that the architect keeps in constant touch with the planning officer concerned to ensure where possible that delay is avoided. It may be, for example, that some further piece of information is required by the planning authority or that some detail has been omitted in error. Prompt attention to such matters by the architect enables the application to be processed with the minimum of delay.

In most cases the architect tries to incorporate within his own concept and design the various design standards set by the planning authority, including such matters as angles of daylight or car-parking standards, and tries to reflect the general policy which the officers have set. This often involves many meetings with the planning officers and sometimes with a separate panel of architects, conservation groups and other interested local people. The architect tries to balance the demands of these various interests with the objectives of the developer and his own understanding of the physical possibilities permitted by the site, so that the building for which the application is made is both socially and economically successful. In addition to obtaining the planning permission, the architect is also responsible for obtaining other approvals, such as building regulation approval and the fire certificate.

8.3.2 Building design

It is generally understood that the architect is responsible for the aesthetic appearance of buildings but it is perhaps less generally understood that he has also to consider the functional aspects of a building and indeed its economic viability. This involves a thorough understanding not only of the mechanics of construction, but also of the features that are demanded by the occupier. He considers the cost—benefit relationship of including within a specification such features as air conditioning, lofty eaves or additional thermal insulation. In making such judgements, he may need to consult other members of the development team such as the quantity surveyor and the estate agent, but an experienced architect brings to the task the benefit of a store of accumulated knowledge.

An important aspect of many developments is the relationship between the gross area of the building and the net area of lettable space within the building. This is particularly so in the case of an office building where great care is required to ensure that staircases, service areas, lift shafts, and the like are designed in such a way that they waste as little space as possible.

There are many factors that directly affect the economic viability of a building and it should not be assumed that the cheapest, meanest form of construction is to be preferred. A successful building needs to combine economic design with a good quality of construction, layout and finish not only because it may be superficially more attractive to a prospective occupier, but also because it facilitates the best use of the space and reduces costs of servicing and maintenance.

We referred above to the fact that planners are sometimes required to have more regard to the social impact of their decisions. The same is true in the field of architecture. Massive monuments to the name of the architect are frowned upon, greater emphasis is placed upon the way in which a new building, or indeed a refurbished building, fits into an existing group of buildings and the extent to which it is functional and provides for a flexible use. Bearing in mind the increasing incidence of technological change, thought is also being given to the extent to which buildings should be designed for a shorter economic life and to ways in which they can be improved or altered to ensure that they are more economical in the use of energy. There is, however, little incentive to produce a short-life building unless substantial savings in cost can be achieved.

8.3.3 The control of the building contract

Subject only to the overall control of a project manager, the architect is the member of the development team principally responsible for the management of the building contract. He has the most direct relationship with the building contractor and controls the access of others to the site. All members of the development team, including the client developer, should inform the architect of their intention to visit the site so that he can make the necessary arrangements with the contractor. Random site visits and casual discussions with the contractor can often lead to confusion as to instructions and to additional costs.

The following are some of the more important aspects of this part of the architect's role:

(a) Organization, arrangement and recording of periodic site meetings to inspect work and resolve problems.

(b) Issuing to the contractor additional instructions of variations.

(c) Ensuring, at all times, that the contractor is supplied with all drawings and other details needed to allow construction to proceed smoothly.

(d) Helping to overcome constructional problems on site that arise either as a result of the contractor not understanding a part of the contract drawings, or some unforeseen technical problem.

(e) Monitoring the quality of workmanship and ensuring that a proper standard is maintained.

(f) Issuing periodic interim certificates of value in accordance with the building contract and arranging for their payment by the client developer.

(g) At the appropriate time, issuing the certificate of practical completion subject, if necessary, to a list of minor items of work still requiring attention and any defective work still to be remedied.

(h) Preparation of the 'snagging list' during and at the end of the defects liability period, listing items of defective work to be remedied by the contractor.

(i) Settlement of details of final account and issuing a final certificate.

The architect is also responsible for keeping the development team informed of the progress of the development project. As we have described in Chapter 5, this may involve the preparation of a development timetable which can be discussed at project meetings and where necessary revised. This timetable enables the developer client to measure the progress of the project and helps other members of the development team to see the way in which the project is proceeding so that they can ensure that any plans or details for which they are responsible are prepared in time.

8.4 THE QUANTITY SURVEYOR

The quantity surveyor is responsible for preparing estimates of building cost, preparing Bills of Quantities and, during the period of construction, for preparing valuations of work upon which the architect bases his periodic interim certificates and his final certificate.

Prior to the start of construction, he may be asked to advise on the cost and merits of alternative forms of construction and generally to guide the developer in planning the cost of the building project. He is often asked to prepare an estimated cash flow, showing the way in which he expects payments to be made to the building contractor during the building contract. Thereafter at project meetings he has to report on the cost of construction and measure actual payments against the estimated cash flow. He must be able to explain why the actual cash flow differs from the estimate and prepare revised estimates for the remainder of the project. This provides an additional check to the way in which the project is proceeding and enables the client developer to organize his development finance more effectively.

If during the building project, consideration is given to possible variations in design, the quantity surveyor is responsible for estimating their cost so that the development team can decide whether or not they are merited.

8.5 THE VALUER AND THE LETTING/SELLING AGENT

The roles of the valuer and the letting/selling agent are often combined as many firms of chartered surveyors and estate agents encompass both tasks, but in fact the tasks are quite distinct.

8.5.1 Valuation

The task of the valuer is to provide estimates of rental and capital value. To do this, he must have a thorough understanding of the relevant letting or selling market and where appropriate the investment market. He must also have a knowledge of the way in which such taxes as capital gains tax and development land tax may affect the development.

Estimates of value may be required for a number of reasons, including the calculation of loss of rent to be used in deciding upon the level of damages resulting from delayed completion to be included as part of the standard JCT building contract (see Chapter 5). However, perhaps the most important valuation is the initial valuation of the project that is needed to assess the correct land price. Drawing information from other members of the development team, such as the architect and quantity surveyor, the valuer arrives at a residual value for the site by comparing:

(a) Estimated rental and capital value with
(b) Estimated development cost (including interest on borrowed capital) and allowing for
(c) The time taken to obtain planning permission, negotiate the building contract, carry out the building construction and dispose of the completed development and
(d) The developers' profit.

In Chapter 2 we described both conventional and cash-flow methods of appraisal. We showed that the residual site value is arrived at by comparing estimated income and cost, and the calculation is 'checked' by taking the estimated residual site value as the assumed site purchase cost and calculating a development yield and a development profit.

As the project proceeds, the initial evaluation may need to be revised to take account of additional information and more precise estimates of cost and income. This process will continue throughout the project so that at all times the outcome of the development is monitored. Care must be taken

to ensure that in estimating rentals or sale figures or investment yields the latest trends in the marketplace are adequately
reflected.

8.5.2 Agency

The main task of the letting/selling agent is to identify potential occupiers and to organize and implement the disposal to
them of the completed development, whether this be by sale
or by lease. We have looked at this in some detail in Chapter
6, but the following is a summary of some of the more
important aspects of the agent's role:

(a)   The identification of potential occupiers.
(b)   The assessment of the rent or price that occupiers will
      pay.
(c)   The assessment of market conditions and possible
      changes that may arise during the development period.
(d)   The analysis of the requirements of occupiers.
(e)   The organization and implementation of a marketing
      strategy.
(f)   The monitoring of the effectiveness of the marketing
      strategy.
(g)   The negotiations of lettings or sales.

It is most important that the agent has a thorough understanding of the product that he is selling. It is advisable,
therefore, that he is included as part of the development
team from the outset, even if he has not been involved in
the acquisition of the development site. This enables him to
contribute helpfully to the discussion of the characteristics
of the buildings that are being constructed to ensure that
they reflect the requirements of the market.

8.6 OTHER MEMBERS OF THE DEVELOPMENT TEAM

So far we have selected only some of the members of the
development team — perhaps those with the leading roles.
There are, however, others and they include the following.

8.6.1 The structural engineer

Working closely with the architect and the quantity surveyor, the structural engineer assists with the design of the structural elements of the building, calculating loads and stresses and advising upon how the design of the building should be modified to accommodate them. His advice is more likely to be required in the larger and more complex buildings such as, for example, a major shopping centre with first-floor car parking and loading areas superimposed with several floors of offices.

8.6.2 The electrical engineer

Such specialist advice is only likely to be required in the larger and more complex buildings. The amount of electricity required to serve a building can vary considerably with different forms of heating, lighting and machinery and complicated problems can arise where a large building is to be demolished.

8.6.3 The air-conditioning consultant

Air conditioning has become a common part of many office buildings and covered shopping centres, although recent increases in energy costs have prevented its use in some provincial office schemes. Where it is included, it is often advisable to appoint a specialist consultant to design the system and to liaise with the architect to determine the way in which it can best be incorporated within the overall design of the building.

8.6.4 The landscape architect

As greater stress is placed upon the quality of the environment that surrounds buildings, there is more often the need to employ a specialist landscape architect to design the non-built areas of a development. Indeed many residential developers have found that well-landscaped roads, gardens and walks enhance the value of the dwellings and that the additional value outweighs the additional cost.

8.6.5 The interior designer

The detail of the interior of offices, shops or residential buildings is of fundamental importance and, in some cases, an interior designer may be employed to assist the architect with these matters. In particular such skills have been used to add to the appearance of the reception areas and common parts of office buildings and to give particular character to covered shopping malls.

8.6.6 The accountant

From time to time an accountant may be co-opted to the development team to advise upon the impact of a particular scheme on the overall position of the development company, or to advise on the details of the financial arrangements and the incidence of taxation.

8.6.7 The solicitor

The services of a solicitor are needed at various stages throughout the development process, starting with the acquisition of the development site and including the drafting and settlement of leases and contracts of sale. The solicitor also advises on the legal implications of financial agreements such as sale and leasebacks. A developer may establish a policy of using standard forms of lease or contract, prepared by the solicitor, to simplify disposals and the subsequent management of properties held for investment.

While this list is by no means exhaustive, we hope that it shows the variety of skills that are required within the development process. Each of the roles has been described separately, but they may overlap with one adviser taking on two or more tasks. The architect, or indeed the valuer, may also be responsible for dealing with applications for planning permission; the valuer and the agent may be one and the same; the architect may prepare the landscape design and, in some simple projects, the architect may handle all negotiations with the contractor without the use of a quantity surveyor.

8.7   APPOINTING AND MANAGING THE DEVELOPMENT TEAM

In order to be really effective, each of these separate roles must be combined within the development team. Indeed one of the most important functions of the developer is to be able to select and bring together a team of advisers who complement each other and work well together.

8.7.1 Appointment

However well the developer knows his advisers there should be some formal exchange of correspondence, giving formal instructions and setting down the basis of charges so that the amount of fees and the way in which they will be paid can be incorporated in project cash flows.

The task of each adviser must be clearly defined both at the start and during the development process. Each adviser must know the limits of his own responsibility and authority. The methods and procedure to be adopted for reporting to the client must also be agreed.

As a general rule, much is gained from appointing the principal members of the team as early as possible, thus enabling the impact of their advice to be felt from the start and avoiding the necessity of making fundamental changes in plan once the development is underway. It may be, for example, that the letting agent advises that 21-ft eaves-heights are essential for a warehousing development, whereas the architect may have been planning to build to only 18 ft. Such a difference of view needs to be discussed at the outset, rather than left until the change of policy causes delay and additional cost.

8.7.2 Team leader

In many cases, the client developer will wish to lead the development team himself but this is not always so. The client developer may, in fact, be an occupier or perhaps a landowner with little or no experience of development. Small projects may not merit a separate team leader, one of the development team taking on the additional task. In such a case the selection depends upon the personality and experience of the people concerned. In larger projects, however, it is best to appoint a separate team leader in order to ensure a balanced overview of the development process, and also to ensure that the advice of each member of the team is properly scrutinized. The team leader is sometimes referred to as the project manager. His basic discipline may be that of an architect, quantity surveyor or valuer/agent, or indeed it may be related more directly to building and contracting. Where the development is being sponsored by someone other than a development company, a development company may be asked to take on the role of project management on the basis of a fee, either fixed or related to the profit of the development.

8.7.3 Project meetings

The development team needs to meet regularly and it is advisable, from fairly early on in the development process, to arrange a fixed programme of meetings. All the principal members of the team should attend these meetings. From time to time additional members need to attend. It is often helpful for written reports to be prepared by each adviser and circulated a few days before the meeting. The developer depends heavily upon his advisers and needs to be sure that their advice is given with confidence. Greater thought is often given to advice which has to be committed to paper, and by circulating it prior to the meeting, the other members of the team have the opportunity of considering it and preparing their comments.

The principal advisers should attend the project meeting even if they have nothing to report, so that they can keep themselves thoroughly up to date with the progress of the project, comment on advice given by others, deal with unexpected questions that arise and ensure that no one is being delayed by lack of information from them.

8.7.4 In-house or external advisers

Developers normally maintain a very small in-house staff relying upon selected external advisers. Over a number of years, a developer often forms a close relationship with his principal advisers, preferring to work with people he knows. This may sometimes lead to the advisers becoming so closely involved with the development company that they are almost a part of the staff. In the past this has been particularly so with certain firms of architects.

Many developers themselves are qualified in one of the main professional disciplines allied to the development industry. They may, for example, have originally been practising architects or, more commonly, surveyors and estate agents. Some of the larger development companies, and indeed institutional funds, have fairly extensive in-house staffs but nearly all of them also rely upon employing outside advisers. Outside advice has principally been sought for the selection of sites, the obtaining of planning permission and the implementation and disposal of the project itself. There is, however, some indication that the principal development companies and institutional funds are now also interested in seeking outside advice in the formulation of development policy.

8.8 THE LOCAL AUTHORITY DEVELOPMENT TEAM

Local government reorganization was accompanied by development of the theory and practice of corporate management techniques. The management team of chief officers led by a chief executive typifies the new local authority top-management structure. The awareness and sense of the importance of corporate identity as well as departmental responsibility reduces and, in many cases, removes the need to expound the advantages of a development team to handle local authority development work.

Local authorities have a long history of success in carrying out major development work in pursuit of their statutory functions whether in the field of public authority housing, education, highway construction, public leisure and recreation, or the social services, and so on, and close co-operation between different local authority departments in handling this work has always been necessary. But if an authority ventures into the field of speculative commercial, industrial, residential or other development, there are certain subtle differences if for no other reason than that the local authority is no longer carrying out the development entirely on its own behalf with only its own requirements to consider. In the field of speculative development the customer plays a prominent role.

When carrying a speculative development project through to completion including ultimate letting or other disposal, the professional skills required and the administrative arrangements are in essence similar to those needed by the private developer. Local authorities differ in size, they do not all have identical departmental management structures and the relative strength of departments varies between one authority and another. However, as a general rule it is likely that the average local authority has available more staff 'in-house' than the average private developer, and certain commonsense adjustments have to be made in administrative and report-writing arrangements to cater for the organizational character of a local authority. It is otherwise unnecessary to add anything to the foregoing comments on the management of a development project.

There is a different emphasis in the composition of the development team when, as is likely to be the case, the activities of the authority are restricted to land assembly and servicing and disposal. The task is to decide the land-use allocations within the growth area, to programme the land acquisition and provision of infrastructure and site disposals; to deal with the methods of site disposal and arrangements for approving development schemes and making any necessary choice between competing bids for sites; to prepare estimates of development costs and revenue and cash flow; and to ensure that as far as is practicable they are adhered to, and to arrange for the necessary reports to be submitted to the authority which should at all times be aware of the progress of practical implementation and the financial implications. The work of the development team is closely correlated with all the relevant activities of the authority. In particular the team works within the framework of the overall planning and transportation policies and the resources available to the authority, and of course the members of the team are in their daily work concerned with all the other activities of the authority.

The composition of the land-development team depends

to an extent on the size and importance of the development programme and subsidiary teams are often established to deal with individual projects. The Chief Executive often leads the team, the permanent members of which are the Planning Officer, the Engineer responsible for highways and transportation, the Finance Officer and the Estate Surveyor and Valuer. Other local authority officers, such as those responsible for education, leisure and recreation and the social services, are called in for consultation whenever appropriate. Specialist consultants are retained on any topics in respect of which comprehensive advice is not available within the local authority staff resources.

At the outset when setting up a development team, it is vital to set out the objectives to be achieved and to clearly establish the responsibilities of each individual member of the team and to ensure that it is clearly understood precisely where the power of decision-making lies. Reports which might have to be submitted to various local authority committees should in no way obviate the necessity for regular comprehensive reports to be prepared covering the whole of the work of the development team. Where different members of the team may from time to time come into contact with the prospective customers (purchasers or lessees), there must be a clear understanding as to who is able to authorize any work requested by the customers and what arrangements have to be observed for maintaining overall financial control and recovering the extra expenditure. The responsibility for financial control, for dealing with all the various legal documents and for obtaining all the necessary statutory and other approvals, including appropriate committee approvals, are some of the matters which it is vital for every member of the development team to understand.

CHAPTER 9

The betterment problem

9.1 INTRODUCTION

In the post-war period there have been a number of attempts to deal with 'the betterment problem', that is the extent to which the community at large or the individual private owner should determine and benefit from the gains in value arising from the development potential of land and buildings. The legislation that has sought to confront this problem has been of two kinds. First there has been legislation concerned with the public control of land use. Secondly there has been legislation designed to recoup for the community all or part of the development value of land.

The Town and Country Planning Act 1947 established a formal system of land-use control and, although that system is not without its critics, it has been accepted and extended by both the major political parties and is now firmly entrenched as an 'institution'. Most of those concerned with development in the public and private sectors accept the general concept of development control, however much they may disagree on matters of detail. There has been, and is, much less agreement on the extent to which central and local government should intervene in the development market and on the taxation of increases in development value, sometimes referred to as the 'taxation of betterment'.

In 1947, as part of the Town and Country Planning Act of that year, the Labour Government established a development charge of 100% to be paid upon the realization of development value, subject to a once-and-for-all payment of compensation. In 1953 the Conservative Party repealed the financial provisions of the Town and Country Planning Act and no further legislation for the taxation of development value was introduced for a period of over 10 years. In 1965, however, capital gains tax was introduced by the Finance Act 1965. It was not designed specifically to tax gains in land values but such capital gains were caught in its net at a rate of 30%.

In 1967 with a Labour Government once more in power the Land Commission Act was introduced. Its aims were to secure that the right land was available at the right time for the implementation of national, regional and local plans, and ensure that a substantial part of the development value created by the community returned to the community and the burden of the cost of land for essential purposes was reduced. A central agency, the Land Commission, acted as both tax-collector and land-buyer, and the rate of tax, or betterment levy as it is known, was 40% and it was planned that in time it would rise to 50%. The tax was levied on the sale and leasing of land and on the realization of development value by the carrying out of a project of material development. Increases in current use value continued to be taxed by capital gains tax. In the event, not much tax was collected and not much land was acquired. In 1970 the Labour Government fell from power, and in 1971 the new Conservative Government introduced legislation abolishing the Land Commission Act in its entirety.

In 1973, however, the Conservative Government of Mr Heath, spurred on by the unfavourable public reaction to the property boom of 1971—2, made proposals to introduce a development gains tax. Before the legislation could be introduced Mr Heath fell from power, but in 1974 the incoming Labour Government introduced the development gains tax in the Finance Act of that year. The tax was levied at income-tax rates on development value realized by a sale, by the granting of a lease at a premium and in certain cases on the first letting of a building following a project of material development but not on the carrying out of such a project. This was the first time that the two main political parties had followed a common policy. The marriage was short-lived, however, for in September 1974, just before the October election, the Labour Party published its White Paper entitled *Land*, and in this two objectives were set out:

(a) To enable the community to control the development of land in accordance with its need and priorities.
(b) To restore to the community the increasing value of land arising from its efforts.

A comparison can be made between these and the almost identical aims of the Land Commission Act, but on this occasion two vehicles were proposed to obtain the objectives. Having learned from the earlier attempt of the unpopularity of a central agency, the local authorities were selected to be the effective agency (Wales being the exception). The vehicles were, of course, the Community Land Act 1975 and the Development Land Tax Act 1976.

9.2 THE COMMUNITY LAND ACT 1975

9.2.1 The Act

Although it has been repealed the Community Land Act was another milestone on the road towards a solution to the vexed problem of how best to secure for the community the positive control of development land and deal with the appropriation of betterment value. It is useful to remember some of the more important provisions.

The implementation was largely in the hands of the local authorities who had wide powers of acquisition and were under a positive duty to consider the desirability of acquiring land for development by themselves or others whenever a planning application for relevant development (i.e. other than certain excepted categories of development) was made. The Secretary of State had power to designate certain types of relevant development and thus place local authorities under a positive obligation to acquire all the land needed for designated relevant development and ultimately it was intended that on the Second Appointed Day there would be a general duty for the local authorities to acquire all land for relevant development. In short the ultimate objective was to take all development land (other than that within the restricted, exempt and excepted categories) into public ownership.

An interesting facet of the legislation was the setting up of the Land Authority for Wales which within the principality enjoyed the same duties and powers as the local authorities elsewhere.

An important principle of the Community Land Act was the retention by the local authorities of a portion of the development land tax levied on private development when such land was acquired and passed through the Community Land Surplus Account before disposal for development purposes. The local authorities retained 30% of the surplus although, in effect, until such time as the land account was in surplus 100% of the development tax was retained by the local authority. A public authority acquiring land for its own use received the full benefit of development land tax which was deducted from the compulsory purchase price.

The authorities had a duty to maintain a register of all land acquisition, holdings and disposals which passed through the land accounts. The information on the register included a description of the land, the nature of the interest held by the authority, the process under which the land was acquired, descriptions of planning permissions and also the existing use of the land and details of any proposals for development. Brief information relating to land disposals also had to be given.

9.2.2   Subsequent legislation

The Community Land Act was finally repealed in the Local Government Planning and Land Act 1980 which itself contains various provisions relating to the positive control of development land.

Local authorities, subject to the authorization of the Secretary of State, have power to acquire compulsorily:

(a)   Any land which is in their area and which is suitable for and is required in order to secure the carrying out of one or more of the following activities, namely, development, re-development and improvement.

(b)   Any land which is in their area and which is required for a purpose which it is necessary to achieve in the interests of the proper planning of an area in which the land is situated.

This power of acquisition, if sensibly authorized and used,

should be adequate to enable local authorities to exercise a prudent positive control over the development land.

The Land Authority for Wales has continued in being albeit with somewhat amended functions. The Secretary of State has power to set up Urban Development Corporations and also to designate enterprise zones, both powers intended to introduce some muscle into the attempts to solve the problems of the inner cities.

Land registers, open to public inspection, have to be compiled and maintained by local authorities and a wide range of other public bodies giving details of land in their ownership which in the opinion of the Secretary of State is not being used or is under-used and the Secretary of State may direct an authority to dispose of any land on the register. This is an attempt to overcome problems, often found in inner city areas, due to large acreages of unused land in the ownership of public authorities.

The Secretary of State has power to direct a local authority to make an assessment of land in its area available and suitable for residential development. This is no doubt to enable him to deal with the complaints often made by developers about shortages of land despite the belief of the local planning authorities that sufficient land allocations have been made in their development plans.

All in all local authorities do have available to them wide powers which, subject to the Secretary of State's authorization, enable them to play an active and positive role in the development sphere quite apart from their substantial powers of control in their capacity as local planning authority.

There is no general consensus of opinion as to the extent to which local authorities should become involved in the property market either with a view to actively taking part in the implementation process, or as long-term investors with the intention of securing future increases in land values for the benefit of the community. It is interesting to note that there are certain matters upon which there is an identity of view. The right of an owner-occupier of a house to own the freehold is generally accepted. There is a wide measure of general agreement that very large-scale development projects involving land acquisition from many owners and the provision of substantial infrastructure by public authorities are in practice best promoted by some form of public agency, even though the extent and degree of involvement of that agency might be debated: hence the New Towns Acts and the Town Development Act 1952 and the Urban Development Corporations, for example. At the opposite end of the development scale there is also general agreement that public authorities should not as a matter of policy become involved in the very small development projects; this was reflected in the exempt and excepted development provisions in the Community Land Act.

In the first edition of this book it was said that legislation relating to the taxation of development values or the general involvement of public authorities in the property development process is usually short-lived. Indeed the repetitive cycle of enactment amendment and repeal is a cause of concern to many who feel that a reasonable period of stability is highly desirable. This is as true in 1982 as it was in 1977.

9.3 THE DEVELOPMENT LAND TAX ACT 1976

Despite, or perhaps because of, the complicated nature of much of the detail of this Act, it is helpful to grasp the simplicity of the basic concept, even if this at first means some oversimplification. Too much attention at the start to the finer detail and nuances of the legislation can lead to confusion and misunderstanding.

Development land tax is a tax payable upon the realization of development value. This simple statement poses three questions:

(a)   What is the rate of tax?
(b)   What is development value?
(c)   How and when is it realized?

9.3.1 The rate of tax

The present rate of tax, subject to certain concessions to which we refer below, is 60%.

9.3.2 Development value

In simple terms development value is the difference between the value of a field as a field and the value of a field as a housing site. Suppose, for example, that Mr Brown has a 5-acre field which has an agricultural value of £5000. He sells it to Mr Smith for residential development for the sum of £50 000. In simple terms the development value that he realizes is the difference between £50 000 and £5000, that is £45 000. It is the difference between the price received for the land and its agricultural value.

The value of the field as a field on the assumption that no development will ever be permitted is known as the 'current use value', and so long as the value realized is greater than the current use value, development value is realized. This is so whether or not planning permission has been obtained. Equally, so long as a planning permission has not been implemented, the current use value will not reflect the value of the right to implement that permission.

Examine these two statements in relation to the above example. Even if Mr Brown had not obtained planning permission for the residential development of his land, by disposing of it for a sum (£50 000) which is higher than the current use value or agricultural value (£5000), he is deemed to have realized development value; and even if Mr Brown had obtained planning permission for the residential development of his land, its current use value would not reflect that higher value so long as the planning permission had not been implemented.

9.3.3 The realization of development value

Development value is most commonly realized by a sale, a lease or the carrying out of a project of material development. Taking again our simple example of Mr Brown, if he sells his field to Mr Smith, that is a disposal by sale. If he grants to Mr Smith a ground lease, that is a disposal by way of lease and is known as a 'part-disposal' in so far as Mr Brown is disposing of only a part of his freehold interest. Both are disposals for development land tax purposes and both will attract development land tax whether or not planning permission has been obtained. If Mr Brown, having obtained planning permission for residential development, carries out the development himself, the start of the project of development is deemed to be a disposal and development land tax is assessed on the development value that is deemed to be realized. The market value, or price, for the deemed disposal is calculated on the basis of a residual valuation or by comparison with similar land sales.

Once the project has been started, the current use value is uplifted to the development value of the project itself. In our example this would mean uplifting the agricultural value of £5000 to the residential value of £50 000. This new current use value is reflected in any subsequent disposal.

A project is deemed to have been started when any of a list of 'specified operations' is begun. These specified operations are listed in Part I of Schedule 1 of the Act and include, for example, the digging of a trench which is to contain the foundations of a building and the laying of any underground main or pipe to the foundations of a building. It should be noted that we refer specifically to 'projects of material development'. Excluded from material development are certain minor additions and alterations, including extensions within one-third of the original cubic content, certain changes of use and the erection of buildings for agricultural forestry. These categories of development excluded from material development are set out in Part II of Schedule 4 of the Act.

9.3.4 Exemptions and concessions

The Act contains a number of exemptions and concessions. Some have a general application and others only apply in special cases. The following are of general application.

Section 1 of the Act provides that no development land tax at all is payable on projects of material development started before the 1 August 1976.

Section 12 of the Act, as now amended, provides that the first £50 000 of realized development value in any one financial year is not subject to development land tax at all.

Section 2 provides that on a deemed disposal, that is, the carrying out of a project of material development, no development land tax is payable on what are known as 'non-major interests'. These are interests in reversion on a lease of 35 years or more, where the rent cannot reflect the value of the development or where the market value of the interest is less than £5000.

There are many more examples of exemptions and concessions for special cases, and these include the following.

Local Authorities and certain other government bodies are totally exempt from development land tax (Section 11).

Even if development value is realized, no development land tax is payable upon the sale of an owner's main private residence plus one acre of land or such area as is required for the reasonable enjoyment of the residence (Section 14).

Provided that the land was owned on 12 September 1974, no development land tax is payable on the erection of a dwelling house provided that it is a single dwelling house and that it is for the occupation of an adult member of the owner's family as their sole or main residence (Section 15).

No development land tax is payable on the disposal of land held as stock-in-trade, provided the interest was acquired on or before 12 September 1974 and at that time there was in force a planning permission authorizing development (Section 16). This exemption is, however, restricted to as much of the realized development value as can be related to the planning permission which was in force on 12 September 1974. Where, therefore, there is a subsequent planning permission which perhaps increases a residential density, then development land tax may be payable on the difference in development value that can be attributed to that increase in density.

Special provisions for minerals are covered by Section 17. No development land tax is payable on the deemed disposal arising from the carrying out of a project of mineral extraction, and on the actual disposal of mineral land the consideration received is reduced by half of a fraction calculated by deducting from the consideration the non-mineral market value.

Section 19, as amended, contains special provisions for the occupiers of industrial and commercial property. Where such occupiers carry out a project of material development, the payment of development land tax is deferred as long as the occupier continues to occupy the buildings. Liability which has been deferred becomes payable when the property ceases to be used for the qualifying purpose. This contingent liability now ceases if it has not become payable within 12 years from the commencement of the development. The occupier must, however, notify the Development Land Tax Office of the project that he is carrying out.

Certain inter-company transactions are free from development land tax and this is covered by Sections 20—22.

No development land tax is payable on projects of material development carried out by statutory undertakers where the buildings are for the purposes of the statutory undertaker and this is covered in Section 23.

Section 26 refers to housing associations. Certain housing associations will not pay development land tax on the carrying out of projects of material development.

Sections 24 and 25 contain special provisions for charities. First, no development land tax is payable on the disposal or deemed disposal of land after 25 March 1980, and second, where land was acquired by a Charity after 12 September 1974 and before 26 March 1980 to carry out a project of material development for the purpose of the Charity then development land tax liability is deferred until a subsequent disposal.

Section 18 covers what is known as the 'three-year exemption'. Where it can be shown that had the development started immediately after the acquisition of the land, no significant amount of development value would have been realized no development land tax will arise. Indeed in such circumstances, a developer can, prior to the start of the project, apply to the Development Land Tax Office for a certificate of exemption. This concession is only applicable if the development starts within three years from the date of the acquisition of the land.

9.3.5 Notification

The Development Land Tax Office has to be notified of all actual and deemed disposals. As far as disposals by sale and lease are concerned, this happens automatically by the submission of Particulars Delivered. Where a deemed disposal takes place, i.e. the start of a project of material development, the Development Land Tax Office must be notified on the appropriate notification forms not more than 60 days before the start and not more than 30 days thereafter. The penalties for failing to notify are contained in Schedule 8 of the Act.

9.3.6 The assessment of development land tax

We have already referred in general terms to the way in which development value is calculated. Having established the price or where appropriate market value of the land, a 'base-value' deduction is made. This base value is either related to the price paid for the land or its current use value and, in certain circumstances, there may be added the cost of improvements. The taxpayer has the opportunity of selecting the most favourable of three base values and, in nearly all cases, it is prudent to take professional advice.

Where a tax liability arises out of a deemed disposal or the grant of a lease for a rent not exceeding the commercial rent the person liable to development land tax may elect to pay the tax by yearly or half-yearly instalments. The tax will normally be payable by eight yearly or sixteen half-yearly instalments either commencing twelve months after the date of disposal or two years after the date of the deemed disposal. For disposals after 15 March 1983 the number of annual instalments was increased to ten and the half-yearly payment facility withdrawn.

9.3.7 The impact of development land tax on the development industry

In considering the impact of development land tax, it is important to distinguish between the general effects of the economy as a whole and the particular effects of the tax itself. The tax is a factor but not the most important factor affecting the supply of land. Of prime importance is the general level of economic activity and of demand and supply. It is the anticipated change in the level of the tax, rather than the tax itself, that currently affects the supply of land. Other things being equal, at times when land values are expected to rise and the level of tax to fall land is held off the market, whereas at times when land values are expected to fall and the tax to rise land is brought on the market. Political agreement on a rate of tax would help to bring greater certainty to the land market and might be a useful step towards a political consensus. In this connection it is interesting to note in the discussion paper, *A Land Policy for the Future*, published in 1982 by the Royal Institution of Chartered Surveyors, the emphasis on the need for government land policies capable of gaining broad public and political support which would avoid the damaging cycle of enactment and repeal and thus help create conditions of stability and confidence.

The tax is aimed at gains derived from land ownership and not at gains derived from the development of land, although the taxation of increases in land values tends to remove the 'cushion' effect of land ownership within the development process. By so doing, it tends to emphasize the need for a careful and 'professional' approach to the management of the development process.

CHAPTER 10

Postscript

10.1 1977

As we have written this book and discussed it together, we have recognized that further and more detailed studies are needed on many separate aspects of property development. In particular, we would like to see work on such matters as market research, the assessment of risk, project control, marketing and alternative methods of assessing rent (particularly in relation to turnover). Certain techniques have begun to be used but need considerable refinement. These include sensitivity analysis, the evaluation of costs in use and the use of discounted cash flow techniques in financial evaluation.

The development industry is subject to change; indeed conditions and expectations have changed while we have been writing. We cannot forecast how political attitudes will change with regard to such matters as private ownership and the balance between industrial efficiency and the conservation of the environment. What will be the nature of the British economy in the future and how will standards of living change? Will oil revenues form the base for a major industrial change or is that hope 'likely to turn out to be a mirage'?*

To what extent will changes in technology, particularly in the fields of communication and energy, affect styles of living and transportation? What changes can be expected in population size, structure and distribution?

How will the property market be affected by the development of the European Economic Community and the growth in the size and influence of the multi-national companies,

*Professor Jim Ball, Principal of London Business School. *Investors Chronicle*, 11th November 1977.

including those financial institutions which make substantial investments in property?

The answers to questions such as these will determine the extent and manner of land use and the future of the development industry. We advocate constant questioning and debate. 'Detecting mistakes and inherent dangers by critical examination and discussion beforehand is an altogether more rational procedure, and as a rule less wasteful of resources, people and time than waiting till they reveal themselves in practice'.*

10.2 1982

In the mid 1970s we were watching the property market begin to emerge from the collapse of 1974—5. Now, in September 1982, we are watching the market decline from the mini-boom of 1979. In the last five years the financial institutions and, in particular the pension funds, have grown in influence and now dominate to the extent that there is an increasing distinction between their market, the 'prime' market, and the rest. At the same time, an increasing number of questions are being asked from within and outside the pension funds both as to their performance in particular and as to the performance of property in general. This book is not concerned primarily with the former. So far as the latter is concerned there is some disquiet about the overall relative performance of rents and increasing attention is being given to the problems of obsolescence, particularly in industrial and commercial buildings. Finally, there is at least an emerging body of useful research and information on property markets. It has a long way to go but it helps to replace the property myth with some possibility of explicit analysis. As it develops, so must the professions and agencies in both public and private sectors that comprise the property industry. We live in hope.

---

*Bryan Magee discussing the philosophy of Karl Popper in *Popper*, Bryan Magee, Collins, 1973.

Functions of principal authorities in England

Reproduced from *Local Government in England and Wales — Guide to the New System*, HMSO, 1974.

	Metro-politan county	Metro-politan district	Non-metro-politan county	Non-metro-politan district	Greater London Council	London borough
Allotments (a)		x		x		x
Arts and recreation:						
Arts and Crafts, support of	x	x	x	x	x	x
Art galleries	x	x	x	x	x	x
Libraries		x	x			x
Museums	x	x	x	x	x	x
Recreation (e.g. parks, playing fields, swimming baths, etc.)	x	x	x	x	x	x
Tourism, encouragement of	x	x	x	x	x	x
Cemeteries and crematoria		x		x		x
Consumer protection:						
Foods and drugs (composition)	x		x			x
Trade description	x		x			x
Weights and measures	x		x			x
Education (b)		x	x	(c)		x(c)(d)
Environmental health:						
Building regulations		x		x		x
Clean air		x		x		x

	Metropolitan county	Metropolitan district	Non-metropolitan county	Non-metropolitan district	Greater London Council	London borough
Communicable disease control		x		x		x
Food safety and hygiene		x		x		x
Home safety		x		x		x
Litter control	x	x	x	x	x	x
Refuse collection		x		x		x
Refuse disposal	x		x		x	
Rodent control		x		x		x
Street cleansing		x		x		x
Fire service	x		x		x	
Footpaths and bridleways:						
Creation, diversion and extinguishment	x	x	x	x		x
Maintenance	x		x			x
Protection	x	x	x	x		x
Signposting	x		x			x
Surveys	x		x			x
Housing	(c)	x	(c)	x	x(f)	x(f)
Local licence duties (e.g. dog and game licences)						
Collection(g)		x		x		x
Markets and fairs		x		x		x
Planning:						
Advertisement control		x		x		x
Building preservation notices	x	x	x	x	x	x
Conservation areas	x	x	x	x	x	x
Country parks	x	x	x	x		x
Derelict land	x	x	x	x	x	x
Development control (processing of planning applications) (h)		x		x		x
Development plan schemes	x		x		x	
Listed building development		x		x		x
Local plans		x		x		x
National parks (b)	x(j)		x(j)			
Structure plans	x		x		x	

	Metro-politan county	Metro-politan district	Non-metro-politan county	Non-metro-politan district	Greater London Council	London borough
Police (b)	x		x		(k)	(k)
Rate collection (l)		x		x		x
Smallholdings	x		x		x	
Social services (b)		x	x			x
Traffic, transport and highways:						
Driver and vehicle licensing	(m)	(m)	(m)	(m)	(m)	
Highways (n)	x	(o)	x	(o)	x(p)	x(p)
Lighting —						
footway	x	x	x	x	x	x
highway	x		x		x(q)	x(q)
Parking —						
off-street	x	x(r)	x	x(r)	x(s)	x
on-street	x		x		x(t)	
Public transport	x(u)		x(v)	(v)	x(u)	
Road safety	x		x		x	
Traffic regulation	x		x		x	
Transportation planning	x		x		x	

Notes:

(a) In areas where there is a parish council that authority will be responsible.

(b) Agency arrangements not permissible.

(c) The councils of non-metropolitan districts and inner London boroughs whose areas serve primary schools are minor authorities for the purpose of appointing managers of these schools, except in areas where there is a parish or community council (or, in England, a parish meeting) which can act as minor authority. Where the area serving the school comprises two or more of the authorities mentioned above, they act jointly as a minor authority.

(d) Education is a borough function in outer London. In inner London education is provided by the Inner London Education Authority which is a special independent committee of the Greater London Council.

(e)   County councils have certain reserve powers to provide housing subject to a request by a district council and/ or the approval of the Secretary of State.

(f)   The London Boroughs are responsible for the provision of housing. The Greater London Council inherited a stock of dwellings from the London County Council, but the bulk of these have been transferred to district and London borough councils (though the GLC retains responsibility for improving the transferred property, where necessary, to a satisfactory standard). The GLC retains a strategic housing role, which includes such functions, as slum clearance (now largely completed), provision of retirement houses outside London, providing for exchanges between tenants, and helping mobility in London through its right to nominate tenants to a percentage of vacancies in ex-GLC housing.

(g)   Most local authorities collect local licence duties through the agency of the Post Office.

(h)   Some matters are reserved to the county councils but the district councils receive all planning applications initially.

(j)   Two joint planning boards have been set up to administer national park functions in the Lake District National Park and the Peak National Park. For other national parks these functions are administered by a special committee of the county council mainly concerned which may include representatives of the other county councils and the district councils for the area of the national park.

(k)   Greater London and certain areas immediately adjacent are policed by the Metropolitan Police force. This force is responsible directly to the Home Secretary.

(l)   Rate demands issued by the district councils include precepts from county and parish councils; those issued by the London borough councils and the City of London include precepts from the Greater London Council.

(m)   The function of licensing vehicles and drivers is now vested in the Secretary of State for Transport. The issue of most licences has been centralized, although Public Service Vehicle and Heavy Goods Vehicle licences are dealt with at the Department of Transport area offices.

There are a limited number of local authority local vehicle licensing offices which deal with a very restricted number of exceptional cases. Arrangements for the issue of private car and motor cycle licences are unchanged.

(n) The Secretary of State for the Environment is highway authority for trunk roads.

(o) District councils may claim the right to maintain unclassified roads in urban areas (this power is distinct from the powers to act under agency agreements).

(p) The Greater London Council is highway authority for all principal roads in London other than trunk roads (i.e. the main strategic road network), while the London boroughs are highway authorities for non-principal roads.

(q) Highway lighting responsibilities in Greater London are divided on the same basis as highway responsibilities.

(r) Subject to the consent of the county council.

(s) Subject to the consent of the appropriate London borough council.

(t) On the application of the appropriate London borough council.

(u) The metropolitan county councils and the Greater London Council are the passenger transport authorities and there are passenger transport executives responsible for day to day administration.

(v) Non-metropolitan county councils are responsible for the co-ordination of public transport in their areas but in some cases district councils run transport undertakings.

Index